Core Instructional Routines

Go-To Structures for Effective Literacy Teaching K–5

Judy Dodge and Andrea Honigsfeld

Foreword by Tanny McGregor

HEINEMANN
Portsmouth, NH

Heinemann

361 Hanover Street

Portsmouth, NH 03801–3912

www.heinemann.com

Offices and agents throughout the world

The authors and publisher wish to thank those who have generously given permission to reprint borrowed material:

Excerpts from Common Core State Standards © Copyright 2010. National Governors Association Center for Best Practices and Council of Chief State School Officers. All rights reserved.

Genre study table taken from "Steps in the Inquiry Process for Genre Study" in *Genre Study: Teaching with Fiction and Nonfiction Books* by Irene Fountas and Gay Su Pinnell. Copyright © 2012 by Irene C. Fountas and Gay Su Pinnell. Published by Heinemann, Portsmouth, NH. All rights reserved.

Figure 2.15: "Comparison of Traditional and Scaffolded Sustained Silent Reading" adapted from "Exploring Scaffolded Silent Reading (ScSR): Effective Practice for Increasing Reading Fluency and Comprehension" by D. Ray Reutzel, Ph.D., Utah State University. From: http://reading.org/downloads/WC_handouts/Exploring%20Scaffolded%20Silent%20Reading%20(ScSR).pdf. Reprinted by permission of the author.

Credits continue on page ix.

Library of Congress Cataloging-in-Publication Data

Dodge, Judith.

    Core instructional routines : go-to structures for effective literacy teaching, K–5 / Judith Dodge and Andrea Honigsfeld.

        pages cm

    Includes bibliographical references.

    ISBN 978-0-325-05661-6

    1. Language arts (Elementary)—United States.   2. Language arts (Elementary)—Standards—United States. I. Title.

CURR   LB1576.D586 2014

    372.6—dc23

    2014014758

Editor: Holly Kim Price

Production: Hilary Goff

Cover design: Suzanne Heiser

Interior design: Bernadette Skok

Typesetter: Gina Poirier, Gina Poirier Design

Manufacturing: Steve Bernier

Printed in the United States of America on acid-free paper

18 17 16 15 14 PAH 1 2 3 4 5

Contents

Foreword

Words interest me. They live and breathe, grow and ripen. As context changes, variations in meaning breed new connotations. Sometimes a word is so hip and cool it quickly becomes overused. Other times a word carries so much baggage that its usefulness and truth are lost. Take the word *concrete*, for example. I have struggled with this word for years. I know teachers are looking for concrete lesson ideas to reach learners who need to understand concepts in tangible ways. Yet the word *concrete* can also be interpreted as low-level, inflexible, and without rigor. When writing about concrete ways to teach complex ideas, it's a wrestling match: my intent versus the perception of the reader. I've come to the aid of the word *concrete*, knowing that it is still positive, useful, and the best way to describe the practical, everyday lessons that my readers expect.

The word *routine* gets a bad rap, too. It is sometimes used to describe the day-to-day, monotonous patterns of our everyday lives, often perceived as boring and unimaginative. This word has somehow lost its truth along the way. *Routine* needs an ally these days, and Judy and Andrea have come to its rescue! The fact is, routines are the foundational architecture for creativity, and in the classroom they give birth to deeper reading, rich writing, and meaningful conversation.

Want your students to exceed the ELA standards in reading, writing, speaking, and listening? Then core instructional routines are in order. Have great literacy lesson ideas but need a way to organize them within the time frame allotted in your daily schedule? Establish solid routines. Great routines allow for great teaching, and great teaching desperately relies on great routines.

The structure of this book is like a welcomed routine in itself. A solid, predictable structure sets the stage for a multitude of practical ideas, a veritable menu from which the reader may choose. Not only do Judy and Andrea make the often invisible instructional routines visible, they answer the ageless question: What would this look like in *my* classroom?

New teachers need to be introduced to the power of core instructional routines, and they need this introduction sooner rather than later. New teachers: Let Judy and Andrea light the path for you. Experienced teachers: Read and be reminded of the routines that anchor past instructional successes. *Core Instructional Routines: Go-To Structures for Effective Literacy Teaching, K–5* offers all of us the steady, timeless advice we need in these unsteady times of pendulum pedagogy. I invite you to make time for this book in your professional reading routine . . . it's not just your *routine* professional book!

—Tanny McGregor
May 2014
Cincinnati, Ohio

Author of *Comprehension Connections: Bridges to Strategic Reading* (2007) and *Genre Connections: Lessons to Launch Literary & Nonfiction Text* (2011), and coauthor of *Comprehension Going Forward: Where We Are & What's Next* (2011).

Acknowledgments

It is all about the students.

We continue to be amazed by your curiosity to explore, your desire to learn, and your never-ending spirit of inquiry.

Special thanks go to those of you who allowed us to feature your work and to capture the essence of your engagement with literacy in the photographs within this book.

It is also about the teachers.

Because of your commitment to provide the best instruction possible, your students embrace and enjoy their experiences with literacy.

We are indebted to all of you who have implemented routines in your classes, where literacy learning is thriving. Thank you for allowing us into your classrooms and for sharing your lessons, your inspiring learning environments, and your original work with students.

As we were working on this manuscript, it sustained us to know that you share our belief about the importance of routines. Watching you practice routines as a regular part of your literacy instruction further affirmed and guided our work on this book.

Our sincere gratitude goes to educators in the following districts who made specific contributions to this project:

Amityville UFSD, NY: Lisa Zomback

Cherry Hill Public School District, NJ: Violeta Katsikis and Paula Pennington

Diocese of Brooklyn, NY: Christina Cedrone, Lisa Peluso

Diocese of Rockville Centre, NY: Kelley Cordeiro

Douglas County Schools, GA: Brandy McDonald

Eastport-South Manor Central School District, NY: Amy Brown, Erin Marone, Lisa Martinez, Christa VanTronk, Charissa Voss

Elmont UFSD, NY: Elementary teachers

Franklin Square UFSD, NY: Judy Harkins-Diede

Glen Cove Schools, NY: Amy E. Cooke and Rose Doran

Island Trees UFSD, NY: K–2 teachers

Malverne UFSD, NY: Marie Dalton, Caroline Farkas, Jeanine Greco, Colleen Hickey, Marlene Marks, Nicole Mauersberger, Michelle Phelan

New York City Public Schools: Members of the PS 228Q Professional Learning Community (coaches Eileen Hughes, Darlin Diaz, and Leticia Cruz, and the following teachers: Evelyn Garcia, Claudia Martinez, Natalie Moy, Belkis Parache) as well as teachers from other NYC public schools, including Nazima Ally, Vaughan O. Danvers, Kaitlin Doria, and Victoria Najera

North Bellmore UFSD, NY: Ellen Tournour

Patchogue Medford School District, NY: Especially the STYLE coaches, Edd Ohlson, Dana Cerbone, and Anne Logan, and the following K–5 teachers: Nicole Cancellieri, Josephine Castano, Marisa Fontana, Jamie Gluckman, Donna King, Elena V. Kushins, Claudine Loria, Timothy Miller, Christine Pearsall, Danielle Ricciardi, Chris Shaw, Danielle Shine, Catherine Spiller, Sue Stahl, Elisabeth Taddei, Sicilia Valenzuela, and Mary Lou Weymann

Rockville Centre UFSD, NY: Amy Weinstein

South Hampton UFSD, NY: School teachers, especially Colleen Ferran, Nadine Isaacs, Amy Lester, Jorge Maldonado, Ellen Martin, Gregory Metzger, James O'Leary, Kerry Palumbo, Karen Raynor, Ken Sisco, Maggie Stadelmaier, Carol Steiber, Barbara Sutton, and Jessica Zukosky

South Huntington UFSD, NY: Elementary teachers, with a special thank you to Kellianne Roth

Valley Stream UFSD 13, NY: Danielle Dodge

Valley Stream District 30, NY: Joyce Smithok-Kollar

Westbury Public Schools, NY: Natasha Gabrielsen

It is also about leadership.

We are indebted to all the administrators and instructional leaders who supported our work with this project directly or indirectly. We admire and appreciate your dedication to enabling members of your school community to be successful. Special acknowledgments to the following:

Sal Alaimo, principal, Eastport Elementary School, NY

Jared Bloom, supervisor of assessment and technology/office of instruction and curriculum, South Huntington UFSD, NY

Lori Canneti, assistant superintendent of Patchogue Medford School District, NY, and all elementary school principals

John Christie, principal, Dayton Avenue Elementary School, NY

Denise Desjardin, Young Diplomats Magnet Academy, NYC DOE

Timothy Frazier, principal, Southampton Intermediate School, NY

George Guy, principal, A. Russell Knight Elementary School, Cherry Hill Public School District, NJ

Olga Iris Guzmán, principal, PS 228Q, NYC DOE

Jennifer Hart, assistant superintendent, Eastport-South Manor Central School District, NY

Bertha Richard, principal, Southampton Elementary School, NY

Kathy Safrey, director of curriculum in Elmont UFSD, NY, and her administrative team

Edward Talon, principal, Davison Avenue School, Malverne UFSD, NY

Susan Wright, assistant principal, Southampton Intermediate School, NY

It is also about collaboration.

We will always cherish the special opportunity for collaboration that writing this book gave to us. It allowed us to recognize and build upon our individual and collective strengths and expertise as we shared the challenges and pleasures of coauthoring. This joint effort could not have taken place without our friends and families cheering us on.

Thanks to all the practitioners and researchers—cited and quoted in this book—whose work infused and enhanced our own understanding of literacy routines.

A special shout-out to the following literacy and technology experts, who offered their insights and suggestions for this project: Sarah Brown Wessling, Blanca Duarte, and Kim Yaris; and to Taylor Volpe, graduate research assistant at Molloy College, whose attention to detail and technical support during preparation of this manuscript were deeply appreciated.

We would also like to acknowledge colleagues at Molloy College, Rockville Centre, NY, especially Dr. Audrey Cohan and Dr. Maria G. Dove, who provided invaluable feedback and advice on earlier drafts of our manuscript.

Last but not least, our gratitude goes to the entire Heinemann staff, without whom this book would not have been possible, especially our acquisitions editor, Holly Kim Price, our production editor, Hilary Goff, our copyeditor Elizabeth Tripp, and our marketing manager, Eric Chalek. You and your team brought this book to life and helped us share our vision and passion for best practices in literacy.

Credits continued from page ii:

Figure 3.17: "Steps in the Writing Process" adapted from: *Reading, Writing, and Learning in ESL: A Resource Book for Teaching K–12 English Learners*, 5th ed., by Suzanne F. Peregoy and Owen F. Boyle. Copyright © 2009. Printed and electronically reproduced by permission of Pearson Education, Inc., Upper Saddle River, New Jersey; and *Guiding Readers and Writers: Teaching Comprehension, Genre, and Content Literacy* by Irene C. Fountas and Gay Su Pinnell. Copyright © 2001 by Irene C. Fountas and Gay Su Pinnell. Published by Heinemann, Portsmouth, NH. All rights reserved.

"Features of Accountable Talk" adapted from the *Accountable Talk® Sourcebook: For Classroom Conversation That Works* by S. Michaels, M. C. O'Connor, M. W. Hall, with L. B. Resnick. Copyright © 2010. Pittsburgh, PA: University of Pittsburgh, Learning Research and Development Center. Reprinted by permission.

Figure 5.1: "Academic Language Dimensions, Features, and CCSS Goals" adapted from "Framing the Development of Complex Language and Literacy" in the forthcoming publication *Common Core Standards in Diverse Classrooms: Essential Practices for Developing Academic Language and Disciplinary Literacy* by Jeff Zwiers, Susan O'Hara, and Robert Pritchard. Copyright © 2014. To be published by Stenhouse, Portland, ME. Originally published with Academic Language Development Network: http://aldnetwork.org/sites/default/files/pictures/aldn_brief_2013.pdf. Copyright © 2013 by O'Hara, Zwiers, and Pritchard. Reprinted by permission of the authors.

Figure 5.7: "Word Wall Assessment" adapted from "Word Walls: A Support for Literacy in Secondary School Classrooms" by Jennifer Cronsberry. Copyright © 2004 by Jennifer Cronsberry. From: http://curriculum.org/resources/word-walls-a-support-for-literacy-in-secondary-school-classrooms. Reprinted by permission of the author.

Introduction: Routines You and Your Students Can Count On

What Is Changing?

These are exciting times when more and more discussion focuses on how important it is to end teacher isolation, engage all educators in a shared dialogue, and align instructional practices to shared goals. No longer can teachers work alone. No longer can educators stay uninformed about what their colleagues are doing on the same grade level or in other grades. Nor can anyone remain unaware of what is happening during the multitudes of special services—English as a second language, academic intervention, remedial reading, enrichment math, and so on (Honigsfeld and Dove 2010).

We are what we repeatedly do. Excellence, then, is not an act, but a habit. Aristotle

If students are to succeed with literacy, it will require teachers to work together in professional learning communities to talk about their craft, to reflect upon their practice, to discuss student progress, and to continuously improve their instruction (Fisher, Frey, and Uline 2013). Teachers and administrators, coaches and instructional specialists—in fact, the entire instructional staff—will need to come together to discuss what effective teaching and learning look like, what is working and what is not, and what teachers can do to improve their own practice.

It is important for educators who read this book to understand that the routines we suggest emerge from the existing literature on effective classrooms. The most highly regarded research and investigations into effective classrooms are independent of the paradigm that arises from current educational policy. So, whether the Common Core State Standards (CCSS) are retained, modified, postponed, or eliminated, there exists a timeless quality to effective use of classroom time. Simply put, good teaching practice is independent of prevailing policy initiatives, and the routines we suggest will be useful no matter which paradigm is in place when you read this book.

How Can You Collaborate with High Expectations in Mind?

We suggest that faculty in the elementary school engage in exploring the local, state, and national (or Common Core) standards, if applicable. Make sure to read all curricular and standards documents both vertically (to see the expectations for one grade level) and horizontally (to see the grade progressions from kindergarten all the way to fifth grade). Teachers of students who struggle, students with disabilities, and students who are English learners now have a resource that helps them backmap to earlier grade-level expectations so they can plan on building appropriate foundational knowledge and skills that students might lack. By the same token, teachers of advanced or gifted learners may look at target expectations in upcoming grades and plan for enrichment based on those standards.

What Is Going on in a SWRLing Classroom?

We believe the twenty-first-century literacy classroom is one in which students SWRL every day—that is, speak, write, read, and listen. We have seen this acronym in several blog posts and recognize it as a powerful synthesizing idea: it reminds us to balance what we must do each day in our classrooms.

As Jan Burkins and Kim Yaris (2013) blogged after the 2013 International Reading Association Conference, "The best readers and writers are the ones who have had the most practice. How much time do your students spend *actually* reading and writing?" They argue for establishing routines for practicing the four language skills—reading, writing, speaking, and listening—as well as for developing academic language proficiency. If, *daily*, you prompt students to collaborate, ask them to interact with text, and require that they write and communicate ideas clearly, precisely, and with supporting evidence, these skills will strengthen over time because of the consistency of the *routines that you have put into place*.

Why Routines?

Routines are deliberate procedures that a teacher establishes in his or her classroom to enhance a sense of community and to offer structure to all learners. Fisher and Frey (2009) suggest that the routines that we choose for our classrooms will "over time become the habits of a self-directed learner" (63). They become the shared habits of our classroom communities. Students come to know that *this is the way we do things around here*. Kirby and Crovitz (2012) acknowledge the power of routines and rituals, stating, "it's relatively easy to develop routines for what we like to do, but the more difficult tasks require the discipline of routine if they are to occur regularly and reliably" (68). Many others validate our beliefs about the need for routines. For example, Maureen Boyd and Sylvia Smyntek-Gworek (2012) assert,

> In classroom communities where literacy events are well-defined regular practices,
> teachers establish routines that not only provide a structured space with clear
> expectations and norms but also opportunity for creative application of what is expected.
> When students feel safe and valued, they willingly engage, lead, and take risks.   (6)

Further, Ron Ritchhart, Mark Church, and Karin Morrison (2011) discuss the need for making thinking visible through routines, which in turn may be viewed as *tools* (for promoting thinking), as *structures* (to support and scaffold learning), and as *patterns of behavior* (to establish and maintain a context for learning).

So what does it mean to have routines? It means that students can count on certain structures to take place regularly and can expect them to be part of business as usual. For example, students may learn that upon entering this classroom, they will regularly complete entrance cards or write

Figure I.1 Letter to Parents About Class Routines

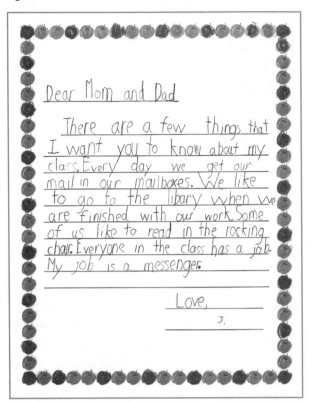

> Dear Mom and Dad
>
> There are a few things that I want you to know about my class. Every day we get our mail in our mailboxes. We like to go to the libary when we are finished with our work. Some of us like to read in the rocking chair. Everyone in the class has a job. My job is a messenger.
>
> Love,
>
> J.

in their academic journals to summarize yesterday's lesson or last night's homework. They may understand that if an interesting question comes up in this classroom during discussion, they can post their question on a bulletin board or the Question Kiosk (see Chapter 1), knowing there will be ongoing opportunities for independent research to discover the answer or to further explore the question. They may look forward to coming to this class because they know they can count on working and talking with a partner because that's a regular part of each lesson. The culture of your classroom will depend upon the expectations that you set and the choices that you make when establishing routines. See Figure I.1 for a second grader's letter to his parents showing how much he values the routines established in his class.

What Are Best Practices Based on Research and Evidence?

While some Common Core advocates call for cold reading of texts, minimal text-to-self connections, and few personal opinions, teachers should not forego what they intrinsically know works with learners. There is seminal research to support activating prior knowledge before reading a new text (Hayes and Tierney 1982; Rosenblatt 1993). Researchers and practitioners also suggest that learners become engaged in a text by making text-to-self connections and making statements of personal opinion (Keene and Zimmermann 1997, 2007). These personal connections lead to greater interaction with the text and, ultimately, greater comprehension for the reader. Struggling learners, in particular, are more successful when teachers encourage them to make these types of connections.

So, how do teachers reconcile the demands of standards-based instruction with what they believe is best practice for teaching English language arts to elementary school students? Teachers should continue to use their clinical expertise, build upon and continue to expand their professional skill sets supported by current research, and provide a *commonsense* approach to literacy instruction. We support our claims with numerous research-based instructional practices, resources we adapted, created, or observed in teachers' classrooms, and authentic input from teachers and coaches around the United States.

How This Book Is Organized

We organized this book into five chapters. With the exception of the first, each chapter focuses on one literacy skill. Keep in mind, however, that although Chapters 2–5 are each dedicated to one literacy skill, many of the routines we suggest engage multiple literacy skills. Students do not develop literacy skills in isolation.

In Chapter 1, we make a case for establishing routines that help activate, assess, and build students' background knowledge in order to maximize their learning of new skills and information. Chapter 2 provides evidence for why reading routines should include whole-class, small-group, and independent reading activities, all of which will lead to greater student engagement, active peer discussions and collaboration, choice opportunities, and student-driven learning. In Chapter 3, we address writing routines that support and propel student thinking and learning. Our routines promote student creativity even as learners are engaged in daily writing practices, mastery of the stages of the writing process, and note taking. In Chapter 4, we offer speaking and listening routines that encourage students to participate in whole-class discussions, talk with others as a means to understand and collaborate in small groups, as well as make group and individual presentations. Chapter 5 encourages teachers to use academic language routines at the word, sentence, and text levels so as to create a culture of robust vocabulary development, curiosity about words and syntax, and proficient use of academic language while listening, speaking, reading, and writing.

All of the chapters have a similar internal organization. Each starts with a brief overview of the goals of the chapter, followed by a graphic organizer that gives you a visual summary of the routines. Then we provide you with research that supports our beliefs and contentions for the suggested instructional routines that follow. We briefly discuss the demands of the CCSS and explore the connections between the standards and our routines. We introduce several routines that we consider essential, some to be practiced daily and others to be used on a weekly or biweekly regular basis. Each chapter also includes a "Scaffolding Toolbox" section. In these sections, you will find a variety of resources to help build essential language and literacy skills in your students. The tools will scaffold and support the routines presented in the chapters and provide access for any learner who needs them. A summary chart featured at the end of each chapter offers recommendations for differentiating instruction for English learners, students with disabilities, and advanced learners. Peppered throughout the text are photographs taken in classrooms we have visited, coach's notes, teacher-2-teacher vignettes, essential resources (under the heading "Check This Out"), samples of student work, and charts for classroom use.

A companion website provides easy access to a list of templates for reference and reproduction. To access the online templates, visit **heinemann.com/products/E05661.aspx** and click on the Companion Resources tab.

Why This Book?

In this book, we offer suggestions for establishing routines that will build consistency, trust, and a sense of safety in your classroom. By showing students what they can expect and count on, you will establish a healthy environment for learning. As mentioned earlier, many of the routines in this book interweave multiple skills. For example, when students are reading, they will be expected to speak and listen to peers as they make meaning from text. In addition, it is likely that after a close reading, students will write brief summaries that require the appropriate use of academic language. With daily and weekly routines that integrate multiple skills, you can feel confident that you are providing instruction that will build skills for students to be successful in school.

While standards and mandated or prescribed curricula tell us *what* we must do, this book will help you decide *how* to establish the necessary routines to do it. Whereas many of the current publications suggest the skills, habits, and dispositions that students will need upon graduation, this book will offer you dozens of routines that will contextualize the standards and answer the question, "What does this look like in my classroom?" It will explore the research behind the routines, providing you with an understanding of *why* certain routines will lead to better learning. It will show you why routines are a necessary part of every teacher's repertoire if we are to help students achieve greater success.

We provide specific suggestions for each set of routines (listening, speaking, reading, writing, and language routines, as well as those for building background knowledge). Some of the recommendations are low-prep; others will require more time to create and implement. You've probably used some of these routines, but you may find a new way to accommodate a specific group of learners.

Contrary to the belief that routines can lead to dull, repetitive, unimaginative, scripted ways of teaching, we believe that the routines here will not only lay the framework for predictable structures, instructional consistency, and skill building but also provide plenty of opportunity for teacher autonomy, creative expression, and nurturing the desire to learn in each child. We, along with thousands of teachers with whom we have worked throughout our combined more than sixty years in the field of education, are convinced that routines can contribute to productive and joyful learning.

Chapter 1

"Background knowledge simply has to become an instructional focus if we want to help students make sense of school. We will lose a generation of learners if we don't act now."

(Fisher and Frey 2009, 20)

BUILDING BACKGROUND KNOWLEDGE

Building background knowledge "should be at the top of any list of interventions intended to enhance student achievement."

(Marzano 2004, 4)

Overview

In this chapter, we

- summarize research support for the background knowledge routines we present
- examine the expectations of the Common Core State Standards for background knowledge
- establish routines for *assessing, activating,* and *building* background knowledge
- present examples, templates, and classroom vignettes along with recommendations from coaches to support the building of background knowledge
- present the anticipation guide as a tool for the scaffolding toolbox
- offer differentiation ideas for building background knowledge for English learners, students with disabilities, and advanced learners.

Building Background Knowledge Routines at a Glance

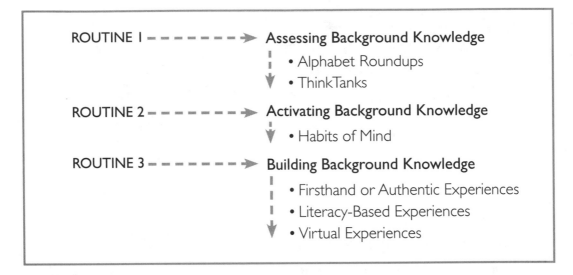

ROUTINE 1 - - - - - - - -➤ **Assessing Background Knowledge**
- Alphabet Roundups
- ThinkTanks

ROUTINE 2 - - - - - - - -➤ **Activating Background Knowledge**
- Habits of Mind

ROUTINE 3 - - - - - - - -➤ **Building Background Knowledge**
- Firsthand or Authentic Experiences
- Literacy-Based Experiences
- Virtual Experiences

What Does the Research Say About Building Background Knowledge?

According to the *Report of the National Reading Panel* (NICHD 2000), "the data suggest that text comprehension is enhanced when readers actively relate the ideas represented in print to their own knowledge and experience and construct mental representations in memory" (14). E. D. Hirsch (2006) reminds us that "the spoken and unspoken taken together constitute meaning. Without this relevant, unspoken background knowledge, we can't understand text" (39). In addition, there is ample research to confirm the popular notion that new information is more easily retained and retrievable if it is linked in our minds with something we already know (Sousa 2001). Clearly, the research supports building background knowledge as a means to better comprehension.

In *What Works in Schools: Translating Research into Action*, Marzano (2003) describes the relationship between learned intelligence and background knowledge. He builds on the work of Cattell and Ackerman, who differentiate between "fluid intelligence and crystallized intelligence" (as cited in Marzano 2003, 133). Fluid intelligence is assumed to be innate and is exemplified by mental procedures and faculties such as abstract reasoning, working memory capacity, and working memory efficiency. Crystallized intelligence, on the other hand, is demonstrated by knowledge of facts, generalizations, and principles—that is, learned knowledge about the world. It is not innate; it can be learned, and it is more strongly correlated to academic achievement. So, when we enhance students' background knowledge (learned knowledge about a specific domain), it is as if we are enhancing their crystallized intelligence, their knowledge about the world. We are, therefore, laying the foundation for greater academic achievement.

In a different line of research, on "dual coding," James Clark and Allan Paivio (1991) describe two ways that we remember: in words (linguistic representations) and in pictures (imagery representations). This theory suggests that these "memory records" are accompanied by a tag or label, in other words, vocabulary terms. Marzano (2003) interprets this accumulation of memory records with tags as the gathering of crystallized knowledge. Further, he suggests, since our vocabulary knowledge is a good indication of our crystallized intelligence, it behooves us to build our students' vocabulary.

Activating prior knowledge is regarded as a research-validated approach for improving children's memory and comprehension of text (Pressley et al. 1989). Additionally, the *Report of the National Reading Panel* (NICHD 2000) shows that readers "access their background knowledge to construct meaning from text. They retain this information in memory and update it as they interpret more text" (2–107). In his research on bilingual and bicultural youngsters, Luis Moll (1992) makes an important contribution regarding *funds of knowledge*, which he describes as "essential cultural practices and bodies of knowledge and information that households use to survive, to get ahead, or to thrive" (21). He suggests that with poor, minority, and bilingual students, we must consider a more sociocultural approach to literacy instruction and background knowledge. That is, we should involve students in socially meaningful tasks that take full advantage of their first-language abilities and make good use of their background knowledge. It is likely they bring with them a foundation for learning based upon prior experiences with their grandparents, immediate and extended family, neighbors, community, and culture.

There are many reasons to have students activate prior knowledge in order to make meaning during learning, not the least of which is that "whenever the learner's working memory decides that an item does not make sense or have meaning, the probability of it being stored is extremely low" (Sousa 2001, 47). David Sousa reminds us just how important background knowledge is to comprehension and retention, and why, if students don't have background knowledge in a particular area, it is incumbent upon us to build it. Marzano, Pickering, and Heflebower (2011) also acknowledge the importance of connecting new learning to students' lives.

What Does the Common Core Say About Background Knowledge?

At first glance, it seems the CCSS do not have much to say about building background knowledge. However, after you examine the research and literature regarding the importance of background knowledge to comprehension, you simply cannot ignore its relevance.

In fact, when David Coleman (2011), one of the lead authors of the CCSS, made a presentation (that was videotaped) suggesting that teachers simply present text to students without activating prior knowledge or generating a purpose for reading, there was a hue and cry from teachers and researchers around the country. In an article for ASCD's *Educational Leadership*, Timothy Shanahan (2012–2013) points out that, as a result of this pushback, Coleman and Pimentel (2012) retreated from their original stance and issued a revision of their position, retracting their admonition against pre-reading (Gewertz 2012). But, as Shanahan (2012–2013) notes, the damage was done, and many teachers and administrators are not even aware of this reversal.

To be clear, there is no longer a warning against activating prior knowledge as we proceed with the Common Core State Standards. We are pleased that the lead authors of the CCSS chose to revise their stance because we believe, as do many others, that setting a purpose for reading by activating prior knowledge ultimately leads to deeper comprehension. In fact, "the brain is biologically programmed to attend to information that has strong emotional content first" (Wolfe 2010, 120). Having students make personal connections to what they are reading can activate strong emotions, making the reading more relevant and, therefore, more memorable.

That said, since close reading (or multiple rereadings to deconstruct the text) is part of the CCSS, you can and should allow students to occasionally wrestle at first with text on their own. In this scenario, you can be assured that your students will be building background knowledge as they reread the same text multiple times, reflecting in writing and discussing format and meaning with peers. However, since students will be confronted with unfamiliar text on their state assessments, with little time for multiple readings or peer reflection, classroom reading practice should also provide them with opportunities to read and interpret text independently.

COACH'S NOTES

Remind your students that in this class we know how important prior knowledge, or background knowledge, is to what we are about to learn. Tell them that it's the glue that will help their new understandings "stick." Then, whenever you begin a new chapter, unit, or concept, start with a routine that assesses and/or activates the background knowledge of your learners.

Building Background Routines

As documented by research—as well as evidenced by successful classroom practices—routines for *assessing, activating,* and *building* background knowledge are necessary for good instruction. While there are many ways to engage with background knowledge, the first commitment you must make is to regularly create opportunities to assess, activate, and build background knowledge in most (if not all) of your lessons. Your students should learn that in your class you will always begin with what they already know. From there, the class will look to fill in gaps in knowledge, make connections, and ask questions about the new information. Ultimately, the students will build new background knowledge through their thinking processes, by their engagement, and because of these classroom routines that remind everyone how important background knowledge is to learning.

When Doug Fisher and Nancy Frey (2009) describe developing background knowledge, they suggest that we "teach with the learning cycle in mind, using an instructional framework that supports how humans learn" (21). Their structured model for teaching (Fisher and Frey 2008), based on the gradual release of responsibility model of comprehension (Pearson and Gallagher 1983), can help guide us to strategically plan our lessons. These lessons should activate and build background knowledge throughout each phase of instruction and include the following elements:

- *a focus lesson,* where the teacher establishes a purpose, models actions or processes, and conducts think-alouds
- *guided instruction,* where the teacher uses cues, prompts, and questions to scaffold learner comprehension
- *collaborative learning,* where students work with partners or in small groups to synthesize background knowledge with new learning
- *independent learning,* where students use what they have learned—now part of their background knowledge—in a new way or continue to build background knowledge by reading or researching further.

These phases are not necessarily implemented in lockstep but, rather, in any sequence necessary to build the background knowledge needed by your learners.

ROUTINE 1 — Assessing Background Knowledge

The first routine you should establish is assessing the background knowledge of your learners before beginning a new unit or concept. Without an assessment, you are unlikely to target exactly what students need in order to make sense of their new learning. This formative assessment should drive your instruction, so that you know which gaps to fill and which students are ready for a challenge. When you assess your learners, you will also be activating their prior knowledge.

When we begin a lesson, most of us brainstorm the concept or topic with students by asking verbal questions at different levels of complexity, by having students complete a K-W-L chart (what you *know*; what you *want* to know; what you've *learned*), or by asking students to reflect in a free-write (see Chapter 3 for a more detailed discussion of freewrites). These quick and easy assessments will give you a view into student misconceptions, vocabulary that students already know, and prior knowledge that students possess. The answer to the critical question, "What do my students already know about this topic or concept?" should inform your instruction.

Doug Fisher and Nancy Frey (2009) suggest additional means for assessing background knowledge, including *opinionnaires* (teacher-provided statements to which students respond that they strongly agree,

agree, disagree, or strongly disagree), *cloze assessments* (essential paragraphs from the textbook with important words left out for students to fill in), and *anticipation guides* (teacher-provided statements based on core knowledge of a unit that students read and judge as true or false). (See the "Scaffolding Toolbox" section later in this chapter for more information on anticipation guides.) Assessments like these will give you a great deal of information about what students know, and they'll help you determine what types of discussions and learning experiences you need to plan for the upcoming unit.

Teacher-2-Teacher

I assess my learners throughout a unit by collecting data—writing samples and homework, exit cards, quick writes and student-generated illustrations, and a checklist of subskills for a particular skill that we are working on. (For example, if we are working on the skill of writing a good paragraph, I use a checklist that includes subskills like indenting, writing a topic sentence, including at least two elaborated details, utilizing good word choice, and using proper punctuation and capitalization.) When I notice that several students are having trouble with the same subskill, I pull a small group together for a minilesson. Meanwhile, the rest of the students continue to work on their reading or writing independently.   **Grade 2 teacher**

ALPHABET ROUNDUPS

One way to assess or activate background knowledge is an alphabet roundup (see Figures 1.1 and 1.2), adapted from Buehl's (2001) sequential roundtable alphabet. You can have your students sit in small groups and give them each a grid with an alphabet taxonomy on it (letters A–Z). Next to each letter

Figure 1.1 Alphabet Roundup About New York

Name: Sara		Topic: New York		
Alphabet Round-Up				
AtLand tic Adrinondale	Bay Border	Climate Coast	Drumlin	East Equater
Forest Finger	Glacier	Harbor Huddson	landform lakes	J
K	Landform	Mouth Mohak Mountain	Nroth	Ocean
Plain Plants	Quote	River	Soarse States States	Tributary
U	Valley	Weather West	X	Y Z

should be enough room to write a term or phrase that comes to mind in relation to the topic. Time them for one minute while each student writes as many words or phrases as he or she can think of. Then, have the students pass their grids clockwise. Reading what their group members have recorded helps spark students' memories and associations. Encourage students not to write the same word on each grid because this will encourage them to read their peers' words and to make new connections. Continue in this way until all group members have had a chance to record on all of the grids. Then give each group five minutes to discuss and then write a group summary statement that will give you a view of what prior knowledge the group members have as well as what misconceptions they hold.

Figure 1.2 Alphabet Roundup About Insects

Name: Aidan		Topic: Insects		
Amazing vision	Bugs	Chrysalis	Dragonfly	Exoskeleton
Fly	Grow	Hoverfly	Insects	Jumps
Kill	Lava	Metamor-phosis	Nocturnal	Odd
Pupa	Quiet	Run	Six legs	Toxic
Unusual	Very still	Wings	X	Yellow
Zoo				

COACH'S NOTES

When you use the alphabet roundup, you might prefer to have your students within each group work with partners to record their ideas. Each pair would pass its grid to another pair within the group. Using partners is especially useful with younger students, ELLs, or other students who might find this task too open-ended. Allowing students to work with a buddy is one way to scaffold struggling learners, and the conversation they have builds their oral language skills as well.

THINKTANK

We have often used a ThinkTank as another effective approach for assessing and activating prior knowledge. We give students the opportunity to put their heads together and discuss, record, and/or illustrate the knowledge and understanding that they already have collectively about a specific topic or problem. Depending upon the size of your class, you might divide it into small groups of four to five students and send them to different corners of the room. (If you have more than twenty students, try to include additional locations for small groups to meet, perhaps in the middle of the room, at a table outside your door, or on a carpet.) At each location, the group members will brainstorm and record what they know about a topic or solve a math word problem on chart paper.

This collaborative activity gets students out of their seats and engages them in content-focused tasks. Two advantages of the ThinkTank are that it is easy to implement and it takes only five minutes. After five minutes, choose one student from each group to share the group members' collective assumptions. (Students can revisit their charts after the unit is over and make any corrections needed in another color to show what they now know to be true.)

You can also use a ThinkTank as a *summative* group assessment, at the end of a learning experience, instead of before it. Given five minutes, the small groups synthesize what they have learned about a topic, recording the key understandings from this unit.

Teacher-2-Teacher

When I use a ThinkTank as a summative assessment for my fourth graders, I have each group write for five minutes on its chart in one color. Then I rotate the groups through a gallery walk (a reading of the other groups' charts), during which they borrow ideas and take notes (on group clipboards) of what they may have forgotten when recording on their own charts. Returning back to its own chart, each group records in a second color any important ideas it previously overlooked.

Grade 4 teacher

COACH'S NOTES

Be sure to use the ThinkTank charts, with their rich vocabulary and content information, for follow-up writing activities. You can ask your students to use the recorded details to write a summary of the topic, to compose an opinion piece, to compare two different ideas or places, or to create an informative or explanatory text.

 ROUTINE 2 **Activating Background Knowledge**

Just because you've assessed your students and found that they possess a certain amount of background knowledge does not mean that they will choose to use it. Unless they have practiced activating their background knowledge as a regular routine in their classroom (e.g., with activities like alphabet roundups and ThinkTanks), many of our students are likely to be passive during a learning experience, preferring to wait and be told how the current lesson connects to other concepts they might already know. Art Costa and Bena Kallick (2000), in their well-known series of books on the habits of mind, remind us that certain habits must be practiced over and over so that learners are "more disposed to draw upon the habits when they are faced with uncertain or challenging situations" (*Book II: Activating and Engaging Habits of Mind*, xiii). Among these sixteen habits are striving for accuracy, persisting, questioning and posing problems, applying past knowledge to new situations, and thinking and communicating with clarity and precision.

In schools where Costa and Kallick (2000) have seen success with students activating their own habits of mind, students talk about, reflect upon, and illustrate the habits of mind that they are focusing on in their personal logs and journals. We recommend choosing even two or three of these habits and cultivating them throughout the year to help learners become more self-directed and responsible. Have your students identify which attributes are exemplified by characters in books they are reading or by historical and biographical figures they are learning about. Talk about what the habit would look like and sound like when being used.

 CHECK THIS OUT

Costa and Kallick's (2000) Habits of Mind: A Developmental Series will provide you with great ideas for teaching students to engage and sustain the types of dispositions needed when learners are confronted by challenges or new problems to solve. Without these habits of thought, as Dewey (1933) called them, students are more likely to call upon what they already know, rather than ponder new possibilities. The New Generation of Science Standards call for a shift to problem solving in all science activities. Costa and Kallick's habits of mind will evoke the kind of thinking necessary to engage in this type of pursuit.

For more information, see these related websites:

        www.instituteforhabitsofmind.com
        www.habitsofmind.org
        www.artcostacentre.com/index.htm
        www.mindfulbydesign.com
        www.ascd.org/Publications/ascd-authors/art-costa.aspx

---

ROUTINE 3 **Building Background Knowledge**

Once you have assessed and activated your students' background knowledge, you may feel challenged if you discover that many of your learners lack sufficient prior knowledge to make sense of an upcoming reading or unit. Now you must plan for routines throughout the year that will develop the building of background knowledge. Because many teachers work in schools with great diversity and a wide range of learner readiness, we focus much of our attention in this chapter on effective routines for building background knowledge.

The best way to build background knowledge is to have a *building-wide* initiative for doing so. Since building background knowledge requires many years, your efforts will have the greatest impact if they are sustained throughout all grade levels. This approach, of course, requires time and planning with colleagues because the best plan is one that requires much reflection and is the focus of building-wide conversations, faculty meetings, and student assembly programs. If you have, or can establish, a PLC (professional learning community; DuFour and Eaker 1998) within your building, by all means, bring this discussion to that group (Fisher, Frey, and Uline 2013). However, if this is not possible, there is plenty that you can do on your own, or with just one other colleague, to develop routines for building your students' background knowledge.

Another way to enhance students' background knowledge is to educate families. At back-to-school nights, at family nights, or in newsletters sent home, tell parents about the many ways they can help their children do better in school. Send a checklist or a one-page description of activities that can boost the learning curve. Recommend to parents that they talk with their children during dinner, in the evening, and while on errands in the neighborhood. Suggest trips to the library, the post office, the grocery store, museums, the bank, the park, and other community sites. These behaviors and actions will increase student vocabulary and provide background schemata for their reading and new learning in school. See Figure 1.3 for a photo of a first grader during a visit to a local fire station.

Figure 1.3 A Visit to the Fire Station

COACH'S NOTES

If a school-wide approach to building background knowledge is not possible, see if you can find just one other colleague in your grade level to work with you. Once other teachers see your students' greater enthusiasm for learning, they will likely want to join you in establishing background knowledge–building routines for their own students.

You can build background knowledge in many ways. We have classified the approaches into three categories: firsthand or authentic experiences, literacy-based experiences, and virtual experiences. When focusing on the routine of building background knowledge, you will want to vary the approach from time to time to meet the needs of different types of learners.

FIRSTHAND OR AUTHENTIC EXPERIENCES

In *Building Background Knowledge for Academic Achievement*, Marzano (2004) reports that the simplest way to build background knowledge is to provide students firsthand experiences that are academically enriching. When you experience something personally, your brain records the experience in several places, encoding the feelings, the smells, the images, the words, and so on. What Marzano refers to as the *direct* approach is the most straightforward—since it includes experiences like mentoring and field trips to museums, art galleries, and places of interest in your community and far beyond—and it also connects to multiple disciplines, life experiences, and literacy development. In *Brain Matters*, Patricia Wolfe, whose work focuses mostly on educational implications of neuroscience and cognitive science, notes that

> concrete experience is one of the best ways to make strong, long-lasting neural connections. . . . [This type of experience] . . . engages more of the senses and uses multiple pathways to store—and therefore more ways to recall—information. This is probably why we remember what we have experienced much better than what we have read or heard. (2001, 118)

Unfortunately, for most schools, these types of experiences are unobtainable because of cost.

One alternative to taking field trips away from school is to bring the outside world into your classroom. There are many cultural and health organizations, animal exhibits and community groups, local farms and museums that can arrange to bring live animals, traveling exhibits, multisensory presentations, assembly programs, and seminars to you. See Figure 1.4 for a photo of a goat visiting an inner-city school so students could find out about *urban farming*.

Students can learn a great deal from visiting experts and their highly engaging, interactive sessions. Your PTA might also sponsor an annual career fair in which parents and community members set up information booths or tables in the cafeteria, gym, or another large multipurpose room for the entire school community to visit. Ask guests to share their tools of the trade, educational background, and details about the daily routines and the requirements of their jobs. Teachers can help students prepare grade-appropriate questions for visitors. Provide students with maps to help them navigate the fair and make the visit more productive.

Figure 1.4 A Goat in an Urban School

Teacher-2-Teacher

Whenever possible, I try to offer students authentic learning experiences. For example, after teaching a unit on the life cycle of owls, I contacted the Theodore Roosevelt Bird Sanctuary of Oyster Bay, New York, to arrange a visit of various live birds to the classroom. This was an effective way for students to apply all of the learned knowledge about these fascinating creatures and make sense of the information. The benefits of this visit were tremendous. Students were engaged throughout the unit, in anticipation of meeting these live creatures. Another example of bringing authentic learning experiences into the classroom occurred during a character education study. As a strong believer in giving back to the community, I was looking for a way to highlight the positive power of volunteers within our community of Long Island, New York. I contacted the Guide Dog Foundation of Suffolk County to arrange a school visit. Two volunteers donated their time and brought two guide dogs to our school. The volunteers explained why and how the dogs were trained and allowed students to experience what it would be like to be blind and use a guide dog. The chosen students were blindfolded and led around the auditorium by the guide dogs. In a class meeting after the assembly, the students expressed to me how they never really knew what the guide dogs did when they saw them in public. Students also shared how their compassion and empathy for people with disabilities increased as a result of the visit. This kind of learning can't happen through lessons taught solely via textbook or computer. When students are exposed to authentic experiences, the benefits are immeasurable. Ellen Tournour, grade 5 teacher

LITERACY-BASED EXPERIENCES

A literacy-based approach integrates language, reading, and writing to help students make sense of their world and to build content knowledge. It involves the following:

- **wide reading programs (like sustained silent reading [SSR] and Drop Everything and Read [DEAR]), as well as daily classroom read-alouds**
- **vocabulary building**
- **research experiences.**

Marzano (2004) also suggests an *indirect* approach to building background knowledge. Similar to our literacy-based approach, his indirect approach includes wide reading programs and vocabulary building and costs much less, in the long run, than do field trips. You may have to purchase reading materials, but many schools have overflowing book rooms that can be mined for this purpose, as well as classroom or library budgets that can assist in these efforts. Consider asking your school's PTA to support your reading program by collecting and donating gently used books or by providing funds to purchase additional high-interest reading material. Then you can create leveled literary book bags developed around content themes to be covered in class. Send them home for reading and sharing with parents, especially with those who might not live in a literature-rich environment.

Since reading is the fastest route (after firsthand experiences) to building background knowledge, we should pay attention to what the reading experts have to add to this discussion. Lucy Calkins and her colleagues (2012) offer a clear picture of what we must do to enhance the reading routines in our classrooms in order to do the challenging work ahead of us. They suggest we conduct frequent read-alouds and model our thinking for students. This builds students' background knowledge about how to approach and deconstruct a text and how to make sense of what they are reading. Along with Allington and Gabriel (2012), we urge you to continue to model fluent, expressive reading using read-alouds to students in *all* grades.

Students need to spend a huge amount of time reading during school, because for many of them, school is the only place they will receive instruction on how to read, listen to fluent read-alouds, or even be encouraged to read. They need to receive direct instruction in reading skills and then a chance to apply these skills to books they are reading independently or in book clubs. And teachers need to provide them with a great deal of feedback and encourage further exploration of the text through discussion and writing. As you can see from these suggestions, reading, writing, and speaking and listening are interwoven in these approaches and work synergistically to build background knowledge in students.

Wide Reading: SSR

Improvement in reading works like that in any other skill: the more students read, the better readers they become. We must create routines for wide reading throughout their day so they can use these literacy experiences to enhance their background knowledge (Allington 1984). The easiest way to insert a block of time in a school's schedule is to set aside a time when everyone in the building is expected to read for SSR. After completing a meta-analysis of over two dozen

SSR studies, Pilgreen (2000) suggests several guidelines for making this type of program a success, including the following:

- Have lots of great reading material at all levels (like comics, poems, newspapers, nonfiction texts, menus, magazines, and travel brochures) so that students can choose what they want to read.
- Do not tie SSR to high levels of accountability (no assignments, just occasional conferences with the teacher).
- Provide staff training (to share ideas for best management of the program).

COACH'S NOTES

During SSR, be sure to offer a wide range of reading materials at many different reading levels. In this way, students can read comfortably at their level, and SSR won't become just another occasion where reading means "failure to understand" for our struggling learners. Remember, this is an opportunity to help students develop a love of reading because they are choosing what they want to read and the reading level is appropriate.

Wide Reading: Independent Reading

Independent reading time is another way to build a wide reading routine into your classroom. During this time, your students can build background knowledge about a specific domain, topic, or concept by selecting from among teacher-chosen reading materials (most often leveled for reading readiness). For example, if you are a first-grade teacher selecting materials for students beginning a unit on the family, you might place the following on a bookshelf for independent reading: stories (e.g., Little Bear books [Minarik and Sendak 1992], *Just Grandma and Me* [Mayer 2001], *Are You My Mother?* [Eastman 1960]), poems (e.g., "As I Was Going to St. Ives," Jack Prelutsky family poems), nonfiction selections (e.g., *Families* [Kuklin 2006, Morris 2000], *The New Baby* [Meyer 2001]), family trees organizers (several diagrams displaying different family makeups), and photographs (of different types of families). (See also the recommended resources under "Check This Out.") During the same week, you might read aloud an excerpt from *The Wonderful Wizard of Oz* (Baum 2014), sharing about Uncle Henry, Aunt Em, and Dorothy as a family unit, and a selection of multicultural family fairy tales, including *Lon Po Po* (Young 1996). Your strategic lesson planning could include a daily ten- to fifteen-minute independent reading time when students would choose their own selections to read and build their background knowledge about different types of families. After each independent reading session, allow students to share something new that they have learned. This will build enthusiasm for future reading and build students' background knowledge at the same time. As Doug Buehl (2011) also points out, "Wide reading is particularly instrumental in building the academic background knowledge that is a prerequisite for learning within the various content disciplines" (150), especially once students reach the upper-elementary grades.

Depending on your students' readiness levels, readings for a family unit might include some of the following fiction, poetry, and nonfiction selections for independent reading or read-alouds.

Fiction

Ada, A. F. 2002. *I Love Saturdays y domingos*. New York: Atheneum.

Cox, J. 2003. *My Family Plays Music*. New York: Holiday House.

Holmberg, B. R. 2008. *A Day with Dad*. Cambridge, MA: Candlewick.

Krishnaswami, U. 2006. *Bringing Asha Home*. New York: Lee and Low.

Lindsay, J. W. 1991. *Do I Have a Daddy? A Story About a Single-Parent Child*. Buena Park, CA: Morning Glory.

Newman, L. 2009. *Heather Has Two Mommies*. Los Angeles: Alyson Wonderland.

Parr, T. 2003. *The Family Book*. New York: Little, Brown Books.

Rylant, C. 1985. *The Relatives Came*. New York: Bradbury

Weninger, B. 1995. *Good-Bye, Daddy!* New York: North-South Books.

Williams, V. B. 1982. *A Chair for My Mother*. New York: Greenwillow Books.

Nonfiction

Adamson, H. 2009. *Families in Many Cultures*. North Mankato, MN: Pebble Plus.

Cole, J. 1999. *The New Baby at Your House*. New York: HarperCollins.

Kent, S. 2000. *Let's Talk About Living with a Grandparent*. New York: Rosen.

Kuklin, S. 2006. *Families*. New York: Hyperion Books.

Morris, A. 2000. *Families*. New York: HarperCollins.

Nelson, J. 2006. *Families Change: A Book for Children Experiencing Termination of Parental Rights*. Minneapolis: Free Spirit.

Rotner, S., and S. Kelly. 2003a. *Lots of Dads*. Brookfield, CT: Millbrook.

_____. 2003b. *Lots of Grandparents*. Brookfield, CT: Millbrook.

_____. 2003c. *Lots of Moms*. Brookfield, CT: Millbrook.

Skutch, R. 1997. *Who's in a Family?* Berkeley, CA: Tricycle.

Poetry

Fletcher, R. 1999. *Relatively Speaking: Poems About Family*. London: Orchard Books.

Greenfield, E. 2008. *Brothers and Sisters: Family Poems*. New York: Amistad.

Hoberman, M. A., and M. Hafner. 2001. *Fathers, Mothers, Sisters, Brothers: A Collection of Family Poems*. New York: Little, Brown Books for Young Readers.

Vocabulary Building

Vocabulary building is another route to building background knowledge. A review of the meta-analysis of vocabulary studies that Marzano (2004) completed concludes that there is a strong relationship between vocabulary knowledge and background knowledge. The oft-cited studies by Hart and Risley (1995, 2003) found that, unfortunately, vocabulary is highly correlated with family income and socioeconomic status (SES). What is most disturbing about this report is that these gaps grow even wider as children grow older. So, when students enter our classrooms, they come with a wide range of literacy skills and background knowledge that continues to widen over the years. Zacarian (2013) describes positive early literacy behaviors as routines "that are like little suitcases ready to carry into school" (33). Now, imagine that some of your young learners from diverse, often impoverished backgrounds, enter your classroom, and instead of carrying *literacy suitcases* filled with prior academic experiences, they carry knapsacks or backpacks filled with oral storytelling, rich language, and their own cultural traditions. What they carry is not necessarily acknowledged in our schools. How frustrating for these children, who often feel so lost. How frustrating for you, as well, as you search for ways to validate what these children know in order to use their experiences for building the necessary background knowledge for success in school.

It is never too late to build a learner's vocabulary. Do your best to tie the new words to experiences that your diverse learners may have already had. Don't assume, for example, that because some of your students don't speak English well, they can't make a connection from one of their previous life experiences to the concept you are teaching. You may need to search for pictures and illustrations from their own cultures that tell stories and help build the connection to new English vocabulary. (For additional information and routines about vocabulary building, see Chapter 5).

Research Experiences

Besides using wide reading and vocabulary building to build background knowledge, we suggest that you incorporate multiple, short research experiences into your curriculum. How many times have your students asked wonderfully intriguing questions during class, and your only wish was that there were enough time to explore the answers? As we feel more constrained by school schedules and curriculum demands, many of us are frustrated that our students' curiosity and wonder are being brushed aside. By embracing these questions and providing opportunities for students to research and explore the ones they are interested in, you will be laying the foundation for lifelong curiosity and, ultimately, learning.

The Question Kiosk is a way for you to honor your students' spirit of inquiry and encourage them to question the world around them. Tied to the routine of building background information, the Question Kiosk invites your students to record and post their questions each day (or as they come up) on a classroom "kiosk" (a bulletin board, easel chart paper, dry-erase board, or project trifold). Create a chart where you can record questions your students generate. Tell your students that there will be several opportunities for them to research answers to the questions that intrigue them the most. See Figure 1.5 for an "I Wonder" chart collaboratively created by curious third graders.

Students wonder about many things every day. It's not unusual to hear young learners say, "Why is the sky blue?" "I wonder how they build skyscrapers," "Are all snakes poisonous?" "I wonder why penguins are never cold," or "I wonder why sometimes we can see the moon during the day and sometimes we can't." As early as kindergarten, our young students can be expected to participate in shared research and writing projects as well as to gather information to answer a question, with guidance and support from adults. In order to encourage our learners' curiosity and inquiry, these short research opportunities should continue throughout the grades.

By acknowledging their questions and encouraging them to create additional inquiries, we increase student engagement, raise students' awareness of their environment, as well as elicit more rigorous thinking from our young scholars. While we don't always have time

Figure 1.5 "I Wonder" Chart from a Third-Grade Class

I wonder...
- what makes lightning.
- Why bad people do bad things that are illegal.
- how soccer was invented.
- Why bees sting.
- how the calendar was made.
- Why night is called night.
- if there are more than eight planets.
- how ABC order was invented.
- Who made Birchwood school.
- how breast stroke got its name.
- Why zebras have stripes.

during class to stop and explore all their wondrous questions, we are committed to making time for short research opportunities. Why not allow your students to choose one of the class-generated questions from the kiosk every other week to research for homework? Alternatively, you could offer this research as a challenge—an extra-credit project—as many of our third-grade teachers choose to do. The next day, form small groups of learners so they can share their new knowledge with one another. Watch their curiosity grow!

See the WonderQuest examples in Figures 1.6 and 1.7 to view how one student summarized an answer to the question, "I wonder what makes a black squirrel black," and another student researched the question, "I wonder why zebras have stripes."

Figures 1.6 and 1.7 WonderQuest Examples

A "WonderQuest": *Write your research question below:*

I Wonder what makes a black squirrel black?

Notes:

1 or 2 copies of pigment genes	common in several towns
2 copies = jet black squirrel	Michigan; Lansing, Detroit
1 copy = brown/black squirrel	Connecticut; Middletown

In a QuickWrite below, use a few of the words above to answer you research question:

A black squirrel has 1 or 2 pigment genes. If it has 2, it becomes the jet-black squirrel.

Common Core Connection: Writing Standard 8 (K-12)

"With guidance and support from adults, recall information from experiences or gather information from provided sources to answer a question."

A "WonderQuest": *Write your research question below:*

I wonder Why do zebras have stripes

Notes: Notes:

The zebras move and run in herds. Zebras live in South Africa and the zoo

In a QuickWrite below, use a few of the words above to answer your research question:

Zebras have stripes to confuse their predators. Their stripes are used as camouflage. Color blind animals may confuse the stripes with tall grass in the savannah.

Common Core Connection: Writing Standard 8 (K-12)

"With guidance and support from adults, recall information from experiences or gather information from provided sources to answer a question."

COACH'S NOTES

You will probably want to add a few of your own questions to the classroom Question Kiosk as you think of appropriate, grade-level questions for your students to ponder and research. After you model how to pose different kinds of questions, students will be sure to provide you with many of their own queries.

VIRTUAL EXPERIENCES

The virtual approach to building background knowledge helps fulfill the expectation that technology be infused into the twenty-first-century curriculum, and it just might become one of your students' favorite ways to learn.

We visited a classroom in Southampton, New York, where students were learning about marine life. The students were engaged throughout the lesson with turn-and-talks that included use of the newly introduced vocabulary, occasions for illustrating what they were learning, and opportunities for handling small instruments and tools. But, clearly, the most exciting moment of the teacher's lesson came when he announced, "Let's go on a field trip!" and all of the students moved excitedly to the tanks of tadpoles and fish and coral that were in the back of the room. As these students observed and reported changes, noted and recorded growth, described properties and compared species, they were completely engaged in their science lesson; several were motivated enough to come back after class to take care of the fish. As they used the discipline-specific vocabulary that had previously been introduced, they were now building their background knowledge.

What made this class so exciting? We realized that *any teacher* could evoke similar enthusiasm by creating a routine of "going on a field trip." In fact, we thought, what could be more exciting for a youngster in the middle of a textbook lesson than to hear, "Grab your passports! We're going on a field trip!" (like Ms. Frizzle in the Magic School Bus series, by Anne Capeci et al. [2006]).

As you're planning your unit, think about what prior knowledge would help your learners make meaning of the key understandings. If you are studying geography and landforms and how they impact recreation and jobs, and your young scholars have never been out of their community, it's time to take a virtual field trip to other parts of the country, or even the world. If you are studying the difference between vertebrates and invertebrates, and your learners have never been to the zoo, it's time to take a virtual field trip. If you're talking about symbols of the US government, and your students have never been to Washington, DC, it's time to take a virtual field trip. If you're talking about plants and trees and what they look like in different seasons, and your class has never been to a botanical garden, it's time to take a virtual field trip.

The students we observed on their classroom field trip seemed as excited as students we have taken on out-of-school field trips. Let your creativity lead you to take your students on exciting and meaningful virtual field trips and watch your students' background knowledge grow as you open their minds to the world around them.

So, how does one teacher take thirty children on such a field trip? First, you need them all to fill out a passport! Create passport pages like the one in Figure 1.8 and store them all in a safe place in your classroom until you need them for your trips. In each one, add a photo and some biographical information to the first page, followed by blank templates that the student will complete for each trip. The passport in Figure 1.8 was created by a first grader on a virtual safari. Have each student write about the visit on the left-hand side and draw an illustration of what he or she saw and learned about on the right-hand side. For students in grades K–1, as well as with struggling learners in the upper grades, use sentence frames, such as the following:

> **Today, we went to** _____.
> **I saw** _____.
> **I learned that** _____.

Figure 1.8 Sample Pages from a First Grader's Passport

Name: ___
Age: 7
School: Saw Mill
Grade: 1

Today I went on a safari.
I saw many wildlife animals
I learned that vultures eat dead zebras.

When planning your unit, make a list of websites and video clips that can transport your students for five minutes to another part of their county, state, country, or world community. Set up the corners or tables in your room with displays, collections, photographs, animal tanks, models, pictures, and all kinds of realia to simulate a real location (a doctor's office, a library, a firehouse, a garden, etc.). Directly teach your students vocabulary that will help them understand the upcoming experience and provide them with sentence frames that will help them make meaning from each experience (One new thing I learned today about ___ was ___. One question I have is ___. I can see that ___ is like ___. I now know that ___ causes ___.). Once this routine is established, most students won't need the sentence frames to produce complete thoughts about their learning in their journals or notebooks.

COACH'S NOTES

Do you remember the days when learning didn't just happen in the classroom? When children knew that third grade meant a trip to a museum in the city or fourth grade meant they were off to visit a restored Revolutionary village? Today's budget woes and security concerns have all but eliminated these rich experiences outside the classrooms.

Today's technologies, however, allow these experiences to take place throughout the year, and they provide learners multiple opportunities to explore and build background knowledge in new ways. Not only do virtual field trips help set content in context, but learners, who work in teams, have been found to express a desire to visit the locations in person after the experiences (Tutwiler, Lin, and Chang 2013). For the best results, you'll need a webcam, a computer with a microphone and speakers, and a strong Internet connection—broadband, LTE, 3G, or 4G will work.

Among other amazing experiences that virtual field trips can provide, teachers and students can discover the wonders of the world, visit museums across the ocean, and explore artwork in exquisite detail. Here are some of my favorite resources for children in K–5:

Skype in the Classroom: https://education.skype.com

Connected Classrooms with Google+: http://connectedclassrooms.withgoogle.com

The Google Cultural Institute: www.google.com/culturalinstitute

Center for Interactive Learning and Collaboration (CILC): www.cilc.org

Collaborations Around the Planet (CAP) Space: http://projects.twice.cc

Google Lit Trips: www.googlelittrips.com

Google Earth: www.google.com/earth

Google Maps: www.google.com/maps

Classrooms Without Borders: https://plus.google.com /communities/105595880115728518300

Blanca E. Duarte, instructional technology specialist, LogicWing

Scaffolding Toolbox: Anticipation Guides

Anticipation guides—also referred to as anticipatory guides—have long been around to help teachers activate prior knowledge, validate students' existing understandings, and preview new material. They also help identify misconceptions and gaps in knowledge that our students possess. Additionally, anticipation guides build curiosity and stimulate student interest in the forthcoming reading (Duffelmeyer 1994; Wood et al. 2008). Anticipation guides are unique in the sense that they help bridge all three phases of working with background knowledge, thus scaffolding learning in multiple ways:

- They *assess* prior knowledge by having students evaluate a teacher-provided list of statements about the topic.
- They *activate* what students already know and make apparent the misconceptions that some students hold.
- They *build* background in several ways: they preview key concepts and introduce vocabulary prior to reading; they provide a purpose for reading; they help students integrate and consolidate new learnings.

For this activity to work, you must give careful directions to the students. Make sure they read each of the statements that you have prepared, or read them aloud yourself to the class. Using one color, younger learners can simply circle *yes* or *no* (or *true* or *false*) regarding each sentence to indicate their agreement or disagreement. Then, after reading the text, they can use a different color to mark their responses a second time. We encourage you to use simple and straightforward statements, as demonstrated in the example in Figure 1.9, based on Edith Thacher Hurd's (2000) book *Starfish*. Your students will be able to focus more on the content rather than on decoding difficult words.

Figure 1.9 Anticipation Guide Based on *Starfish* (Hurd 2000)

Yes	No	Starfish live deep down in the sea.
Yes	No	A starfish has many eyes.
Yes	No	A starfish has no ears or nose.
Yes	No	Starfish crawl faster than snails.
Yes	No	Starfish lay many eggs that look like sand.

A more complex format for upper-elementary grades would contain several columns. In the first column, labeled "Before Reading," have students state whether they agree or disagree with each sentence. After they read the text (independently or by listening to a read-aloud), give them a second opportunity to respond to the statements. They can keep or change their original opinions, basing their conclusions upon the information contained in the text. Have them indicate their final choices for each statement in the "After Reading" column. An example of this template can be found in Figure 1.10, based on Sarah L. Thomson's (2010) *Where Do Polar Bears Live?*

As a follow-up, have students write summaries based on how their ideas have changed. You can offer sentence frames to further scaffold this step: At first I thought ___, but now I know ___.

Figure 1.10 Anticipation Guide Based on *Where Do Polar Bears Live?* by Sarah L. Thomson (2010)

Before Reading (Agree or Disagree?)	Statements	After Reading (Agree or Disagree?)
	1. Polar bears live in Antarctica.	
	2. A polar bear cub is as big as a rabbit when it is born.	
	3. Polar bears get hot very easily.	
	4. Polar bears cool off by jumping into icy water.	
	5. The polar bear's fur is three inches thick.	
Summary Statement:		

Karen Mitchell (2006) has observed that her fourth graders "are motivated to continue reading a selection if they are searching for answers to questions they've formulated in their minds" (66). We have also found that many teachers like to add another box or column on the anticipation guide where students pose their own questions after responding to the guide but prior to reading the text.

Donna Merkley (1996/1997), on the other hand, has found that modifying the classic anticipation guide by adding a third column labeled "I Am Not Sure" allows students to opt out of making a forced selection prior to reading if they do not have sufficient knowledge about a certain topic. In addition, Merkley uses the anticipation guide statements with fifth graders for setting a purpose for reading and for citing proof from the reading to support or refute the statements given to them prior to the reading.

The word choice of the anticipation guide—whether you use agree/disagree, yes/no, true/false, or other word pairs—is up to you. I vary the way I create my anticipation guides to expose my third graders to different formats and vocabulary. I use this tool with both fiction and nonfiction pieces. I combine anticipation guides with many other strategies; turn-and-talk seems to work really well for most students as they discuss what they believe to be true statements prior to reading the selection. They really enjoy defending their ideas. What I appreciate even more, however, is how they learn to go back into the text and cite evidence when they defend their conclusions in a turn-and-talk after the reading is done.

Grade 3 teacher

How to Differentiate Instruction When Building Background Knowledge

Figure 1.11 offers a quick guide for addressing the readiness levels and varied needs of diverse learners. Please note that there are some overlapping suggestions for ELLs and students with disabilities, whereas their unique needs are also considered.

A Final Thought

Clearly, we know that students without sufficient grade-appropriate background knowledge struggle more in school and retain less from their learning experiences than do their peers who possess more background knowledge. Keeping this in mind, you will want to routinely *assess* your learners' background knowledge, *activate* the use of their background knowledge, and provide experiences to *build* their background knowledge. While we have shown you that wide reading, vocabulary building, and research experiences are three literacy pathways to building background knowledge, we have also shown you how firsthand, authentic experiences as well as virtual experiences can enhance your learners' background knowledge. In addition, we have provided you with suggestions for spicing up your class with collaborative activities that assess and activate background knowledge, such as ThinkTanks and alphabet roundups. Moreover, we encourage you to embrace students' natural curiosity and wonder as a route to building background knowledge. The Question Kiosk and WonderQuest will enhance student inquisitiveness while building background knowledge and student engagement. Finally, nothing we have seen will evoke more enthusiasm and build greater background knowledge than going on a field trip. So, whether it's real or virtual, grab your passports and take your students on a field trip!

Figure 1.11 Differentiating Instruction When Focusing on Background Knowledge

ELLs	SWDs	Advanced Learners
• Supply a word bank, definitions, or list of words for their own personal dictionaries. • Search for connections between the new information and the cultural and familial experiences these students already have. • Continue to offer scaffolds and sentence frames when they are removed for others. • Provide these students with more resources and books to peruse and take home about the topics that you will be studying. • Guide group brainstorming tasks by providing written questions and prompts. • Have students use sentence frames you provide to construct summaries from their brainstorming. • Allow these students to work with partners.		• Have these young learners make a classroom anchor chart titled "Things We Know About ___ " while you work with the rest of the class building background knowledge. • Ask for text-to-text or text-to-world connections. • Ask students to consider "What if?" scenarios (What if there were no rain for several months? How would this affect the water cycle and our community?). • Ask these students to create a "How to ___" or "Guide to ___" text to help students who have no background knowledge about the skill or place. • Allow these students to do additional research and make new connections to present to the class. • Have these students create a simple children's book that would help a younger child understand the concept.
• Provide word boxes targeting basic (Tier 1) vocabulary as needed. • Use bilingual glossaries and dictionaries if children are bilingual and biliterate. • Offer native language support through bilingual peer bridges, teaching assistants, and print and electronic resources. • Allow these students to ask questions in their native languages (to be translated into English).	• Follow the specifics of students' Individualized Education Programs (IEPs). • Offer accommodations and modifications based on IEPs.	

Essential Questions for Individual Reflection, Collegial Circles, and Group Discussions

- *What is the central idea running through this chapter that informs your instruction?*

- *Why do you need to assess, activate, as well as build background knowledge?*

- *How can you reconcile the demands of the curriculum with the desire for nurturing inquisitiveness?*

- *How often do you assess prior knowledge when beginning a new unit? What can you use to assess prior knowledge?*

- *What are the most useful and effective routines for building background knowledge?*

- *How can you support your struggling learners when they have little background knowledge?*

- *How can you support ELLs in light of their prior life experiences? How can you validate what they do know about the world?*

- *How can you challenge advanced learners when you discover they already know what you are about to teach?*

Chapter **2**

READING ROUTINES

Because reading has more impact on students' achievement than any other activity in school, setting aside time for reading must be the first activity we teachers write on our lesson plans, not the last.

Donalyn Miller, *The Book Whisperer*

As teachers, we can flood the room with engaging texts, we can share interesting ideas, we can model our own curiosity, we can foster thoughtful conversations. Only they can turn what they hear, see, read, and talk about into knowledge by thinking deeply and expansively.

Stephanie Harvey and Anne Goudvis,
"Comprehension at the Core"

Overview

In this chapter, we

- summarize research and evidence-based support for the routines we suggest
- examine the reading expectations of the Common Core State Standards
- establish routines for reading as a whole class, reading in small groups and pairs, and reading individually
- present examples, templates (available online), resources, and classroom vignettes along with recommendations from coaches to support the implementation of the reading routines
- add text maps (story maps and text structure maps) to the scaffolding toolbox
- offer differentiation ideas for reading instruction for English learners, students with disabilities, and advanced learners.

Reading Routines at a Glance

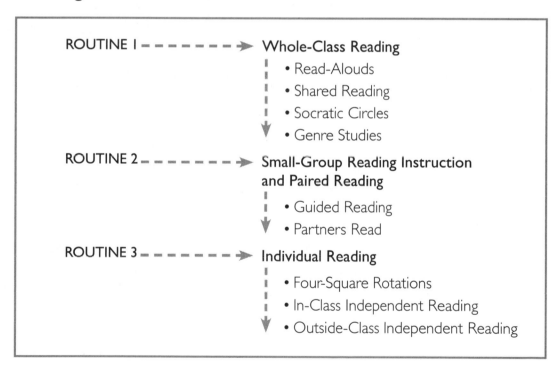

ROUTINE 1 - - - - - - ➤ **Whole-Class Reading**
- Read-Alouds
- Shared Reading
- Socratic Circles
- Genre Studies

ROUTINE 2 - - - - - - ➤ **Small-Group Reading Instruction and Paired Reading**
- Guided Reading
- Partners Read

ROUTINE 3 - - - - - - ➤ **Individual Reading**
- Four-Square Rotations
- In-Class Independent Reading
- Outside-Class Independent Reading

What Does the Research Say About Teaching Reading?

A complete collection of research publications about reading could easily fill a library of its own, so our attempt to share some critical points will not be an exhaustive treatment of the topic. Culling from the most comprehensive sources on the topic, we turned to the findings provided by John Hattie, grounded in fifty meta-analyses—which in turn were based on over two thousand studies on reading. Hattie (2009) emphasizes "the importance and value of actively teaching the skills and strategies of reading across all years of schooling" (129). Since becoming a successful reader "requires the development of decoding skills, the development of vocabulary and comprehension, and the learning of specific strategies and processes" (129–30), Hattie further stresses that reading programs have to be carefully planned, deliberate, and explicit in their teaching of specific skills. Among many other reports, he refers to the *Report of the National Reading Panel (NICHD 2000)* and concludes the following:

> There is much support for the five pillars of good reading instruction: phonemic awareness, phonics, fluency, vocabulary, and comprehension—and attending to all is far more important than whether the program teaches one of the five as opposed to another. The most effective programs for teaching reading are, first, to attend to the visual and auditory perceptual skills. Then a combination of vocabulary, comprehension, and phonics instruction with repeated reading opportunities is the most powerful set of instructional methods. (140)

Somewhat contrary to these findings, Stephen Krashen (2004) reports the results of his own meta-analysis of research on independent reading and concludes that no other literacy activity has a more profound effect on students' vocabulary development, reading comprehension, writing skill development, and overall academic achievement than what he calls FVR (free voluntary reading).

In an article published in *Education Leadership* concerning the core skill of reading, Richard Allington and Rachel E. Gabriel (2012) synthesize decades of research and evidence-based best practices and suggest what every child should experience *every* day. They recommend that each day, students should do all of the following:

- **read something they choose to read**
- **read accurately, which means at a level they can read and understand. (With this type of high-success reading, students will progress in learning to read [Allington 2009; Kuhn et al. 2006]. If struggling readers are presented only with too-challenging texts throughout the day, their independent reading level will not improve)**
- **read and reread something comprehensible, as this is more effective in improving reading than working on isolated basic reading skills**
- **write about what they've read, composing something meaningful and authentic (such as how-to guides or informational texts for other students)**
- **talk with peers about reading and writing**
- **have the opportunity to hear their teacher read aloud, no matter what grade they are in.**

Our beliefs and professional practice are aligned with Allington and Gabriel (2012), as they illuminate one of the most significant obstacles to reconciling good reading instruction with the grade-level demands of the new standards. While students definitely need opportunities to grapple with challenging text during each day in order to succeed with the standards, they also need engaging, comprehensible text at their independent reading level in order to improve their reading skills. Reading text driven by personal interest at a manageable level of comprehension is the surest way to motivate youngsters to read more on their own. And it is indisputable that the more one reads, the better reader one becomes.

In Chapter 1, we discuss how wide reading and sustained silent reading of student-chosen texts are the best ways to grow students' vocabulary and background knowledge. Now, Allington and Gabriel (2012) provide us with one more reason for making sure that the reading routines we choose to use regularly in our classrooms invite students to read frequently at their own level and of their own choice. In addition, investigations by Allington and Gabriel, Guthrie et al. (2006), Ogle (2011), and Malloy and Gambrell (2013) support the idea that classroom time spent independently reading self-selected texts improves personal reading skills.

Jennifer Renner Del Nero (2013), in her introduction to *Teaching with the Common Core Standards for English Language Arts, Grades 3–5*, reminds us that in the face of new standards, we must not abandon what we already know works.

We still need to use small group instruction and differentiate instruction using materials with which they can learn and be successful. However, in whole-class instruction, we need to use grade-level text to be sure that students are exposed to and guided through complex materials. (xii)

Richard Allington's (2006) research supports the same conclusions: students need to be put at their differentiated levels. We concur. A balance of texts at students' independent reading levels and grade level will prepare your learners to be engaged in academic learning in school, to make progress toward meeting grade-appropriate reading goals, to develop a lifelong passion for literacy, as well as to develop the skills necessary to be successful academically.

David Pearson and Elfrieda Hiebert (2013) help us keep our focus on the goal of gaining knowledge and insight from reading by

- **helping students set a purpose for reading**
- **reviewing key ideas from literature and disciplinary areas (themes, topics, insights, and problems from a set of texts)**
- **asking the essential questions: What's new in the text we just read? How does it connect to what we already know about this issue?**

As you read literature throughout the year, continue to add to an anchor chart in your room the themes that you come across. Include themes like friendship, perseverance, love, courage, loyalty, patience, individuality, overcoming obstacles, and so on.

As you read informational text in science and social studies, continue to add to a second anchor chart the themes and topics you explore. Depending on the grade level, your list might include the following: family, communities, animal and plant cycles, the food chain, exploration, geography, traditions, government, exploration, the human body, the rock cycle, the water cycle, weather, sound, machines, magnets, space, freedom, democracy, or rights and responsibilities.

Model and teach students how to make connections among the elements listed on the charts. As you read new text, point out how certain concepts compare and contrast, how there might be a sequence involved, how some of the elements cause positive or negative effects to occur, how several of the elements are related to one another. This is an effective way to help students make sense of all the knowledge they are acquiring and to place their new learning in a broader context.

Finally, in helping us understand what the implementation of the CCSS reading standards should look like at the classroom level, Pearson and Hiebert (2013) note that what we do can either facilitate or hinder our students' learning from complex text. They advise teachers to do the following in order to maximize literacy instruction:

- **Help students appreciate the differences in vocabulary that is found in narrative and informational texts.**
- **Give students the opportunities** *to pursue topics of personal interest.*
- **Ensure that students read** *sufficient amounts of text* **(volume) and also** *read increasingly longer selections* **(stamina).**

In short, you should consider *opportunity, volume,* and *stamina* when you choose the classroom reading routines that you will incorporate into your daily reading instruction.

What Are the Reading Demands of the Common Core?

The reading standards occupy the most prominent, first section of the CCSS and are well supported by research (see CCSS Appendix A) and an extensive list of recommended fiction, nonfiction, and poetry titles arranged by grade level both for independent reading and teacher read-alouds (see CCSS Appendix B).

Let's take a look at the College and Career Readiness Anchor Standards for Reading which are divided into four major sections:

- **Key Ideas and Details:** Students determine main ideas and supporting details, make inferences based on the text, and establish how individuals, events, and other text elements are related to each other.
- **Craft and Structure:** Students examine the text closely and analyze it for word- and sentence-level choices as well as identify text structure, purpose, and point of view expressed in the text.
- **Integration of Knowledge and Ideas:** Students analyze, compare, contrast, and synthesize information from various print and nonprint sources.
- **Range of Reading and Level of Text Complexity:** Students read and comprehend complex literary and informational texts independently and proficiently.

There are three anchor standards and corresponding grade-level standards for the first three strands of the standards, and one remaining standard for range of reading and level of text complexity. These ten anchor standards apply to reading both literature and informational text, as reflected in the grade-level progression charts. In addition, the CCSS contain reading standards for foundational skills, the goal of which include "fostering students' understanding and working knowledge of concepts of print, the alphabetic principle, and other basic conventions of the English writing system" (NGA Center for Best Practices and CCSSO 2010, 15).

The routines presented in this chapter focus on the reading standards for literature and informational text. While we recognize the importance of developing foundational skills (print concepts, phonological awareness, phonics and word recognition, and fluency, as noted by the CCSS), addressing them is beyond the scope of this book.

Reading Routines

We recommend establishing routines for whole-class reading instruction through read-alouds and shared reading and by regularly engaging students in Socratic circle discussions and genre studies. Large-group routines must also be supplemented with routines for small-group reading instruction and opportunities for paired reading through guided reading instruction and a practice we call Partners Read. Finally, reading must also become a routine that students are able to tackle independently. We suggest the following approaches to establish such routines: first, involve students in highly structured reading routines such as the Four-Square rotation we describe in this chapter. Then, give them opportunities to read independently—with and without structures—both in and out of class.

ROUTINE *1* Whole-Class Reading

Your students are seated on the rug or at their desks, ready to learn, perhaps eager to learn or maybe fidgety and distracted. What is one of the most empowering activities in which you can engage your students? Reading, of course! Read to them, read with them, dig deep into the text with them; invite them to question the text, question the author, and question each other. Allow them to enter the text with you, with your guidance, and live inside the text, captured and captivated, wanting to read more!

READ-ALOUDS

In a highly respected and frequently quoted report of the Commission on Reading titled *Becoming a Nation of Readers*, Richard Anderson, Elfrieda Hiebert, Judith Scott, and Ian Wilkinson (1985) note that "the single most important activity for building the knowledge required for eventual success in reading is reading aloud to children" (23). Fountas and Pinnell (2001) introduced interactive read-alouds that incorporate student-to-student interaction so peers can discuss the reading, engage in some deep

Figure 2.1 Fifth Grader During a Read-Aloud

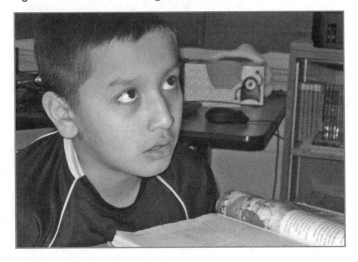

thinking about it, and immediately practice reading strategies that the teacher has modeled. Many researchers and practitioners have also been promoting reading aloud to children of all ages and across all content areas. Notice the attentiveness of the fifth-grade student in Figure 2.1 as he listens to his teacher, Chris Shaw, read a social studies chapter aloud.

Most recently, Debbie Miller (2013) has suggested that reading aloud motivates students, enhances and expands their oral language development, and, at the same time, helps build a community of learners in your classroom. Similarly, Jim Trelease emphatically claims that *we read to children for all the same reasons we talk with children: to reassure, to entertain, to bond, to inform or explain, to arouse curiosity, and to inspire. But in reading aloud, we also:*

- *build vocabulary*
- *condition the child's brain to associate reading with pleasure*
- *create background knowledge*
- *provide a reading role model*
- *plant the desire to read.* (2013, 6)

What are the key components of an effective read-aloud routine? It must have some regular elements, to which we can add and modify, as needed.

Always

1. Ensure students are seated comfortably and are fully attentive to you (or the reader).
2. Read with expression that makes listening engaging and irresistible, with the hope of passing on your love of reading to your students.
3. Use clear annunciation, adequate pausing, and lots of facial expression and animation.
4. Find ways to reread the same text or an extension of the text during guided reading and independent reading.

Regularly

1. Read through the entire selection for enjoyment, especially with shorter pieces.
2. Stop and process; have students discuss what they have heard.
   - Have them make predictions and pose questions they are wondering about.
   - Build theories about the reading.
   - Turn and talk or stop and jot.
3. Take a picture walk (fiction) or text tour (nonfiction) prior to reading aloud to offer a preview of the reading.
4. Invite students to create mental images as you read.
5. Have students build theories in their minds about a character (fiction).

Occasionally

1. Read the same text aloud again, or even multiple times for different purposes.
2. Have students act out parts of the story.
3. Place the read-aloud book at a center for students to "read" to each other by pointing out pictures and retelling what they remember.

Never

1. Test or quiz students on the contents of the read-aloud.
2. Have students do the read-aloud in round-robin fashion.

Don't stop at reading aloud to your students; consider expanding this critical literacy experience through *thinking aloud* or *comprehending aloud* (Zwiers 2014) for them. Through think-alouds and comprehend-alouds, you can allow your students to gain insight into your own meaning-making process and how you, as an accomplished reader, use strategies such as predicting, clarifying, summarizing, and making connections. According to Jeff Zwiers, think-alouds support the development of a range of reading strategies, whereas comprehend-alouds make visible thinking about processing and analyzing the language of complex texts. Review Figure 2.2 for sentence starters you can use to model think-alouds and comprehend-alouds with just about any text. In the younger grades, adapt these sentence starters to match students' readiness levels. Also see the anchor chart (Figure 2.3) prepared for a third-grade class to support visualization with think-aloud and comprehend-aloud sentence stems.

Figure 2.2 Sentence Starters for Think-Alouds and Comprehend-Alouds

Think-Aloud Sentence Stems	Comprehend-Aloud Sentence Stems
Predicting • When I saw the title of this book, I immediately thought of . . . • I predict . . . • In the next part, I think the author . . . *Clarifying* • I was confused when I read . . . • I had to go back to page . . . • I had to think back to what I learned about . . . *Summarizing* • I think this section is mainly about . . . • The most important point the author is making . . . • So I think the purpose of this article is . . . *Making Connections* • This is like . . . • This paragraph reminds me of . . . • The part I just read is similar to . . . • When I read this section, I thought of . . . • I think the author wants me to . . .	*Word or Phrase Level* • I noticed that the author uses the same word here . . . • I am not sure what this word means in the first paragraph, so I will reread this section . . . • I have never seen this word before. Let me see if I can figure out the meaning by reading ahead/looking for some examples/ finding an illustration. • The author begins the sentence with the phrase . . . *Sentence or Text Level* • The author uses a very long sentence in this paragraph. Let me see if I can break it down into shorter sections, such as . . . • In this section, I noticed some sentences are very similar; they have a similar pattern. • I noticed this section has a lot of dialogue and quotes. I wonder . . .

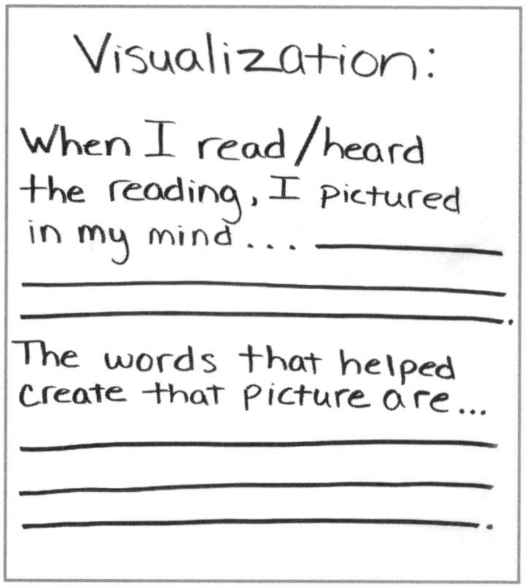

Figure 2.3 Anchor Chart with Think-Aloud and Comprehend-Aloud Sentence Stems

The handwritten chart reads:

> Visualization:
>
> When I read/heard the reading, I pictured in my mind... _____
> _____
> _____.
>
> The words that helped create that picture are...
> _____
> _____
> _____.

SHARED READING

Even though shared reading of large-print text was originally intended for younger learners, and in some classrooms it may be limited to students reading along in unison with the teacher, this practice may be expanded and utilized for achieving broader instructional goals (Fisher and Fisher Medvic 2000; Taberski 2010). During shared reading, your students have the opportunity to join in the process of reading along with you and making sense of the text with you in a large-group or whole-class setting. Jan Richardson (2009) suggests utilizing shared reading time "to teach skills and strategies, increase reading fluency, learn content information for social studies and science, and support developing readers" (7). Whole-class read-alouds and shared reading allow for establishing routines for comprehension strategy instruction and close reading. Barbara Taylor claims,

> [The] major goal of comprehension instruction is to help students use a set of procedures when reading independently that will yield deep comprehension of a text. . . . Research has shown that explicit lessons in the following strategies are most effective:
>
> - summarizing
> - comprehension monitoring
> - use of graphic and semantic organizers
> - use of story structure
> - higher level question answering about text
> - question generation before, during, and after reading
> - use of multiple strategies in the context of reading texts.   (2011, 37)

Based on the grade level you teach, a range of additional reading comprehension strategies will also be necessary. Explicitly teach one comprehension strategy at a time over a particular period of time. Though discussing each of these strategies is beyond the scope of this book, we firmly believe that routines must be established for teaching them. Similar to the gradual release of responsibility framework (Fisher and Frey 2008; also see Chapter 1) and the reading workshop (Fountas and Pinnell 2001), comprehension strategy instruction is most effective when it follows a well-planned, predictable sequence. With each strategy you select for instruction, try this routine:

1. Begin with a minilesson. Introduce the strategy and explain what it is and how it is used.

2. Model the strategy on multiple texts during read-alouds and shared reading sessions.

3. Incorporate teacher-supported practice with the target comprehension strategy during guided reading time.

4. Provide cooperative learning opportunities to apply the strategy while also getting help from peers (for example, literature circles, reading workshop, buddy reading, guided reading groups).

5. Have students practice the target strategy, and monitor strategy use during individual conference time.

6. Leave time to reflect on the strategy use and invite students to evaluate how effective the strategy you taught was for them.

COACH'S NOTES

In early childhood classrooms, shared reading provides the explicit instruction readers—primarily emergent and early readers—need to develop their reading process. The most effective way to approach shared reading is for you to use the same large-print text for several days and follow a gradual release model during each session. Scheduling time for shared reading as the opening to reading workshop promotes the predictable structure that we know children thrive on and feel most comfortable with. If we expect students to construct their own reading process, then we have to provide the experience of shared reading daily. Unless young readers see and hear what readers do and how they think as they construct meaning, they will not be able to employ this challenging process on their own.

Brandy McDonald, NBCT, literacy coach

Shared reading time also provides the ideal context for introducing and practicing close reading, which is one of the hallmarks and most frequently cited shifts of literacy instruction. Nancy Boyles (2013) defines close reading as "reading to uncover layers of meaning that lead to deep comprehension" (37). Rereading the text allows for going to those deeper levels, moving from factual information gleaned from the text to critical reading and text analysis at the word, sentence, and discourse levels. As Sheila Brown and Lee Kappes put it,

Through text-based questions and discussion, students are guided to deeply analyze and appreciate various aspects of the text, such as key vocabulary and how its meaning is shaped by context; attention to form, tone, imagery and/or rhetorical devices; the significance of word choice and syntax; and the discovery of different levels of meaning as passages are read multiple times. (2012, 2)

Close reading invites students to find evidence from the text in response to carefully crafted questions. See the anchor charts that were created with students in Figures 2.4a and 2.4b. In the chart in Figure 2.4a, students identified what close readers do in general, and in the chart in Figure 2.4b, they reflected on their metacognitive processes as close readers of *Esperanza Rising* (Ryan 2002).

Figure 2.4a Close Reading Anchor Chart   **Figure 2.4b** Reflection Anchor Chart for *Esperanza Rising*

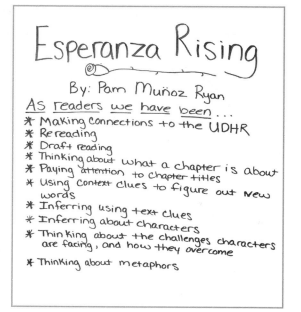

Close Readers Do These Things

1. Talk to each other about what you think something means — James
2. Read the text slowly and more than once.
3. Circle words you are not sure of and try to make sense out of them, visualize, sketch — Caroline
4. Summarize and annotate — Joshua
5. Try to put the text in your own words. — Joshua

Esperanza Rising
By: Pam Muñoz Ryan
As readers we have been...
* Making connections to the UDHR
* Rereading
* Draft reading
* Thinking about what a chapter is about
* Paying attention to chapter titles
* Using context clues to figure out new words
* Inferring using text clues
* Inferring about characters
* Thinking about the challenges characters are facing, and how they overcome
* Thinking about metaphors

Though some questions might prompt for literal responses, most discussion will take place at the analysis, synthesis, and evaluation levels of Bloom's taxonomy (see Chapter 4 for further details on questioning for all levels of Bloom's taxonomy). Not all text will be ideal for close reading, but those with difficult passages call for such analysis. Since close reading often spans multiple days of instruction, one or more of those readings and rereadings should be successfully accomplished through shared reading experiences at the elementary level to offer the necessary support and guidance for students to work with complex text.

When students read closely, they do more than react to or summarize a text. Instead, they zoom in on significant passages and unpack the text by looking at how facets, such as specific word choice, metaphor, or cause-effect relationships, influence meaning. It's important to remember that close reading is one critical way that we come to understand the larger meanings in a text, but doing this exercise out of context or in isolation won't fully develop self-sufficient readers.

Sarah Brown Wessling, English teacher,
Johnston High School Teacher Laureate,
Teaching Channel; 2010 National Teacher of the Year

Inspired by Carol Ann Tomlinson's (2001) equalizer, Judy Dodge's (2006) Bloom question starters, Stephanie Harvey and Harvey Daniels' (2009) comprehension continuum, and others who have organized student understanding on a continuum, we tend to conceptualize close reading as a process of unpacking text on multiple levels. Similar to the organization of academic language in Chapter 5, here, too, we suggest planning close reading activities that uncover meaning at the discourse (text), sentence, and vocabulary (word) levels while also moving students from a factual, foundational, or concrete way of looking at and thinking about the text to a more abstract and critical process. Figure 2.5 offers sample questions that address three different dimensions of linguistic complexity (read the chart vertically) and cognitive complexity (read the chart horizontally). We start close reading questioning at the text level, which supports a global processing of the text. Figure 2.5 includes generic question frames so you can fill in your own text-specific information and create your own close reading questions.

Coach's Notes

You may be disheartened to note that many of your students have a hard time inferring. You may watch as, grappling with text on an unfamiliar topic, they fail to make any inferences about what they are reading. Our task must be to activate or to build their background knowledge and to explicitly teach how to make inferences. Providing a formula such as What I Know + What I See = Inference is helpful for students, as is creating ample opportunities for them to practice inferring with your guidance and support. See Figure 2.6 for an anchor chart from Claudia Martinez's second-grade dual-language classroom.

Figure 2.5 Close Reading Questioning on Three Levels

	Concrete, Foundational, and Factual Questions	Questions That Integrate Language, Thinking, and Text	Abstract and Complex Questions for Critical Analysis
Text Level	• What is the title of this reading? • Look at the headings and subheadings: What do you infer/predict about the reading based on those text features? • Look at the illustration on page x. What details stand out in the illustrations?	• What is the main purpose of this author? What evidence is there that shows _____? • Why did the illustrator choose to offer details on _____? How are those details also depicted in the text?	• What is the theme of this story? What message is the author trying to give the readers? How can you tell? • What is the central idea or underlying message of the text? How can you justify your answer? • How does this story compare with another story we have read?
Sentence Level	• Which sentence introduces the topic? • Which sentence identifies _____? • Which sentence describes _____?	• Which phrase or sentence helps the reader understand what the author means by saying _____? • Can you find examples of where the author _____?	• The text begins with _____. Why do you think the author chose to begin the text with this statement/question? • The text ends with _____. Why do you think the author chose to end the text with this statement/question?
Word Level	• What is the first important word in this text? • What words does the author repeat? • What does the word _____ mean in this text?	• What words does the author use to convince the reader about _____?	• What words stand out as carrying the most important piece of information? • Why did the author choose the word _____ to describe _____?

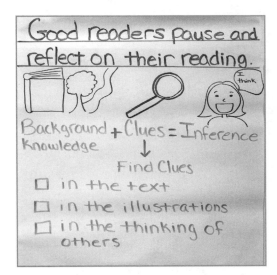

Figure 2.6 Anchor Chart for Making Inferences

 CHECK THIS OUT

More in-depth discussion on the reading workshop can be found in the following seminal resources.

Books

Calkins, L. 2010. *Launch an Intermediate Reading Workshop*. Portsmouth, NH: Heinemann.

Fountas, I. C., and G. S. Pinnell. 1996. *Guided Reading: Good First Teaching for All Children*. Portsmouth, NH: Heinemann.

_____. 2001. *Guiding Readers and Writers Grades 3–6: Teaching Comprehension, Genre, and Content Literacy*. Portsmouth, NH: Heinemann.

Serafini, F. 2001. *The Reading Workshop*. Portsmouth, NH: Heinemann.

Serafini, F., and S. Youngs. 2006. *Around the Reading Workshop in 180 Days*. Portsmouth, NH: Heinemann.

Taberski, S. 2010. *Comprehension from the Ground Up: Simplified, Sensible Instruction for the K–3 Reading Workshop*. Portsmouth, NH: Heinemann.

Websites

http://readingandwritingproject.com

www.readersworkshop.org

www.lauracandler.com

www.scholastic.com/teachers/top_teaching/2009/10/reading-workshop

Video Clips

"Rick's Reading Workshop: Complete Lesson," with Rick Kleine: www.teachingchannel .org/videos/student-reading-workshop-lesson

"Guided Reading with Jenna Complete Lesson," with Jenna Ogier: www.teachingchannel .org/videos/guided-reading-differentiation-system

SOCRATIC CIRCLES

A Socratic circle is a routine for whole-class reading instruction. As described on the International Reading Association's ReadWriteThink website (www.readwritethink.org), a Socratic seminar, or a Socratic circle as it is also known, is a formal discussion, based on a text, in which the leader asks open-ended questions. Students learn to listen to one another, think critically, and articulate their own thoughts and answers in response to what others have said. Used in the elementary grades, the Socratic circle creates a community of young learners who explore together the ideas, issues, and values in the text before them. Many teachers use the Socratic circle one day a week so students get used to reading and responding to literature and nonfiction text in this interactive fashion.

This whole-class approach to reading "promotes team building and appropriate classroom behavior. Students are taught to look at one another when they speak and listen, to wait their turn to respond, and to communicate in a way that shows respect for viewpoints differing from their own . . . and, always, to return to the text to find evidence and support for their ideas" (Dodge 2006, 121). Socratic circles teach students appropriate social skills while building their knowledge through the study of content-rich nonfiction text. They also provide a simple routine for modeling how to do close reading and analyze text.

When using this routine, have students create a large circle with chairs (or desks) around the room. Alternatively, you can create Socratic circles with small groups. Ask each student to write his or her name on a tented index card or piece of folded construction paper. The name cards will add to the formality of the routine, evoking a sense of responsibility to respond to one's peers, rather than just to the teacher. Encourage your students to direct their comments to one another, always using the name of the person to whom they are speaking. For example, one student might say, "I understand what Jason is saying, and I would like to add _____ because on page three the author says that _____." Anchor charts with precise academic language and sentence frames for discussion (like the former example) should be displayed in your room so that students can refer to them when participating in this reading routine.

You can see how the routines often engage multiple skills at the same time. Here, reading skills are enhanced by the use of listening, speaking skills, and writing skills. Students listen and speak in order to make sense of the reading. Following the Socratic circle, have each of your students write a brief summary or complete an "I learned _____" statement to reflect on what he or she has learned through the Socratic circle routine.

See Figure 2.7a, in which PS 228 students are getting ready for a Socratic circle by annotating their reading, and Figure 2.7b, which shows students participating in a Socratic circle.

Figure 2.7a Second Graders Annotating Their Reading

Figure 2.7b Students Participating in a Socratic Circle

GENRE STUDIES

Different kinds of texts place different demands on readers. Reading a book that is within our control but offers just a small challenge enables us to expand and enrich our in-the-head strategic actions. For example, the first time we read a book that flashes back in time or follows multiple generations across a long period of time, we learn how to use those structures to understand and enjoy the book. It is essential for students to experience a variety of rich texts—fiction and nonfiction—if they are to acquire the reading strategies they need. (Fountas and Pinnell, *Genre Study*)

Text types and genres have been discussed long before the CCSS. Genres are commonly defined as "categories or kinds of writing, with distinctive features or rhetorical elements that speak to their purpose" (Fearn and Farrnan 2001, 227). We subscribe to the way Nell Duke, Samantha Caughlan, Mary Juzwik, and Nicole Martin (2011) organize the reading and writing genres for a focused study into five major categories. These categories are established based on the purposes of the genres. In Figure 2.8, we provide examples that we have seen in classrooms to help you get started with genre studies in your own classroom. Please note that in these examples, reading and writing in the various genres are combined or integrated.

Figure 2.8 Categories of Genres and Their Authentic Purposes

Genre Group	Purpose	Genre Types	Examples from the Classroom
Narrative Genres	Sharing and making meaning of experiences	• Fictional narratives, historical narratives, personal narratives, memoirs, family narratives, community narratives • Science fiction, fantasy	Students read and write about real and imaginary events (such as writing a story about a family celebration).
Procedural Genres	Learning how to do something and teaching others	• How-to texts • Manuals for classroom or school procedures • Directions for games or activities	Students read how-to texts. They produce similar texts (such as one that explains the steps to play a game they developed as a culminating project for a unit of study).
Informational Genres	Developing and communicating expertise	• Reports, research projects, guides, informational booklets, informational websites	Students read informational texts and online sources. They produce similar texts (e.g., a guidebook or website about a topic they are researching, such as the community in which they live).

continues

Figure 2.8 Categories of Genres and Their Authentic Purposes, *continued*

Genre Group	Purpose	Genre Types	Examples from the Classroom
Dramatic Genres	Exploring meaning through performance	• Plays, skits, readers theater scripts • Poetry	Students read plays and scripts as well as write and perform short skits on a topical issue, such as bullying.
Persuasive Genres	Affecting change	• Persuasive essays, magazine articles, formal letters, persuasive speeches, advocacy projects, pamphlets, posters, fliers	Students read articles and write a letter to the principal or school board requesting a change of a school rule or policy, such as the use of electronic devices.

There are several ways to introduce and sustain genre studies in the K–5 ELA class. Here are two of the most frequently used methods:

1. Engage in genre studies through a teacher-directed, explicit, deductive approach, where you introduce each genre and analyze it for its characteristics. Students read widely in each genre and they produce writing based on the knowledge and skills you have taught.

2. Implement genre studies through teacher-led inquiries. Among others, Fountas and Pinnell (2012) also suggest that you try a student-centered approach to genre studies. Students get immersed in reading exemplary texts to discover similar characteristics of a target genre during carefully directed exploratory lessons. This practice connects studying a variety of genres to the writing process and daily writing experiences.

Kindergarten through grade 5 learners who participate in instructional routines for reading and writing—specifically for genre studies—that are inquiry-based in nature are best described by Fountas and Pinnell:

By engaging deeply and constantly with a variety of high quality texts, they build an internal foundation of information on which they can base further learning. They learn how to develop genre understandings and can apply their thinking to any genre. (2012, 5)

Our perspective for genre studies is designed to promote literacy development through high levels of student engagement by integrating reading and writing in each genre. We depart from the genre study procedure suggested by Fountas and Pinnell (2012) somewhat, to immerse students in each target genre and to combine reading and writing experiences. Try this procedure for genre study as a routine in your ELA instructional framework:

1. Collect	• Collect a set of mentor texts in the genre to read aloud. • Be selective; use high-quality, authentic picture books or shorter texts (when possible). • Collect books (at a range of difficulty levels) to place in a genre basket in the classroom library—books students can choose to read independently. • Collect multiple copies of books for genre book clubs (books of interest to the grade level) and guided reading groups (must be at the appropriate level for the group).
2. Immerse	• Immerse students in several clear examples of the genre, also referred to as touchstone books (Troia 2007). As you read these mentor texts aloud, encourage students to think about, talk about, and identify common characteristics. • Invite students to select the genre for their independent reading. • Provide multiple copies of texts in the genre for book clubs and guided reading groups. Help students think about genre characteristics.
3. Study	• After students have read several examples, have them analyze characteristics that are common to the group of texts. • List the genre features they notice on chart paper or on an interactive whiteboard. Make sure that students are able to distinguish between characteristics that are always evident and those that are often evident.
4. Define	• Define the genre. Use the list of characteristics generated by the class to collaboratively create a short working definition (rather than offer one to your students).
5. Teach	• Teach specific minilessons on the important genre features on the list, using the mentor texts and adding new readings to the initial text set.
6. Read and Revise	• Expand student understandings during individual conferences about their independent reading, and facilitate group share sessions. • Encourage students to talk about the genre in their book clubs, guided reading discussions, reading conferences, and any other appropriate instructional contexts. • Add more characteristics to the class charts and revise the working definition of the genre if needed.
7. Write in the Genre	• Follow the writing process steps to facilitate the transfer of skills and understanding from reading to writing. • Encourage students to use the mentor texts and the genre traits. • Allow students to write in the author's voice before they find their own voices.

Adapted from Fountas and Pinnell (2012, 17).

One unit that not only taps into all four ELA skills but also highlights nonfiction is a biography unit. I time it to occur in January, and, as a class, we read a biography of Dr. Martin Luther King Jr. During this unit, students have access to other biographies of varying Lexile levels as well; nevertheless, once the shared reading piece is concluded, students then discuss and establish the components of a biography and are subsequently tasked with writing one themselves. I give them a set of questions and several days to each interview an adult of their choice; suggested subjects are parents, grandparents, and teachers in the school. By their own request, students have even interviewed school administrators. Once the interviews are completed, the biography writing begins, and then students present their finished work to the class. Lisa Peluso, grade 4 teacher

COACH'S NOTES

Remember to introduce your students to mixed-genre or multigenre reading and writing as well. At the elementary level, great mentor texts for multigenre reading and writing are the Magic School Bus series (www.scholastic.com/magicschoolbus) and Magic Tree House series (www.magictreehouse.com), in which scientific, informational writing is mixed with science fiction or historical narratives.

ROUTINE 2 Small-Group Reading Instruction and Paired Reading
GUIDED READING

Guided reading—a small-group reading instructional routine that should be used with all readers—serves three fundamental purposes, as described by Anita Iaquinta:

- **to meet the varying instructional needs of all the students in the classroom, enabling them to greatly expand their reading powers (Fountas and Pinnell 2001)**
- **to teach students to read increasingly difficult texts with understanding and fluency**
- **to construct meaning while using problem solving strategies to figure out unfamiliar words that deal with complex sentence structures, and to understand concepts or ideas not previously encountered. (2006, 3)**

The primary purpose is to co-construct meaning about the text with guidance from the teacher and to practice strategies so students can ultimately read independently. Guided reading is often combined with the Four Blocks approach (Cunningham, Hall, and Sigmon 1999), which includes guided reading, writing, self-selected, independent reading, and word work. During guided reading instruction, the rest of the class is engaged in independent work, which allows you to give all of your attention to one group.

Teacher-2-Teacher

When having guided reading groups or small-group instruction, consider using a visual that lets students know that they will not be able to talk with you unless they are part of the group. In the past I've used Shrek ears or even a crown. Students see this on my head and know that unless there is an emergency, they will not be able to interrupt me during this period. Edd Ohlsen, K–5 teacher on special assignment/peer coach

The guided reading routine that we suggest consists of three (expandable and adaptable) stages. Such a format has also been proposed by Charles Temple, Donna Ogle, Alan Crawford, and Penny Freppon (2013) and others.

Stage 1: Before Reading

Introduce and briefly discuss the text selected for instruction with your guided reading group. Use anticipation guides, questions that set the stage for the reading, and other pre-reading strategies of your choice.

The instructional purpose of this stage is for your students to
- enter the guided reading with curiosity and excitement
- preview text features or illustrations to get an overall understanding about the upcoming reading
- make predictions based on the cover the book or title of the reading
- ask questions
- use their (activated) prior knowledge to make sense of the new text more effectively
- get hooked at the beginning
- prepare and focus.

Stage 2: During Reading

As your students read the whole text or an excerpt selected for guided instruction with you, observe them for reading strategy use, and offer strategies that promote both their comprehension and critical thinking skills.

The instructional purpose of this stage is for your students to
- read the whole text or a specified selection to themselves either silently or softly whispering
- stop and process what they have read
- select, collect, and organize notes

- engage in a discussion about the reading
- develop new reading skills or enhance existing ones
- employ multiple reading comprehension strategies to make meaning
- request help from you as needed
- make meaning by reacting, responding, and associating
- interact and engage with the text.

Stage 3: After Reading

Engage your students in responding to the reading selection through whole-group discussions, think-pair-share and other paired activities, writing, or acting out aspects of the story. Return to the text, especially the challenging sections of it, to review the reading strategy used to make sense of the reading.

The instructional purpose of this stage is for your students to

- discuss what they have read
- offer their personal response to the reading and make connections between what they read and what they know
- revisit their predictions and talk about the similarities and differences
- reflect on or explain their strategy use
- synthesize what they have learned and apply the learning in a new way or reorganize the information and create something new to internalize and transfer the information.

COACH'S NOTES

Prior to conferring with students, have them use a graphic organizer to collect "evidence" of their reading goal. For example, students use sticky notes to record which tricky words they chunked into smaller words and where they found them. At the reading conference, students refer to these notes and take the lead, explaining their progress toward their reading goal and supporting it with the evidence collected. This technique allows students to take on more responsibility for their growth as readers. Students lead the reading conference and pave the way for their own learning.

Violeta Katsikis, literacy teacher coach

Guided reading groups tend to consist of students who are approximately on the same reading level. This type of homogeneous grouping ensures that the selected readings are easily tackled by all members of the group and that the reading comprehension strategies employed are meaningful for the group. We suggest you keep a running record of individual reading behaviors during guided reading time not only to make guided reading instruction manageable but also to collect formative assessment data that can lead to regrouping students as their reading needs change.

Teacher-2-Teacher

I group my class into four guided reading groups based on students' ability levels from benchmark assessments, and I differentiate instruction depending on a group's proficiency level. For groups with lower reading levels, especially ones including beginner ELLs, I front-load information—introduce vocabulary and provide more background knowledge—to prepare them for reading. With these students, my instruction includes a shared reading: I read aloud to model fluency and ask questions to check for students' comprehension. I would advise any new teacher to create a dynamic anchor chart of reading skills that can become a reference tool for reviewing and applying previously taught skills at various teachable moments during guided reading.

Joyce Smithok-Kollar, grade 2 teacher

PARTNERS READ

Managing group work effectively may be challenging for some teachers. In our years of experience, we discovered that many of the same teachers who found working with multiple groups difficult often found working with partners very satisfying. As long as you suggest a very structured framework for your students to follow, you should be successful using partner work in your classroom. The Partners Read routine is one such structured paired activity. It invites buddies of the same reading levels to work together to find meaning in their reading. You can easily move from pair to pair providing necessary guidance for each of these groups (occasionally grabbing two groups at the same time, replicating the type of instruction that you would provide in small homogeneous groups during guided reading). You can scaffold the Partners Read routine with printed questions to offer support or challenge to appropriate groups. This reading routine can be used daily or several times a week with partners. Consider using it whenever you present new social studies or science informational text to your students. After modeling how to closely read a portion of the article or a section of the textbook yourself, invite students to work with you on the next portion. Then, pair students of the same reading levels so that they can continue making sense of the reading together. This gradual release of responsibility (Fisher and Frey 2008) will prepare your students for success with the routine.

Follow these steps for Partners Read with any piece of text:

1. Student partners (or the teacher) divide the reading into chunks depending upon the grade level (i.e., sentence by sentence, paragraph by paragraph, section by section, page by page).
2. Partners assign themselves the first two chunks, and each reads *both* portions *silently*.

3. During a *second reading* of only *his or her own* portion, each student creates and writes *at least one* important question that is answered by the text (a text-dependent question).

4. Then the student who has been assigned the first chunk reads it out loud to his or her partner and poses the prepared question(s).

5. The listener searches the text to answer the question. Discussion between the two partners is where meaningful learning takes place, as they analyze the text and support their ideas with evidence. Back and forth, they discuss their findings.

6. Next, both partners record the question, the answer around which they find consensus, and the line or page number where they found this answer.

7. Students switch roles, and then repeat steps 4, 5, and 6 with the second chunk of text.

8. If the task is complete, the teacher will bring the whole class together and share questions and answers with all of the class members.

9. If the reading has not been completed, the partners continue with the next two chunks, proceeding through all of the steps above, until the teacher ends the session by bringing the class together for a group share.

COACH'S NOTES

When your students begin to partner read, be sure to co-develop with them a list of meaningful text-dependent questions to help guide their exploration of the text. At first you should scaffold their reading by having them choose questions from the following list. Later, older students will be able to generate their own questions. An anchor chart of these questions can serve as reference for those who still need them.

- What one word, phrase, or sentence illustrates the central idea?
- What word(s) stand out? Why do you think the author uses them?
- What does the word _____ mean? What other words provide clues?
- One of the themes of this story is _____. What evidence of this can you find in this story?
- What does the author want his readers to know about _____? Why do you say this?
- What have you learned by reading the captions on the page?
- What text features does the author use to help you make sense of this topic?
- What text structure does this reading follow: problem–solution, comparison–contrast, cause–effect, sequence, description–main ideas–details?

The Partners Read routine was inspired by the work of by Donna Ogle (2011). In *Partnering for Content Literacy: PRC2 in Action,* she goes into great detail about how learners can develop academic language while they actively make sense of content area reading when using the PRC2 framework (whose acronym stands for partner reading and content, too; xiv). Other reading researchers and practitioners suggest paired reading and reading dyads, as well (Frey and Fisher 2013; Fuchs, Fuchs, and Burish 2000; Miller et al. 2013). When students are encouraged to use buddies for reading, reading becomes less of a struggle for below-grade-level readers. Partners have the opportunity to work out their thinking with someone else, but they don't feel intimidated by doing it in front of the whole class.

ROUTINE 3 Individual Reading

The following three routines for individual reading will take you and your students from a highly structured framework to more and more independence, encouraging reading to become both an in-school and out-of-school habit.

FOUR-SQUARE ROTATIONS FOR SOCIAL STUDIES OR SCIENCE

The Four-Square rotation for social studies or science lessons is a routine for individual practice and growth in reading informational text (as well as fiction) and developing content area literacy. This routine addresses students' desire for choice, while it also addresses the need to instill greater independence in our learners as they work to improve their skills. The Four-Square rotation allows teachers to differentiate instruction by offering students choice in the way they work, leveled materials for comprehensible input, and a range of product options. Offering students four tasks to be completed in any order they prefer, the Four-Square rotation provides opportunities for students to do the following:

- read text independently at their instructional level (to increase fluency)
- read text at their grade level and practice answering text-dependent questions (with more rigorous informational text)
- analyze documents (charts, time lines, tables, photographs, political cartoons, graphs, etc.)
- build knowledge through content-rich nonfiction
- write pieces grounded in evidence from the text
- create visual tools (that answer questions, summarize their learning, serve as prewriting activities, or function as study tools)
- become intrinsically motivated through choice.

Each task should be designed to take approximately twenty minutes to complete, so most teachers choose to have students work on two tasks per day. They use the Four-Square rotation routine for either their science or their social studies unit. Some teachers we have spoken with have decided to borrow some reading time from their literacy blocks because so much of the Four-Square activities focus on reading. They feel it is a fair exchange of time.

Task 1 is for independent reading. Designed to build background knowledge and content knowledge, this task requires that you gather as many texts (both fiction and nonfiction), excerpts, or picture books as you can on the topic of study, making sure to provide texts at various reading levels. In the Eastport-South Manor School District, both elementary library media specialists actively worked to gather leveled materials, scouring their databases and their libraries for multiple resources. They provided teachers and students access to materials appropriate to many levels of readiness. In Figure 2.9, two fourth graders choose from among the many options provided for task 1.

Task 2 is an independent reading and writing task with nonfiction text. Your students will read a grade-level informational text that you have selected and respond to it by answering text-dependent questions or by summarizing the reading.

Task 3 gives students the option of working alone or with a partner to analyze a document related to the topic (the document can be an excerpt from a speech, a political cartoon, a graph, a chart, a map, a photograph, etc.).

Task 4 provides a creative opportunity for students to design a visual tool, to produce a Foldable (a piece of paper that can be folded into infinite shapes to help graphically organize ideas), or to generate a study tool. In Figure 2.10, a fourth grader designs illustrations and hashtags to highlight key concepts he learned about his topic.

Figure 2.9 Fourth Graders Choose Books for Independent Reading (Task 1 in Four-Square Rotation)

Figure 2.10 A Fourth Grader Designs Illustrations and Hashtags (Task 4 in Four-Square Rotation)

When you discuss the format of the Four-Square rotation with your class, be sure to mention the following information:

- how often the class will engage in this routine
- how much time will be given for each task to be completed
- what student accountability looks like

To introduce the Four-Square rotation to your class, follow this multistep approach:

1. Discuss the structure and design of the Four-Square rotation routine.
2. Cocreate a list of expectations for how students are to work.
3. Model how each of the tasks must be completed.

Your students must be able to work for at least twenty minutes independently before you begin a teacher-led small group as a fifth rotation, should you choose to do so. These small teacher-led groups might be homogeneous, skill-based groups (similar to guided reading groups). This will allow you to work with small groups of learners who have the same needs. Consider running only one or, at most, two small groups a day until your students become more independent. If you are tied up with one group, you will not be available to the rest of your students.

As part of the list of expectations that you generate with your class, be sure to brainstorm ways students can get help if you are off limits for a time. (Suggest that students use class resources, anchor charts, learning partners, or a daily chosen "student teacher" when they require assistance and you are not immediately available.) Younger students may require your attention and ability to facilitate the groups, as needed, in which case you won't be able to spend a long time with one particular group.

If you do choose to work with guided groups, leave some time afterward to circulate and facilitate the work of the rest of the class as the students continue with their independent tasks. Don't hesitate to call the whole class together (and stop all work) at any point when you think that the rules and expectations need to be reviewed or perhaps even revised.

Finally, always follow the Four-Square rotation with a student self-evaluation of that day's work. See Figure 2.11 for an example of Four-Square rotation with literacy tasks applicable to social studies or science. We have also included a selection of the actual tasks that Erin Marone, Lisa Martinez, and Amy Brown prepared to run the Four-Square rotation routine during a unit on Native Americans (see Figure 2.12). In Figure 2.13, you'll see an example of one student tracking progress with the Four-Square rotation as well as his self-evaluation.

Teacher-2-Teacher

*Erin Marone, my library media specialist, helped me gather books at my students'
independent reading levels and collected nonfiction articles at grade level. Working together
made the preparation for my Four-Square rotation routine on the topic of forming a new
nation much easier than if I had had to find all of the resources by myself. Working with
another staff member cuts down your planning time dramatically.*

*My students were very motivated, on task, and engaged in these social studies activities.
I was able to support students who needed extra support while my more advanced
students were able to independently complete two or three of the choice tasks in each
rotation. Love this activity!*

Charissa Voss, grade 5 teacher

Figure 2.11 Four-Square Rotation—Social Studies or Science

1. Independent Reading • Fiction and nonfiction • Texts provide background knowledge about social studies or science topic • Teacher-provided texts at different reading levels • Student choice • Independent reading levels	**2. Independent Reading/Writing Task with Nonfiction Text** • Respond to a provided text: textbook, nonfiction article, or document • Answer text-dependent questions about grade-level informational text • Summarize
3. Independent Critical Analysis Task (Option: Alone or with a Partner) Using appropriate language of the discipline, analyze provided text: • chart • graph • map • time line • political cartoon • photograph	**4. Creation of a Visual Tool/ Other Activity (Choice)** • Foldable or other visual tool • Vocabulary-building activity • Annotated visual/illustration/poster • "Smart card" on the topic—a student-generated study tool

Figure 2.12 Sample Four-Square Rotation: Native American Unit

Square #1: Independent Reading

Directions: At this station you will be browsing or reading through the nonfiction books about the Algonquin or Iroquois. Choose one book about the Iroquois and one about the Algonquin. Please complete the chart for each book. When you are finished, you may read or look through additional books.

Subject:	Title:	Author:	Reflect: What was the central idea of the book? Provide one or two details that support the idea.
Iroquois Check when complete.			
Algonquin Check when complete.			

Square #2: Articles from the Virtual Reference Collection

Name: _____

Number: _____

Directions: You must choose one article on the Iroquois and one article on the Algonquins to read. Fill out the chart below for each article.

Topic:	
Article Title:	
Author:	
Events:	People:
Key Terms:	Key Facts:

Additional Information (quotes, references, etc.):

Square #3: Timeline

http://marjorieintegratedproject09.wikispaces.com/Iroquois+Six+Nations+Confederacy

1. Which happened first, the Iroquois conquering Illinois or the Iroquois being attacked by Americans?

2. About how much time passed between when the League of the Iroquois was founded and a peace treaty was negotiated with the Algonquins?

Square #4: Student Choice Boards

Name: _____

Number: _____

Directions: Select an activity from one of the boxes below to complete using the information you gathered from your articles, documents, and books on either the Algonquin Native Americans or the Iroquois.

How were the Iroquois and the Algonquins similar? How were they different? Create and complete a "Foldable" comparing the Iroquois and Algonquin tribes.	Explore the culture of either the Iroquois or the Algonquins by writing a poem or a jingle/song using descriptive language to bring their culture to life.	Imagine you were living among the Iroquois or the Algonquin tribe. Write a newspaper article reporting on an important event in Native American history. Remember to create a headline!
Become an illustrator by drawing four important pictures highlighting the Iroquois or Algonquin culture. Below the pictures make sure to include a brief caption and a hashtag or subject.	**Student Choice Board:** *Which one will you choose?*	Create a Facebook profile for an Iroquois/Algonquin tribe member. Describe your hobbies, likes, and dislikes. Fill in your status with cultural and gender-specific activities you would be participating in.

Figure 2.13 Four-Square Rotation Chart with Student Responses

My Four-Square Rotation Chart

Task #1: Independent Reading I completed: *The Constitution of the United states*	Task #2: Independent Reading/Writing Task With Non-Fiction Text I completed: *The United States Bill of Rights*
Task #3: Independent Critical Analysis Task /Analyzing Documents I completed: *Northwest Territory* *The system of Check and balances*	Task #4: (Creation of a visual tool) I completed: *The Three Branches of Government (poster)*

My name: *Joelle*   Date: _____

Self-Evaluation: Circle One and write a brief explanation:
I think I earned a smiley face because I did 4 tasks. I also think this and I was on task.

IN-CLASS INDEPENDENT READING

First and foremost, create the time and space to read for enjoyment every day in class (Krashen 2011). Make a range of engaging fiction and nonfiction books, magazines, poetry, graphic novels, newspapers, comic books, and so on available for students to reach for. Model independent reading and let them see you "buried in a book." (See Figure 2.14 for a picture of a student engrossed in a book.) Or take out your iPad or tablet reader and let them see you hooked on reading on your device.

Figure 2.14 A Fourth Grader Buried in a Book

A critical component to establishing a successful independent reading routine is to set concise and challenging expectations and immerse students immediately in the reading process. Students practice their independent reading routine as soon as they are introduced to the program, so it becomes second nature. A multistep series of checkpoints is implemented and must be completed before they graduate to the next independent reading book. Each student must complete graphic organizers, comprehension questions, and reading responses prior to taking a comprehension quiz on the computer. Accomplishments are celebrated and shared with the class weekly to motivate and encourage friendly competition and ensure productive daily independent reading sessions.

Marisa Fontana, grade 4 teacher

Among others, Debbie Miller, Barbara Moss, Nell Duke, and Ellen Oliver Keene (2013) make a compelling case for the implementation of scaffolded silent reading (ScSR), which includes a range of appropriate supports and teacher monitoring of the reading. D. Ray Reutzel, Cindy Jones, and Terry Newman (2010) also suggest a makeover for the traditional practice by adding student accountability through completed reading response assignments and time for teacher-student conferencing about the reading. Figure 2.15 summarizes the similarities and differences of the key characteristics of the traditional approach and the more current, scaffolded approach to silent reading.

Figure 2.15 Comparison of Traditional and Scaffolded Sustained Silent Reading

Key Considerations	Traditional Sustained Silent Reading	Scaffolded Sustained Silent Reading
What is your role?	Model for students how to read self-selected books silently.	Teach book selection strategies to make sure your students choose appropriate books for independent reading.
How do you set up the class library?	Store and display books in a variety of ways around the classroom.	Store and display books by genre and according to levels of reading difficulty.

continues

Key Considerations	Traditional Sustained Silent Reading	Scaffolded Sustained Silent Reading
How do you motivate your students?	Offer your students free choice of reading materials, allowing them to stay with the same genre as long as they wish to do so.	Use a genre selection wheel or other tool to limit reading selection to a certain genre each day and to ultimately encourage wide reading across genres.
How do your students select books based on the level of text difficulty?	Allow students to freely choose the level of difficulty of reading materials.	Make sure students choose texts at their independent reading levels with your support.
How do you monitor individual reading?	N/A	Use brief individual student reading conferences.
How do you make students accountable?	N/A	Have students read aloud to you and answer your questions. Have students set personal goals for completing the reading of a book within a time frame. Make sure students complete one or more response projects.

Adapted from Miller et al. (2013, 14).

Text Markups

During scaffolded silent reading, have students develop the habit of using a simple system for coding the target texts. After you model and students practice using annotations, students will appreciate how text coding will make their thinking visible: as your students read, they will interact with the text, using an established set of markups to critically respond to the reading. There are some standard notation systems available using symbols (see Buehl 2009), or you can make up your own. Color coding, underlining, or circling text features or using sticky notes will also promote active reading, thinking about the text, and conducting text-level analysis and reflection at the elementary level.

= Confirmed my thinking

+ Added to my thinking

△ Changed my thinking

In my reading room, I have a reminder posted for students to use for text markups. The notations came about in response to some of my students having a difficult time revising their preconceived notions. They could identify particular facts learned during reading but struggled to reconcile these after reading. The intention of the notations was twofold: to invite students to monitor their own thinking and to celebrate the changes in thinking that readers often experience, particularly in informational text. I presented the three signs (=, +, and △) in conjunction with sign language visual cues during read-alouds and shared reading. Kindergarten through third-grade students were quick to incorporate the vocabulary, the signs, and the notations into class discussions, partner readings, and independent responses. In addition, the students themselves began to transfer the notations to fiction text. They came to understand that as they added to and changed their thinking, they were learning. I have also found that a number of other notations can be used, such as the exclamation point for something important and the question mark for something not understood.

Dana Cerbone, K–5 teacher on special assignment/peer coach

Marginal Notes: Noticings and Wonderings

A more elaborate way of annotating readings is through marginal notes that can be written directly in the margins of the text or on sticky notes. Try this: On the left-hand side, have students jot down what they notice about the words, the sentences, the paragraphs, or the text as a whole. Keep the notes factual and brief and encourage these marginal notes to be connected to what the students already know. On the right-hand side, have students write down what words or phrases they found particularly interesting or unusual, or even which sentence made them curious. Jotting down noticings and wonderings is a powerful strategy to strengthen your students' language awareness. As students share their noticings and wonderings, you can support them with appropriate sentence starters initially. See Figure 2.16 for sentence starters to discuss noticings and wonderings and Figure 2.17 for examples from a second grader in response to reading about Siberian huskies for a research project.

Figure 2.16 Sentence Starters to Support Reporting on Noticings and Wonderings

Noticings	Wonderings
• When I read the first sentence, I noticed … • When I got to the second paragraph, I knew … • When I was reading this text, I noticed … • After finishing the whole text, I realized/ noticed …	• I was wondering what the author meant by saying … • I am curious why the author used the word/ phrase … • I wonder why … • I am not sure what … • When I read that word/phrase/sentence/ paragraph, I started thinking about how …

Figure 2.17 Second Grader's Notes About Siberian Huskies

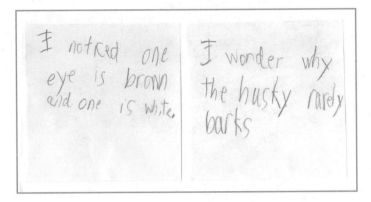

OUTSIDE-CLASS INDEPENDENT READING

For many teachers, the routine of independent reading is one that is completed outside of class and school. Students may choose any book (or magazine) they want to read, preferably at their independent reading level. Reading at this level is important because it builds fluency and the necessary stamina for future reading assessment tasks. Generally, accountability for this routine comes in the form of a parent-signed reading log or, simply, a list of the number of pages an individual student has read. However, there are other ways to determine that students have been reading independently and, more importantly, that they have been making sense of what they've read.

In Figure 2.18, you'll find a fiction tic-tac-toe choice board that focuses on essential story elements. Students choose two tasks that address characterization, setting, plot, conflict, or theme. In Figure 2.19 you'll find a nonfiction tic-tac-toe choice board, where students choose two tasks that address text structure, central idea and supporting details, syntax, or vocabulary. The students must make a tic-tac-toe line by going through the center box. This design allows teachers to strategically place activities that are balanced (a writing activity with a drawing activity, for example, or one task on theme with another on characterization). Each of the tasks on the choice board reflects important concepts and skills that students need to build. Before you give students this board to use independently, however, model each task and complete one as a whole class. See some student responses to tic-tac-toe choice boards in Figures 2.20 through 2.22. In Figure 2.20, a fifth grader responds to a nonfiction choice board by summarizing his reading and generating his own questions for further reflection. In addition, in Figure 2.21, he chooses two sentences that the author uses and combines them into one. Finally, in Figure 2.22, he chooses one of the text features (captions) and explains how it helps him learn the information.

Figure 2.18 A Fiction Tic-Tac-Toe Choice Board

Describe how the setting of the story impacts its development in at least two different ways.	**Choose one event** and discuss its impact on the main character.	**Discuss the two sides of one conflict** that is present in this reading.
Find one example in the text that shows evidence of one of the themes discussed in class: (i.e., loyalty, friendship, perseverance, honesty, kindness).	Complete your independent reading each night. Choose two after-reading tasks to make a tic-tac-toe by going through this center box.	**List two attributes** of the main character and provide evidence from the text for each (including page numbers).
Find two important quotes. Explain their significance in the development of the story or how they reflect a particular character's attributes.	**Write a postcard from the point of view of** _____ to _____.	**Create a time line** showing the change over time of the main character.

Essential understandings: story elements (characterization, setting, plot, conflict, theme)

Figure 2.19 A Nonfiction Tic-Tac-Toe Choice Board

Summarize tonight's reading. Include what is most important about the topic. **Generate your own question** about the topic.	**What is the central idea** of the reading? What does the author want you to understand?	From the reading, **pick out two sentences** that the author uses. **Combine them into one.**
Choose one new vocabulary word that you don't know. Based on context clues, what do you think the word means? Which words give you a clue to the meaning?	Complete your independent reading each night. Choose two after-reading tasks to make a tic-tac-toe by going through this center box.	**Complete the provided graphic organizer** about the main idea and supporting details.
What is one of the features of this nonfiction text that helps you learn the information? How is it useful?	**Make a personal connection** to something you just read.	**Describe the problem and/or the solution** discussed in your text.

Essential understandings: nonfiction elements (text structure, central idea and supporting details, syntax, and vocabulary)

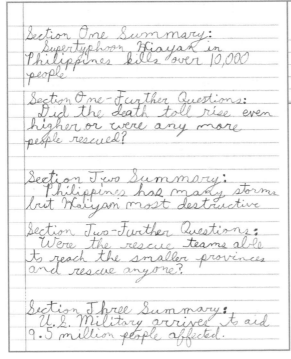

Section One Summary:
Supertyphoon Haiyan in Philippines kills over 10,000 people

Section One—Further Questions:
Did the death toll rise even higher or were any more people rescued?

Section Two Summary:
Philippines has many storms but Haiyan most destructive

Section Two—Further Questions:
Were the rescue teams able to reach the smaller provinces and rescue anyone?

Section Three Summary:
U.S. Military arrives to aid 9.5 million people affected.

Section Three—Further Questions:
How can I help the people that were affected by Haiyan?

Figure 2.20 Joey's Response: Summarize and Generate Questions

Look at how Joey's thinking evolves as he responds to three different prompts from the Nonfiction Tic-Tac-Toe Choice Board.

Figure 2.21 Joey's Response: Sentence Combining

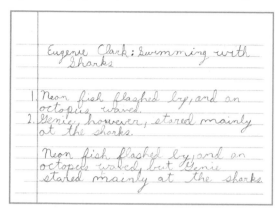

Figure 2.22 Joey's Response: Text Feature

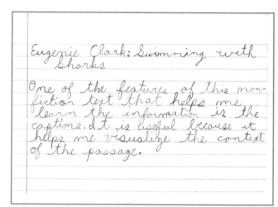

Scaffolding Toolbox: Story Maps and Text Structure Maps

For fiction, there are many story maps you might be familiar with. The one we suggest is shown in Figure 2.23. This story map format scaffolds students' comprehension of a story as well as their writing. By the time your students have answered all of the questions provided, they will be able to construct a summary of the story that clearly describes the beginning, middle, and end.

As you discuss the text structure of informational texts, you will need to shift your focus. Nonfiction text does not have a beginning, middle, and end the same way narrative genres do. Rather, it follows one of at least six predictable text structures that might be challenging to observe. To assist your learners in making sense of their informational texts, teach them to associate each text structure with a visual or graphic representation that aligns with the internal organization of the text. Initially, provide a graphic organizer for the text structure of a specific reading (see Figure 2.24). As your students become more proficient with the graphic organizer you have given, invite them to create their own text map to help them follow the progression of ideas in their reading.

Figure 2.23 Story Map Template

Story Map Template

Name: _____

Title of the Story: _____

I can write about Beginning, Middle, and End

At first. At the beginning,		Who are the characters? (main, minor) What is the setting? (when, where)
Then, Later on, Next,		What is the problem? (conflict) What does the main character try to do about the problem? How does the main character feel about the problem? What event is the climax of the story?
Finally, In the end, By the end of the story.		How does the problem get resolved? How does the main character change from the beginning to the end of the story? What lesson does the main character learn?

Visit the book's companion website at heinemann.com/products/E05661.aspx for blank templates, provided in Microsoft Word and PDF formats, of the graphic organizers we present here. We encourage you to customize these text structure maps by adding information unique to the texts you are working with, such as titles, headings, and labels. If necessary, offer students partially completed text structure maps to guide their own thinking and organization of ideas. Also, see the sentence frames that are aligned to these six text types in the "Scaffolding Toolbox" section in Chapter 3. They will help your students write about their reading with appropriate academic language. Using both scaffolding tools together might provide effective support for your most needy students.

Figure 2.24 Nonfiction Text Types with Text Structure Graphic Organizers

Text Type	Text Characteristics	Suggested Text Structure Maps
Description	Text describes or defines information.	Description web 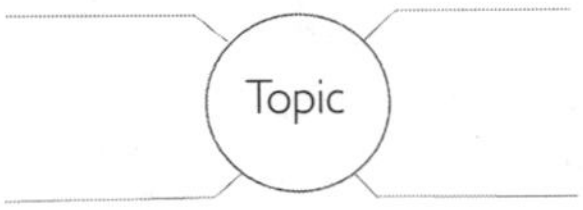 Description flowchart 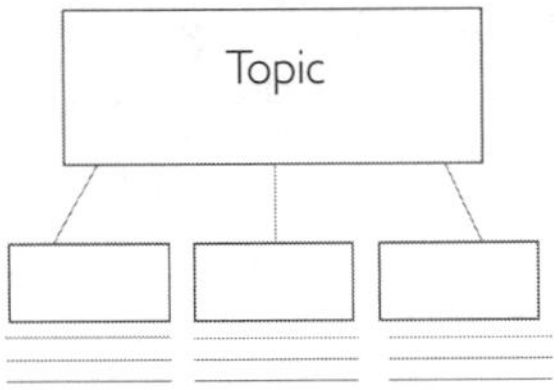
Comparison–Contrast	Text presents similarities and differences between people, ideas, events, facts, concepts, texts, processes, etc.	Compare-and-contrast double T-chart 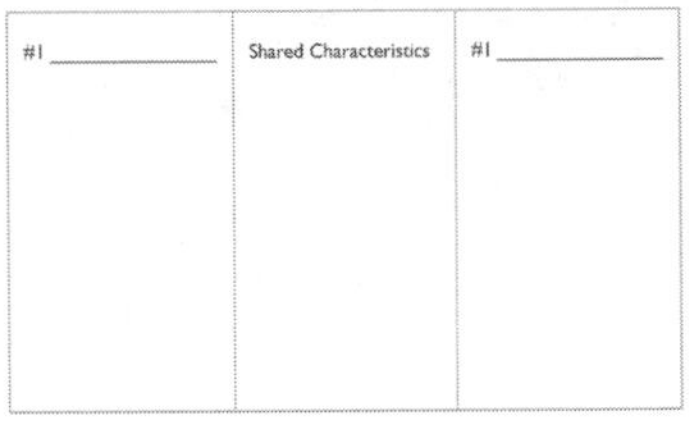 Venn diagram 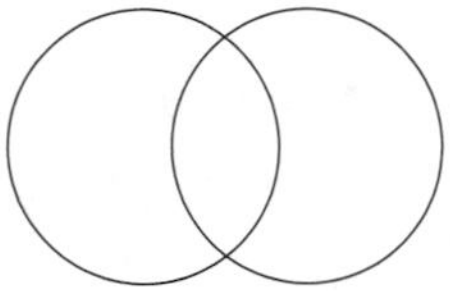

continues

Text Type	Text Characteristics	Suggested Text Structure Maps
Cause–Effect	Text describes how one or more events lead to specific consequences.	**Cause–effect map** Cause Effect **Cause–effect flowchart** Cause → Effect #1 / Effect #2
Sequence/Chronology	Text presents a chronological order of events.	**Sequence map** First Next Then After Finally **Sequence flowchart**
Problem and Solution	Text presents a problem and one or more solutions.	**Problem-and-solution outline** Problem — Who / What / Where / When / Why Solution — End result/Resolution to the problem **Problem-and-solution chart** Problem — What happened? / Solution — How did it get resolved?

continues

Figure 2.24 Nonfiction Text Types with Text Structure Graphic Organizers, *continued*

Text Type	Text Characteristics	Suggested Text Structure Maps
Opinion or Persuasion	Text presents the author's opinion and/or is written to persuade the reader.	Persuasion map Opinion outline

---

✔ **CHECK THIS OUT**

Graphic organizers are essential scaffolding tools that support processing text on all grade levels. Here are some websites with additional downloadable graphic organizers:

> www.eduplace.com/graphicorganizer
> http://freeology.com/graphicorgs
> www.graphic.org
> www.writedesignonline.com/organizers

How to Differentiate Reading Instruction

Figure 2.25 offers a quick guide for differentiated practices to address the readiness needs of diverse learners. Please note that there are some overlapping suggestions for ELLs and students with disabilities, whereas their unique needs are also considered.

Figure 2.25 Differentiating Reading Instruction

ELLs	SWDs	Advanced Learners
• Model and read aloud more extensively for ELLs and SWDs. • Reread target text with students during guided reading and engage them in strategic meaning making. • Use graphic organizers and scaffolded tasks for higher levels of engagement in all your reading routines. • Devote ample time to pre-reading activities to build or activate prior knowledge. • Vary the grouping configurations for guided reading to avoid letting students feel stigmatized. • Use the language experience approach (LEA) to allow students to see their own experiences written into a story, which, in turn, can be read and used for a range of instructional purposes. • Use supplemental reading materials and videos or other visual input to support reading comprehension.		• Encourage them to prepare a self-chosen read-aloud to present to the class. • Encourage them to prepare a few questions ahead of time in order to guide an upcoming Socratic circle (instead of having you lead it). • Challenge them to compare the text they are reading with other texts they have read or to make real-world connections in a persuasive way. • Ask them to prepare five-minute book talks to encourage others to read their favorite books, as described in Jim Trelease's *The Read-Aloud Handbook* (2013). • Use the Junior Great Books program with these students. While the literature used by JGB would benefit your entire class, these students will thrive with the challenge provided by the quality text and the types of questions asked. • During a Four-Square rotation, have these students *compare and contrast* two documents for their analysis, rather than simply analyze one.
• Teach reading skills in conjunction with the other modalities (speaking, listening, and writing) to enhance students' communicative competence. • Incorporate culturally relevant themes and topics that allow students to see themselves in the text. • Use multicultural literature that allow ELLs to make more meaningful connections. • Foster and build on literacy in the native language if possible (for example, encourage independent reading in both the native language and English).	• Employ explicit instruction complete with teacher explanation and modeling of target reading skills. • Offer immediate corrective feedback. • Teach reading skills in conjunction with self-monitoring strategies. • Help students generalize their learning to new learning. • Provide reading materials that these students can achieve independent success with. • Use guided reading instruction time to address these students' literacy development needs through targeted interventions.	

A Final Thought

Educators know that students must be able to read complex text with greater acuity. Achieving such success, however, is no small feat. It will require your determination and ingenuity to motivate students to read more and more *every day*. It will necessitate that you plan lessons that engage your learners with *more informational text* as well as with literature. It will warrant more time for reading *during class* than you may have provided in years past. However, as you dedicate yourself to improving your students' literacy and begin embedding some of the suggested reading routines into the fabric of your classroom, you'll see your students' interest, stamina, and reading acumen flourish.

Essential Questions for Individual Reflection, Collegial Circles, and Group Discussions

- *What is the central idea running through this chapter that informs your instruction?*

- *Why is it important to provide ample opportunity for your students to read at their independent reading levels even though grade level assessments might be at higher levels?*

- *How will you fit the recommended routines into your daily and weekly literacy instructional practice?*

- *How can graphic organizers support meaning making during reading?*

- *How often do students read independently in your class? How often should they be reading to develop literacy competencies?*

- *What elements should be part of your reading routines?*

- *What challenges do you anticipate as you implement the suggested reading routines?*

- *How can you support your struggling learners and ELLs as you expose them to increasingly complex varied text?*

- *How can you challenge advanced learners while continuing to provide support for on-grade learners as well as struggling learners?*

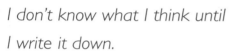

Chapter 3

WRITING
ROUTINES

I don't know what I think until
I write it down.

Joan Didion

How do I know what I think until
I see what I say?

E. M. Forster

Overview

In this chapter, we

- summarize research support for the writing routines we present
- examine the writing expectations of the Common Core State Standards
- establish routines for (1) daily writing activities, (2) the writing process, and (3) note taking for research
- present examples, templates, and classroom vignettes along with recommendations from coaches to support the implementation of the routines
- add sentence frames to the scaffolding toolbox
- offer differentiation of writing instruction for English learners, students with disabilities, and advanced learners.

Writing Routines at a Glance

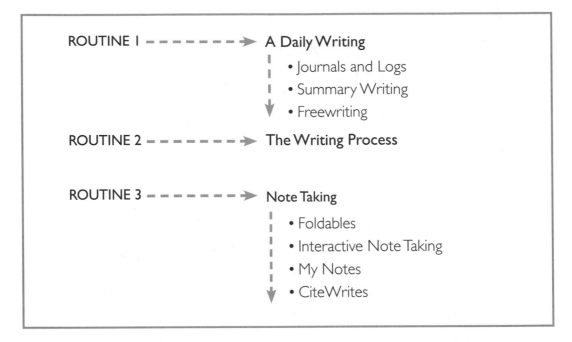

ROUTINE 1 ----------> A Daily Writing
  • Journals and Logs
  • Summary Writing
  • Freewriting

ROUTINE 2 ----------> The Writing Process

ROUTINE 3 ----------> Note Taking
  • Foldables
  • Interactive Note Taking
  • My Notes
  • CiteWrites

What Does the Research Say About Teaching Writing?

We are sure that you wonder about the types of instruction needed to improve the quality of writing produced by your students. Both pioneering research studies and very recent ones should guide your decision in selecting the most effective instructional routines.

Over twenty-five years ago, Hillocks (1986), and then more recently, Graham and Perin (2007), conducted comprehensive reviews of writing interventions with students in grades 3 to college and with students in grades 4 to 12, respectively. The two reports shared some of the same findings about what *did* and *did not* improve student writing: they both noted that explicit instruction in sentence combining, studying exemplary modes of writing, and inquiry-based writing instruction had a positive impact, and, on the flip side, they concluded that grammar instruction was *not* beneficial for improving writing.

The differences in their findings are also intriguing. In the earlier study, Hillocks reported improvement in student writing when writing guides or scales were utilized; Graham and Perin, on the other hand, reported positive outcomes for a range of additional interventions including teaching the process approach for writing, teaching strategies explicitly, teaching summarization, engaging students in prewriting activities, offering structured peer assistance, setting product goals, and utilizing word processing.

Some studies focused only on special populations. For example, Gersten and Baker (2001) limited their investigation on effective writing instruction to students with disabilities in their review of previous research and identified five instructional elements that resulted in positive outcomes for struggling writers:

1. Explicit teacher modeling of the writing process and composing strategies
2. Peer collaboration and teacher conferencing to gain informative feedback
3. Use of procedural prompts (e.g., graphic organizers, mnemonics, outlines, checklists) to facilitate planning and revising
4. Limiting barriers produced by poor text transcription (e.g., dictating)
5. Self-regulation (e.g., self-statements and questions) (as cited in Troia 2007, 135)

Many of these findings are also aligned to research outcomes of studies conducted with students who do not have any classifications, confirming that both general education teachers and those working with special populations might be able to use similar approaches.

Most recently, Steve Graham, Debra McKeown, Sharlene Kiuhara, and Karen Harris (2012) conducted a systematic review of writing intervention research and found that the following explicit instructional practices had positive effects on students' writing performance: instruction in strategies, self-regulation with strategies, text structure, creativity or imagery, and transcription skills (how to move from speech to the systematic representation of language in written form, such as understanding sound-letter correspondence). In addition, they noted that procedures for scaffolding and supporting students' writing are also highly effective, such as performing prewriting activities, obtaining peer assistance when writing, establishing product goals, and assessing writing.

When Gary Troia (2007) reviewed research on writing instruction, he suggested something similar to the basic premise of this book: "a major step in implementing strong writing instruction is establishing routines for (a) daily writing instruction, (b) covering the whole writing curriculum, and (c) examining the valued qualities of good writing" (37). The three routines in this chapter will help you focus on making writing a daily occurrence for students; it will support the implementation of any comprehensive writing program that you may use in your school; and it will also include the study of exemplary written work such as mentor texts (Dorfman and Cappelli 2007).

What Are the Writing Demands of the Common Core?

If students are to make knowledge their own, they must struggle with the details, wrestle with the facts, and rework raw information and dimly understood concepts into language they can communicate to someone else. In short, if students are to learn, they must write. (NCWASC 2003, 9)

Ten years after this imperative from the National Commission on Writing in America's Schools and Colleges, the urgency of teaching students to become effective writers has not diminished. Writing—often considered the most difficult of the four language skills—must be incorporated into daily routines in meaningful and engaging ways. The College and Career Readiness Anchor Standards for Writing (NGA Center for Best Practices and CCSSO 2010) are divided into four major sections:

1. Text Types and Purposes: Students learn to produce opinion and argument pieces and also write in informative and explanatory and narrative structures.

2. Production and Distribution of Writing: Students engage in the writing process and share their final product in multiple ways; they also learn to use technology across all genres.

3. Research to Build and Present Knowledge: Students take an analytical approach to both literature and nonfiction; engage in collaborative and independent research; and present their findings.

4. Range of Writing: Students participate in a variety of writing experiences across the subject matters in the elementary grades.

The grade-level progression charts that accompany the ten anchor standards offer much-needed details on how to translate the rigorous goals into age- and grade-appropriate expectations.

Writing Routines

When writing becomes routine in your classroom, students see that you value writing and that you are going to help them become better writers. Students must develop a routine for writing, as a daily activity, not a series of isolated assignments (Fountas and Pinnell 2001). With practice, they will be able to communicate their thoughts and ideas more logically and coherently. Over time, this skill, which is generally the most resisted by students, will become less onerous to them. In fact, with the right support and encouragement, your students who were formerly averse to writing will even begin to anticipate what they will write about when it is time to freewrite or journal.

Writing to learn as a routine helps students clarify their thoughts and engage in critical thinking. Taking notes, creating summaries, and writing opinion pieces evoke different levels of thinking from the learner. While taking notes asks students to analyze and record information they deem most important about a concept, creating summaries requires them to synthesize—often from several activities, text readings, and class discussions—the essence of what they have learned. Writing opinion pieces calls for learners to evaluate the topic under study and to take a stand, providing reasons to support their claim. Take a look at the fourth graders engaged in writing to learn in Figures 3.1a and 3.1b.

The goal here is to create in your classroom an environment where everyone always writes. The students write notes, questions, reflections, and summaries. They write to think; they write to organize ideas; they write to learn and remember; they write to record notes to study from later on. They write short pieces. They write long pieces. They write on demand; they write using the writing process.

We recommend you establish the following three routines to foster students' writing development.

Figure 3.1a A Fourth Grader Writing a Summary Statement   **Figure 3.1b** A Fourth Grader Taking Notes

ROUTINE 1 Daily Writing

Donald Graves said, "If you provide frequent occasions for writing, then students start to think about writing when they are not doing it. I call this a state of constant composition" (National Writing Project and Nagin 2006, 22). Since writing is the most difficult of the literacy skills to develop, it must be practiced regularly across the curriculum and throughout each day. To develop this skill, you must establish daily routines, providing students multiple opportunities to write. The three daily routines that we suggest are (1) journal writing and writing in logs; (2) summary writing; and (3) freewriting.

Obviously, you won't use all of these routines each day. Choose appropriately—depending upon your curriculum and your lesson objectives—from among the different options. The goal is to ensure that your students are writing abundantly using at least one of them every day.

JOURNALS AND LOGS

Keeping journals and logs in the content areas helps students formulate opinions, process new learning, and develop further understandings about a topic. Since "knowing is a process" (Bruner 1966, 72), we see these records as the knowledge warehouse where critical thinking takes place. Students record observations, opinions, essential understandings, questions, ideas, and important facts so that they can reorganize and make sense of the information. You can establish a separate notebook, a separate folder, or one section of a binder as a repository for daily writing. While you do not need to grade these daily entries, we advise that you periodically collect these records and respond to students in writing. There are many types of journals and logs to choose from for your daily routine. One we find particularly effective is dialogue journaling, where the student corresponds with a parent or other family member, or even a classmate or the teacher. See Figures 3.2a and 3.2b for excerpts from two third graders as they used one of their dialogue journals to plan a playdate and seek parental permission.

Figure 3.2a Dialogue Journal Page from Xavier

Dear Ben,

I want to have a playdate with you. I want to have a playdate with you because we haven't had any playdats in a while. I also want to try to have a sleepover with you too. When we have a sleepover we are so going to have alot of fun.

Figure 3.2b Dialogue Journal Page from Ben

Dear Mom and Dad,

Me and Xavier never had a sleepover. So we would like to go to his house. As you can see.

Teacher-2-Teacher

Although kindergartners enter school with a wide range of reading and writing ability levels, we begin the routine of keeping a class journal by the second week of school. The journal accompanies our class "pet," a stuffed bunny named Francis. The students take turns taking Francis home each night, and they must create an illustrated journal entry telling us what happened when Francis went home with them. Initially, some children are able to write only a word or two to accompany their illustration, but eventually most are able to complete one sentence. As part of our daily morning routine we review Francis' travel journal, with the student presenting his or her journal entry to the class. This is followed by a "warm" critique, which I introduce as "Things that I love about this, by Mrs. Cordeiro." I tell the child the things I love about the entry, which always includes a reminder that we head each page with our first and last names, we use uppercase and lowercase letters as appropriate, we start each sentence with an uppercase letter, we end each sentence with a member of the punctuation family, and we always have manners when we speak and write. First I point out which elements the student has included and tell him or her how much I love this. If the student has forgotten any of these elements, I ask, "What might make this sentence just a little bit better?" By October the students know the routine by heart and say it along with me.

Kelley Cordeiro, kindergarten teacher

When deciding what type of daily entry your students should make in their journals or logs to enhance their content acquisition, consider opinion logs, science observation journals, or history journals, which evoke both creativity and critical thinking.

Opinion Logs

Since students in elementary classes are expected to compose opinion pieces in all content areas from the time they enter school, we suggest you engage them in a daily practice of stating their opinions, not only during class discussions, but in writing as well. Establishing a personal opinion log helps writing and thinking about opinions to become a habit. Since students in an active classroom environment have frequent opportunities to speak and exchange ideas, express thoughts, and state preferences orally, a subtle shift in practice will make such communication transfer into writing instruction as well.

The personal opinion log—just as any other type of journal or log you might choose to use as your daily routine—might be a regular marble notebook (decorated and personalized) specifically designated for stating opinions. Other options include using loose-leaf pages, index cards on a book ring, or electronic media, such as the NoteBook app on the iPad or Evernote on a Mac or PC. Students can keep track of their opinions on a variety of content-based, literacy-related, and authentic, real-world topics.

Maintaining an opinion log serves multiple purposes and helps students do the following:

- **learn to state preferences**
- **formulate opinions using suggested sentence frames or words or phrases**
- **develop ownership of opinions by putting them in writing**
- **make choices and justify them**
- **make connections to content area learning**
- **express their opinions in a more structured format**
- **reflect on and re-evaluate opinions held previously (since they remain available in the log)**
- **notice how opinions change over time.**

See Figure 3.3 for a completed personal opinion log on musical instruments.

As students progress through the grades, the requirement for stating opinions will get more complex. It is apparent that students need to use

Figure 3.3 Opinion Log on Musical Instruments

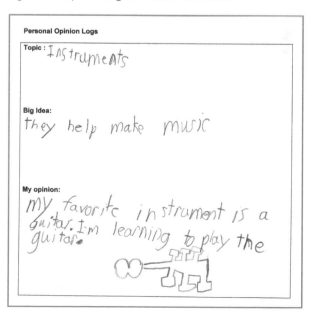

increasingly sophisticated language, apply a more carefully planned organization to their ideas, and incorporate more complex content in their writing.

The following sentence frames reflect the varied sentence structures your students will grapple with, depending upon their grade and readiness levels. Opinion logs should be used once or twice a week so that students get into the habit of formulating opinions, justifying them, and engaging in the process of *coming to know*.

COACH'S NOTES

As needed, offer your students grade-appropriate sentence stems to state an opinion on the topic or to respond to the big idea identified in their personal opinion logs.

I like _____.

I like _____ because_____.

I prefer _____ to _____ because _____.

I think _____ is necessary/important* because_____.

I believe _____ is beneficial/dangerous* because _____.

For example, _____.

I used to believe/think/feel _____, but now I believe/think/feel _____ because _____. In addition, _____.

In my opinion, _____ leads to _____. Then, _____ _____.

*Replace these adjectives with ones that best match the topic, the big idea, or the content of the lesson. Alternately, encourage students to use their own adjectives from the Opinions Matter Adjective Chart (see Figure 3.4).

Figure 3.4 Opinions Matter Adjective Chart

helpful	useful	valuable	effective
beneficial	positive	practical	worthwhile
necessary	crucial	needed	essential
important	critical	vital	significant
optional	possible	promising	likely
dangerous	ineffective	less important	not necessary
unlikely	unacceptable	poor	unsatisfactory
awful	terrible		

Writing Like a Scientist

Many of the teachers we work with use journal writing as their preferred classroom routine and as a way to record examples of the many types of writing utilized in the academic disciplines. Used regularly with thoughtful prompts and questions, as well as freewrites and directed freewrites, these academic journals become a record of your students' thought processes and growth over time about the world of science.

Writing like a scientist implies that the learner has the ability to ask questions, gather information and data, analyze data, describe behavior, make connections, draw inferences, and predict future outcomes. This becomes especially important when scientists have conducted an investigation and want to share it with others. They must be able to communicate these ideas with enough clarity and precision so that others can replicate their study.

However, writing like a scientist involves more than simply following the scientific method in carrying out an experiment and writing up a lab report. Science literacy includes speaking, listening, presenting, interpreting, reading, and writing about science. Being scientifically literate requires that a person have an essential understanding of key science ideas, along with a fluency in the language and terms used to describe them (Connecticut State Department of Education 2004).

One noteworthy science journal that engages learners' curiosity about phenomena in the world is the **observation journal**. As an extension activity, or as a homework assignment, have your students record their observations of the world around them and relate their experiences to the content they have learned in class. Using science process skills, your students will observe, classify, measure, collect data, record information, take notes, interpret, predict, and communicate using words, content-specific vocabulary, numbers, and sketches.

To make science come alive, encourage students to look for evidence of science phenomena in their environment. For example, once kindergartners have learned about the properties of objects, they can look for artifacts at home and draw pictures of them in their journals, labeling the properties they can identify (provided on an anchor chart, glued in their journals from cut-out words, or written by themselves using learned vocabulary). A third grader who has learned about different states of matter might show evidence of the changing states in his world by recording a picture of his ice cream melting in the sun and explaining in words what is happening. A fifth grader who plays the guitar and has learned about sound might draw a labeled diagram to illustrate how the sounds of her guitar travel through her ear. The journal writing can be done either in class or for homework in the upper-elementary grades. Most importantly, however, make time for your students to share their findings with their peers in order to stimulate more curiosity and wonder. See Figure 3.5 for a fifth grader's science observation journal entry—complete with several detailed sketches and carefully written notes—written after an investigation at a hermit crab station.

A second, and more concrete, way to use the science observation journal is to gather and display a range of scientific objects, artifacts, relics, bones, seeds, shells, leaves, plants, animals, rocks, and so on, in a "**science museum**" (a shelf or cart) to be used for student exploration. Then, at a specified time (or during center time), students can visit the science museum to record their findings

Figure 3.5 Science Observation Journal Entry

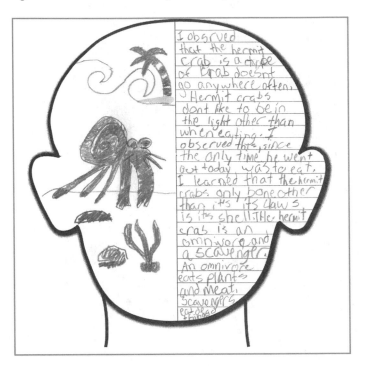

I observed that the hermit crab is a type of crab doesn't go anywhere often. Hermit crabs dont like to be in the light other than when eating. I observed this, since the only time he went out today was to eat. I learned that the hermit crabs only bone other than its its claws is its shell. The hermit crab is an omnivore and a scavenger. An omnivore eats plants and meat. Scavengers eat dead things.

in their journals. Given a checklist of required and optional activities (see Figure 3.6, for example), students will record observations using all of their senses, use tools to measure and weigh their artifacts, sketch and label what they observe, and, depending upon the grade level, note a connection, describe an adaptation, provide a comparison, or make an inference.

Teacher-2-Teacher

I teach science in the elementary grades, and I always include a routine for writing like a scientist. My students love to explore my science table, where I gather, among other things, gourds, pumpkins, rocks, empty crab shells, plants, magnets, seeds, fish, and even an occasional guinea pig. My kindergartners draw pictures of what they observe and label their illustrations using vocabulary from our class-generated anchor charts. My older students jot questions they wonder about as well as answers they discover through research or subsequent lessons. In their journals, my fifth graders write reflections and illustrate the steps of experiments or demonstrations that we have done in class. Sometimes, I ask them to write summaries of nonfiction articles or science current events that we find in newspapers. Their science journals grow throughout the year as they become more attuned to the world around them.   Elementary science teacher

Figure 3.6 Guiding Questions for Science Observation Journal

My observations:

☐ What does the artifact look like? Draw and label its parts.

☐ What questions can I ask about the object?

☐ What properties (color, hardness, odor, sound, taste, etc.) can I observe?

☐ Is it a solid, a liquid, or a gas?

☐ How can I measure it? What tool will I use to measure it? What does it measure?

☐ This is a list of words that come to mind as I look at this object:

☐ What connection can I make? (Make a comparison with something else. Suggest a group to which this object belongs. Provide one fact and offer one opinion. Relate it to something else we have learned about.)

☐ Optional: What inference can I make about this object? What might have happened to make it look like it does?

Writing Like a Historian

Historians are questioners. They ask questions, make connections, engage in deep thinking, and offer plausible explanations about the past:

- **What happened in the past? (also responding to related who, where, when, and how questions)**
- **Why did something happen in the past?**
- **Who was affected?**
- **Why does it matter today?**
- **How did something take place in the past? How can we learn more about it today?**
- **How can we explain it?**

Routinely asking questions like a historian requires the highest levels of analytical thinking, something young children are prone to develop naturally when allowed: by age four, most questions they ask begin with *Why?* By kindergarten, they love to recall and retell what happened to them and offer details about how something happened. Nurturing these skills in the early grades help young learners develop the more advanced skills needed for historical analyses later on in their schooling.

In a publication written over four decades ago, Jerome Bruner (1966) observed, "We teach not to produce little living libraries on that subject, but rather to get a student . . . to consider matters as an historian does, to take part in the process of knowledge-getting. Knowing is a process not a product" (72).

Like the science journal we discussed earlier, the **history journal** may serve as a record of students' thought processes and growth over time about historical events, explanations about them, and connections made to the present. In the elementary grades, writing like a historian may take several forms and perspectives. For example, in grades K–2, you can engage your students in shared writing and research projects based on a grade-appropriate social studies topic. For example, view the chart created by a second-grade class after taking a neighborhood walk to discover the places of interest in the community (Figure 3.7).

Starting in third grade, short, carefully structured research projects can be conducted in smaller groups, in pairs, and, eventually, independently. You can also encourage students in these grades to write from the perspective of people living in a particular time period or

Figure 3.7 Shared Writing on a Second-Grade Social Studies Topic

culture. They can create a historical character and show their understanding of an event or time period by writing in that persona, under the heading "My Story." Writing in the first-person singular will help your students see events in the past through the eyes of those who lived a long time ago while offering a personal point of view about those events (Mandell and Malon 2008). When students write with the voice of someone who has firsthand knowledge of a particular experience, the writing will resemble many of the primary sources that your young learners will encounter later on when studying social studies and history.

First-person writing invites students to place themselves in a time period of history, in the culture of a civilization, or in a scene from a book. By imagining themselves in these situations, students are invited to feel empathy and to consider the factors that led to particular circumstances. Using critical thinking skills during this routine, students analyze events, recognize cause-and-effect relationships, make judgments about a particular state of affairs, and, further, attempt to persuade others of their point of view. Used regularly, this approach helps students wrestle with complex ideas and come to a deeper understanding of the significance of historical events, circumstances, or literary happenings.

In Figure 3.8, we present several formats of journal entries and provide examples from multiple classrooms to give you ideas for incorporating this type of writing into your instructional routine. Figure 3.9 has a fourth grader's historical journal entry written in the first-person perspective of someone who was alive on July 4, 1776! You must agree that he had quite a story to tell.

Figure 3.8 Variations on First-Person Writing Journal Entries with Classroom Examples

Formats	Examples from the Classroom
Diary Entry	As a child living in the city, write three diary entries that describe your daily life, including what your neighborhood is like, what type of transportation you use, and what your home is like.
Historical Autobiography/ Personal Account	Write a brief autobiography of your life and describe three conditions that impacted your life during the time period we are studying.
Captain's Log/Log Book/ Account	Writing in the persona of Christopher Columbus/Lewis and Clark, write three log entries about your trip, including why you decided to make your voyage/trip, problems you faced during the journey, what you found when you landed/arrived.
Postcard/Letter	As a child living through the Civil War, write a postcard that includes three details about what life has been like for you and your family living in the South, defending your home.
Personal Narrative/ Memoir	Write a personal narrative about your life as a colonial child (memoir). What type of schooling do you have? What are your chores? What is life like for you and your family?
Dear Abby Letter	Write a letter to Dear Abby (or Dr. Phil or Dr. Laura) describing in detail the conflict you are having (as a character in this book), and write Dear Abby's (or Dr. Phil's or Dr. Laura's) letter in response, offering you advice.
Speech	Give a speech to nominate your favorite community worker for an award from your local chamber of commerce. Provide at least two reasons that this person is so important to your community.
Tweets	Send three tweets about an event you are witnessing; describe what you are observing; what caused it to happen; and how it is impacting your life.

Figure 3.9 A "My Story" Diary Entry for July 4, 1776

Monday, July 4, 1776

Dear Journal,

'Tis my birthday today. They just signed the Declaration of Independence! Mama and I are very happy that we are finally going to get freedom. I got this journal for my birthday from my older sister Meg.

Mama let me choose what we're going to have for dinner. I chose Johnny cakes and fish for dinner. I had Johnny cakes and a bit of stew for supper.

Since it was my birthday we all did not have to do our chores so Papa went out and fed the chickens the cows and he chopped the wood. Then he made a nice warm fire. We all sat around it and we talked and talked until 2:00 in the morning! Then I went to bed.

I woke up that morning to the cry of Meg. She was in tears because she found out that her beau had joined General Washington's army.

I had already seen the note from him when I went to get a cup of tea. I was not as devastated for I did not see him too much. Meg on the other hand saw him all the time.

I creaked open the door. I asked her what the matter is **although I already knew.** She responded, "Michael, he left to go join General Washington's army!"

I said, "Oh that is terrible," **although it wasn't.** "I'm sure he will write you letters." She said she would like that.

Another type of entry that you might choose to assign as part of your history writing routine is "**Extra! Extra! Read All About It!**" Writing entries with this heading, students imagine they are reporters at the scene of a particular historical event. By role-playing interviews with eyewitnesses or by personally reporting from the scene of an event, our budding journalists provide us important details about what has happened in our past.

As they write in the third person, students will learn to organize their thoughts by responding to the five W questions. By reorganizing these details into a piece of "journalism," writers synthesize their understanding about the content. You can provide guiding questions to scaffold your fledgling journalists' work and keep them focused on key questions as they describe a significant event (see Figure 3.10 for guiding questions and Figure 3.11 for a student example).

Figure 3.10 Guiding Questions for "Extra! Extra! Read All About It!" Entries

What happened?

Who was involved?

Whom did it affect?

Where did the event take place?

When did the event take place?

Why did it happen? *or* Why is this important? How did it happen?

Figure 3.11 "Extra! Extra! Read All About It!" Native American Newspaper Report

Extra! Extra! Read All About It!

Name of Newspaper: *Native American News*

News Subject: Starving in Winter

Headline: American Indians are hungry and there is no food!

Article: It is winter time and there is no food for the Native Americans. The deer and bears and birds are gone so they can't eat. People are getting sick from no food and the cold weather. All of the animals are hibernating and the lake is frozen solid. Everyone is getting very cold. The only relief is when a family of bears comes out. They are killed and eaten which makes everyone feel better.

SUMMARY WRITING

It is not surprising that Marzano, Pickering, and Pollock (2001) presented summarizing as one of the nine most effective teaching strategies for increasing student achievement. When you ask students to stop and think about the essence of a lesson or a reading, you put them in control of their own learning and ask them to use critical thinking skills. Rather than being passive, they are engaging in making decisions about the information, asking themselves, "What should I include? What should I delete? What is most important to record in my summary? How can I reword this reading in as few words as possible while retaining its essence?"

Little learning occurs as a result of instruction alone, as Rick Wormeli (2005) reminds us in *Summarization in Any Subject*. Without time to reflect on and process the newly acquired concepts through an activity like summary writing, students are unlikely to retain the information presented.

Summaries come in many forms, but all of them have the objective of helping students reduce the information into its meaningful essence. A summary routine might be as simple as having your students use your three chosen vocabulary terms to sum up a lesson, essentially a directed freewrite (see the Directed Freewrites section later in this chapter). To vary your routine a bit, teach these alternative summaries:

- **Five Ws + H Summary: In Figure 3.12, a third grader uses this type of summary for a nonfiction piece of text about the Statue of Liberty.**

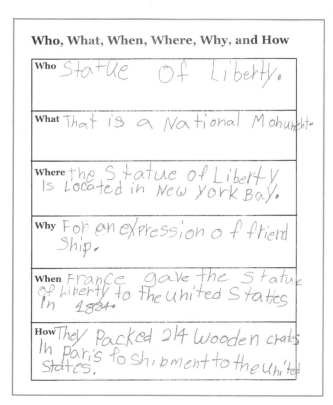

Who, What, When, Where, Why, and How

Who Statue of Liberty.

What That is a National Monument.

Where the Statue of Liberty is Located in New York Bay.

Why For an expression of friend Ship.

When France gave the statue of liberty to the United States in 1884.

How They Packed 214 Wooden crates in Paris to shibment to the United States.

Figure 3.12 Third Grader's Five Ws + H Summary About the Statue of Liberty

- Somebody Wanted . . . , But . . . , So Framework: In Figure 3.13, a first grader uses this framework to summarize the story of *The Fisherman and His Wife* in a Foldable. Nazima Ally created the more sophisticated matrix template somebody wanted . . . , but . . . , so . . . , then . . . to help her fourth-grade students summarize and compare several nonfiction selections (see Figure 3.14).
- What's the Gist? Summary: This activity invites students to synthesize new learning in a social studies or science class after reading informational text.

Figure 3.13 First Grader's Somebody Wanted . . . , But . . . , So . . . Foldable on Fiction Story

Figure 3.14 Fourth Grader's Scaffolded Somebody Wanted . . . , But . . . , So . . . , Then . . . Matrix on Three Nonfiction Texts

Students will summarize each of the text for Module A, unit 1 and then write a comparative paragraph using linking words.

Somebody	Wanted/Needed	But	So	Then
Sam Marshall	wanted to share his love of tarantulas with the world	people were afraid of tarantulas	Sam Marshall travelled to different countries to research tarantulas and show people more about them	the world learned more about tarantulas and how they are important to the planet.
John James	Wanted to find out if birds come back to the same nest ever year	John James didn't know the answer to his question	He put a thread on one of the baby birds to mark it	Then next spring came the bird came back with the mark and John James answered his question
Frog Scientists	Need to find out why the world's amphibians are dispreeing	There was to many reasons for example here are some reasons habait loss global warming fungus/constrution	They went to study them more	They made mechine to stop the fugus

FREEWRITING

A freewrite is a routine that encourages the *process* of writing. For primary students it looks like the opportunity to stop and reflect upon something they have just learned, by drawing, labeling, using inventive spelling, and/or writing about the concept or topic. With older students, the usual requirements of writing are eliminated, and they do not need to worry about spelling and grammar; they just write nonstop for a brief period in order to synthesize their thoughts and get them down on paper. Without a great deal of structure, students feel freer to jot, note, and record their ideas or even draw pictures to show their understanding of a concept. See Figures 3.15a and 3.15b for a first grader's freewrite on a significant life event (losing his first tooth) and a most expressive drawing that accompanied the writing.

Fluency builds over time, as student writers increase the number of words they can write on their own. While unconcerned about the usual demands of a polished piece, students build stamina and learn to get into the flow of writing. Jim Wright, best known for his work with RTI (response to intervention), shared an effective routine for increasing fluency in writing, which was first espoused by Natalie Rathvon (1999). (See the following "Coach's Notes" section for a description of this intervention.)

Figure 3.15b Lost Tooth

Figure 3.15a Jacob's Freewrite About Losing a Tooth

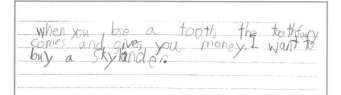

COACH'S NOTES

Natalie Rathvon, *author of several books on special education and evidence-based interventions, suggests a simple-to-use self-monitoring intervention that improves student fluency in writing. We suggest that you implement this practice along with your routine of freewrites and directed freewrites. Twice a week, after an approximately five-minute freewrite (this amount of time can increase over the course of the year), have students count up the number of words they have written and have them chart their own rate of fluency (words written per five minutes, for example). Gather the scores of all your students (anonymously) and chart the results on a class chart. Together, set a goal for increasing the number of words that students will write the next week. The routine of writing frequently will build their fluency. Setting a class goal will motivate all of your students.*

Directed Freewrites

Once your students have become more fluent and comfortable with freewriting, you will want them to develop their facility with directed freewrites. These short writings are more focused, and students must use specific vocabulary and/or meet certain requirements. For example, you might ask your students to answer a text-dependent question, note a comparison–contrast relationship, or use three specific vocabulary terms in their writing. Move from freewrites to directed freewrites and back again to vary the amount of independence and structure that you provide to your learners.

See Figure 3.16, in which a fourth grader was required to use the three mathematical terms *multiply*, *partial product*, and *product* to explain how to solve 63 × 17 in her directed freewrite.

You can point out word wall terms (by attaching sticky notes) that must be included in the writing. In this way, you develop not only the routine of writing, but also the routines of using a word wall as well as using important disciplinary vocabulary when communicating orally or in writing.

From a study skills standpoint, these brief, three- to four-minute writing activities that should punctuate your daily lessons serve to enhance retention. By having the learner use the new information in a directed

Figure 3.16 Fourth Grader's Directed Freewrite in a Math Class

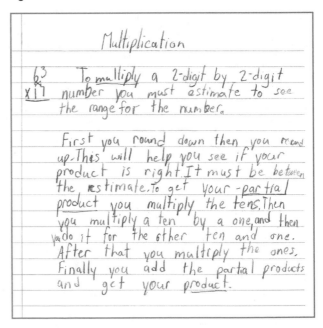

freewrite soon after hearing it, you will increase the likelihood that transfer and later retrieval can take place. By providing additional time for your students to make sense of, to elaborate upon, and to assign value and relevance to the new information, you increase the chance of long-term storage (Sousa 2001). Without such encoding, students are unlikely to remember much of what has been covered during classroom lessons.

Burris and Garrity (2008) suggest that in addition to aiding retention, directed freewrites can help determine prior knowledge, spark student interest in writing, expand student thinking, as well as assess student understanding, growth, and readiness. Clearly, this routine has the potential for providing meaningful, yet quick, formative assessment in a jam-packed curriculum. As described in Burris and Garrity's book, students write for three minutes and then share for two minutes. How can you resist a routine that takes just five minutes but can have such a powerful impact on learning?

COACH'S NOTES

How many times have you wondered why students don't remember what you "covered" in your lesson? Research shows us that we need to slow down and allow our students to reflect periodically in writing (or talk with a peer) about what they have just learned. Try this out and see what your own "action research" proves.

ROUTINE 2 The Writing Process

Although the scope of this book cannot encompass a detailed review of process writing, we would be remiss if we did not briefly describe the process and its important relationship to the Common Core. Undoubtedly, the expectation of the CCSS is that students will use the writing process to plan, draft, revise, edit, proofread, and then publish much of their writing. It is interesting to note that studies show that students who learn the writing process score better on state writing tests than those who receive only specific instruction in the skills assessed on the test (IRA/NCTE 2013). Although this is certainly not the only reason to use the writing process, it does suggest the compelling argument that implementing such a process routinely can only help students improve their writing.

Implementing the multistep writing process over the course of

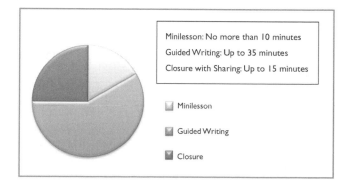

Minilesson: No more than 10 minutes
Guided Writing: Up to 35 minutes
Closure with Sharing: Up to 15 minutes

- Minilesson
- Guided Writing
- Closure

several days builds students' writing skills, their confidence, and their independence over time. It provides you the opportunity to conference with individual students, overcoming one of the principal complaints we hear in our workshops from teachers: "When can I find time to work with individuals or small groups?"

Teacher-2-Teacher

"Good afternoon, writers!" That's how I address my students at the beginning of writing workshop and throughout the lesson. It helps them see themselves as writers and develop confidence and pride from day one. We also have a ritual: The whole class gathers on the rug and we put on our "writing crowns." The boys and girls overlap their hands over their heads to make a writing crown and echo a few statements that I chant: "I am a writer. I use capitals. I use punctuation. I stay on one topic. I am a writer." With that, the children lower their crowns onto their heads. The mantra always begins and ends the same, but the middle sentences reflect what the students are working on during their writing time (e.g., I can add details. I label my pictures. I use spaces.).

Mary Lou Weymann, kindergarten teacher

 CHECK THIS OUT

Explore the following print resources for more information on the writing workshop and the writing process.

Calkins, L. 1986. *The Art of Teaching Writing*. Portsmouth, NH: Heinemann.
———. 1994. *The Art of Teaching Writing*. 2nd ed. Portsmouth, NH: Heinemann.

Cleaveland, L. B., and K. Wood Ray. 2003. *About the Authors: Writing Workshop with Our Youngest Writers*. Portsmouth, NH: Heinemann.

Fletcher, R., and J. Portalupi. 2001. *Writing Workshop: The Essential Guide*. Portsmouth, NH: Heinemann.

Fountas, I. C., and G. S. Pinnell. 2001. *Guiding Readers and Writers Grades 3–6: Teaching Comprehension, Genre, and Content Literacy*. Portsmouth, NH: Heinemann.

Graham, S., C. A. MacArthur, and J. Fitzgerald, eds. 2007. *Best Practices in Writing Instruction*. New York: Guilford.

Harris, K. R., and S. Graham. 1996. *Making the Writing Process Work: Strategies for Composition and Self-Regulation*. Cambridge, MA: Brookline Books.

Leograndis, D. 2008. *Launching the Writing Workshop: A Step-by-Step Guide in Photographs*. New York: Scholastic.

During each writing workshop, or writing block, present an initial five- to ten-minute minilesson to the entire class. A minilesson is a short lesson focused on a specific principle or procedure (Calkins 1986, 1994). These brief lessons focus on one of the following:

- **management of the routines and procedures of the writing workshop**
- **strategies and skills for using the conventions of English**
- **how writers use their skills. (Fountas and Pinnell 2001)**

Then, students will participate in the guided portion of the writing workshop that includes working independently on their writing during a sustained period of time with or without your immediate support. At this point, some students may be using their writing notebook to jot down ideas for writing projects or to develop an idea. Other students might be revising or editing a piece of their writing and they may choose to conference with a peer and use a checklist for editing or revising (see Fountas and Pinnell 2001). At this time, you may choose to work one-on-one with certain students, providing feedback to these writers and guiding them in setting future writing goals.

COACH'S NOTES

According to Brookhart (2013), the most effective feedback is immediate, descriptive, nonjudgmental, and specific. Conferring with students one-on-one, about either how well they met a learning goal or what specifically they need to work on to meet the learning target, guides students to be responsible for their own learning. Instead of correcting every mistake, the conferrer responds to no more than two specific fixes (pushes) at a time. Make sure not to simply say, "Good job," or "Write more," but review with the students what they have accomplished and what specifically they need to work on next to reach their goal. Conferring on specific targets, with descriptive feedback, and not overwhelming students with multiple fixes helps students zero in on exactly what they need to work on to build the foundation toward successfully reaching their overall learning target.

Paula Pennington, literacy teacher coach

Next, you might pull together one or two small, temporary groups to work on specific skills. Only those students who need the help will be part of these groups. Therefore, you can see how the writing workshop is an important routine for a differentiated classroom with diverse learners and multiple readiness levels.

Another part of the writing workshop block in grades 3–5—which Fountas and Pinnell (2001) suggest should typically last about an hour—is *investigations*. During this time period, students explore a piece of literature or a content area topic in depth, using reading, writing, media, and technology. They are expected to present orally, to perform, or to create a display to share what they have learned. This research can be done independently, with a partner, or with a small group. Also see the description of SOLE research projects in Chapter 4.

It is important to bring the entire class back together each day after the writing workshop time so that students can share what they have written. This is a time for you and other students to provide feedback, and for the writer to share what he or she has learned and applied. After a student has gone through all of the steps in the writing process and has thoroughly polished a piece of writing, it is time to publish the finished product and honor this accomplished writer! See Figure 3.17 for an overview of the steps in the writing process.

Figure 3.17 Steps in the Writing Process

Steps	Purposes	Practices Aligned with College and Career Readiness Standards
Prewriting	• Activating prior knowledge • Generating and gathering ideas • Encouraging wonder and curiosity • Building background knowledge • Identifying purpose and audience • Using thinking skills • Noting main ideas and details	• Partner talks • Brainstorming • Seed journals • Freewriting • Anchor charts • Ideas from in-class and off-site field trips or the Question Kiosk • Note taking • WonderQuests
Drafting	• Getting ideas down on paper without concern for form, conventions, or organization	• Freewrites • Quick writes • Idea webs • Science, English, or history journals
Revising	• Revisiting the piece with fresh eyes • Paying attention to organization, language, and audience • Re-creating	• Self-revising checklists • Peer evaluations • Sentence combining • One-on-one conferencing with teacher
Editing and Proofreading	• Making changes and corrections that conform to conventions • Mechanics, sentence fragments, punctuation, spelling, etc.	• Self-editing checklists • Partner evaluations • Editing stations
Publishing	• Creating a final copy • Going public	• Blogging • Publishing to approved sites on the Internet • Creating classroom books • Sending letters • Framing poems • Making books

Adapted from Peregoy and Boyle (2012) and Fountas and Pinnell (2001) by permission of Pearson and Heinemann.

Teacher-2-Teacher

I find that the most effective way to conference with students about their writing is to coach them one on one. The first step is to make a tool kit for each unit. I include my writing pieces and folder, several small guided reading books, correction tape, extra paper for students to write on, and mentor texts. I also create a class roster and attach it to the several types of conferences that I could have. This way I ensure that I teach differently each time I meet with a student or a small group. Here are some of the ways that I confer:

- Explicitly: Show student how to become a better writer through a strategy or craft technique (then release the student to try it on his or her own).

- Implicitly: Show students a strategy or craft technique that helped me as a writer.

- Using a Mentor Text: Show students how an author or illustrator used a strategy or craft technique in his or her writing.

Edd Ohlsen, K–5 teacher on special assignment, peer coach

ROUTINE 3 Note Taking

The introduction to the CCSS (NGA Center for Best Practices and CCSSO 2010) suggests that students become "self-directed learners, effectively seeking out and using resources to assist them, including teachers, peers, and print and digital reference materials" (7). One way to help create independent learners is through establishing a regular routine for taking notes that will contribute to the data-gathering phase of the research process required in grades 3 and up. Once basic skills are acquired, the research process is more likely to turn into a rewarding, enriching experience. We recognize that engaging young learners in meaningful research tasks—as required by the CCSS—will present several challenges, yet nurturing students' natural curiosity for learning cannot be underestimated. In one visit to a kindergarten class, we observed a teacher who wanted to find out what topics the students were interested in researching. Always eager to understand the world around them, the kindergartners asked questions such as these:

- How come gravity does not pull a plane out of the sky?
- Why is it nighttime on the other side of the earth when it is morning here?
- Why doesn't the human body last forever?
- Are there more boys than girls in the world?

Yet, we agree with Boch and Piolat, who so keenly note that

primary schools, secondary schools, and universities provide their students with no (or very little) help in acquiring the skills needed to successfully develop these two essential write-to-learn functions: (1) taking notes to stabilize the knowledge to be acquired . . . and (2) taking notes to effectively resolve problems. (2005, 102)

Note taking as a daily practice is rather difficult for most students to master. This should not surprise us, when we consider that learning to take notes well undoubtedly takes as much time as learning to write in a relatively experienced way (at least fifteen years!), according to Scardamalia and Bereiter (1991). Without this skill, many students are unlikely to be successful at retrieving information later that they formerly learned in their classes. In addition, the research required by the CCSS presumes that students will develop note-taking skills. Even if you teach the earliest grades, you can begin the process of guided note taking on a daily basis. Boch and Piolat (2005) suggest that a matrix-like structure for recording information is more beneficial than the outline structure or a linear representation of ideas. These graphic organizers, or charts, help students make stronger connections as well as retain new learning. This makes sense since the brain is a pattern seeker, and a matrix, or chart, allows us to notice patterns by sorting and comparing information visually. See Figure 3.18 for a note-taking template developed by Kelley Cordeiro for *Everybody Eats Rice* (Dooley 1992). Students using a matrix can compare several items and categories since the information is organized visually.

Figure 3.18 *Everybody Eats Rice* Note-Taking Matrix

Family	Country	Meal Cooked	Customs
Darlington			
Diaz	Puerto Rico		
Tran			
Krishnamurthy	India		
Hua			
Bleu	Haiti		
Carrie and Anthony's family			

Note-taking formats are numerous, and they vary in their effectiveness with different grade levels. We have found Foldables, interactive note taking, "My Notes," and CiteWrites to be beneficial variations with elementary students.

FOLDABLES

Foldables help prepare primary students for the more rigorous note-taking expectations that start in grade 3. By folding paper in almost infinite ways, you can create graphic organizers (essentially, three-dimensional charts or matrices) that help students organize ideas and retain them better. One example might have the main idea written on the outside, along with an illustration. Supporting details or evidence (with a noted page or line number) could be written under the folded tabs. See Figure 3.19, in which a first-grade student shows his understanding of patriotic holidays in a Foldable.

✔ CHECK THIS OUT

According to the foremost authority on the subject of Foldables, Dinah Zike, a Foldable is "a 3-D, student-made, interactive graphic organizer that takes complicated data and information and makes it visual and kinesthetic." See her website for more information and examples: www.dinah.com/faq/faq.php.

Foldables can be used to help little ones retell a story, describe a character, show a cause-and-effect relationship, note a problem and its solution, illustrate the sequence of a cycle, or record main ideas and details. Although there are many ways to design a Foldable activity, your students might begin with an illustration, add vocabulary from an anchor chart or a word bank, and then complete a sentence frame for writing practice. We can't say enough about how the students, and their teachers, love using Foldables to organize ideas and begin to take notes. Research confirms the positive effect that spatial organization has on making stronger connections. Using Foldables for students to see ideas and their connections is a great way for youngsters to begin the long journey toward independent note taking and study skills. After reading two different nonfiction articles on anti-bullying, a fourth-grade student took notes to create a Foldable on ways to prevent conflicts in school (see Figure 3.20).

Figure 3.19 The Front Page and Inside page of a Foldable on Patriotic Holidays

Figure 3.20 The Front Page and Inside Page of a Foldable Entitled "How Can We Prevent Conflicts in Schools?"

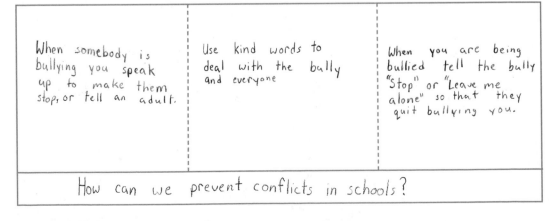

Although it's tempting to use the Foldable just for low-level recall or pictures and vocabulary, it is more powerful when used to show relationships or critical thinking: cause and effect, comparison and contrast, sequence, change over time, and so on. By adding an essential question along the bottom of the Foldable (start by gently folding an 8½ -by-11-inch paper in half vertically, and then creasing it after leaving a half-inch for writing the question along the bottom), you can raise the rigor of the activity. Students are expected to use the details or facts within the Foldable to answer a higher-order thinking question. They can write their response on the back of the Foldable. For example, a primary class might create a Foldable to describe three characters. On the front would be the names of the three characters and either a picture or symbol that relates to each character. Inside, students would list either the traits for each character or, in the case of older students, the character traits as well as evidence with page numbers from the text for each trait. The essential question on the bottom might be "What makes a friend a friend? Use the sentence frame (on the back of the Foldable) to respond."

A friend is someone who _____.
I would like to be friends with _____ because _____.

Or, for a bit more rigor, the question might be "What makes a friend a friend? Compare two of the characters and tell which one you would prefer to be friends with and why. Use the sentence frame (on the back of the Foldable) to respond."

While _____ [character 1] is _____, _____ [character 2] is _____.
I would prefer to be friends with _____ because _____.

(Learn more about sentence frames later in this chapter.)

INTERACTIVE NOTE TAKING

It has been well established that note taking is a critical routine for students to develop in school. Since note taking takes many years to refine, it is incumbent upon every grade-level teacher to make taking notes a priority and a regular part of lessons. While there are numerous ways to teach note taking, some formats are more effective than others when used with learners in the classroom. One of the most engaging methods we have used when building this routine is interactive note taking.

The first time we came across the concept of interactive note taking, it was part of the *History Alive! Notebook* developed by Teachers' Curriculum Institute (TCI) (1999). Recognizing the enthusiasm of secondary social studies students who took notes in this responsive, hands-on manner, we became determined to simplify the concept and make it easier to implement across the curriculum on an elementary level (TCI 2013). Visiting the TCI website (www.teachtci .com), you can see the developers also noted that elementary students would benefit from this interactive approach.

Interactive notebooks can be powerful tools for implementing the writing standards as well as for differentiation. With the growing diversity in classrooms today, you are likely to welcome a tool that addresses these differences. During the interactive phase of learning (Buehl 1995; Costa and Garmston 1994), students must learn to take notes and organize information. You may have noticed that when students simply copy notes, they do not learn the information. Instead, they must actively do something with the information provided to make sense of it and to construct meaning for themselves. Combining elements of multiple intelligences, study and organizational skills, choice, and right-brain and left-brain processing, interactive notebooks foster critical thinking in students, while addressing the fact that all students learn differently. The left page–right page format of the notebook will remind you to stop your lesson periodically and provide opportunities for students to do something with the information in order to process it. See Figure 3.21 for guidelines for developing an interactive notebook or interactive note taking.

Figure 3.21 Guidelines for Developing an Interactive Notebook or Interactive Note Taking

Guidelines for Developing An *Interactive Notebook*

Interactive Note Taking

- The Interactive Notebook will have a left-side, right-side orientation

- The first page(s) of the notebook will contain the Table of Contents

Left-side pages	Right-side pages
Teacher *input* Notes gathered from video, PowerPoint, or Internet site Note-taking: Class notes or text notes List of terms, definitions, content Content information/reading/text provided by the teacher Charts, maps, documents, graphic organizers *provided by teacher*	Student *output and engagement* Integration of terms/content to process for long-term memory Evidence of student processing Questioning of the text—students generate their own questions Use of higher-order skills to make meaning from information Student reflections, connections, evaluations, re-organization of information, illustrations *(Option: can be done as H.W.)* Charts, maps, graphic organizers *created by the student*

Request that students bring the following materials:
Colored pens
Colored pencils and highlighters
Glue stick
A pad of sticky notes

Assessments:
Notebooks will be collected and graded periodically
A class-developed rubric will be used for evaluation
Among the assessment criteria will be: organization, connections made, thoroughness and neatness/visual appeal

Adapted from: <u>History Alive! Interactive Student Notebook Manual</u>; TCI; 1999

The notion of *interactive* note taking immediately suggests that students are doing more than simply copying notes off the board or from a Power-Point presentation. Indeed, your students are responding and reacting to the notes or presentation by reorganizing the information and constructing meaning for themselves. The constant goal of our brain is to turn data into meaning (Jensen 1996). By using the interactive notebook or the process of interactive note taking, you will provide students multiple opportunities to do so.

The left-side pages of the notebook are where students gather notes from your presentation, text, magazine article, website, or teacher-created handouts. The right-side pages are where the students show evidence of their thinking processes, where students reorganize the provided information using creative formats, create their own graphic organizers, reflect upon the information by giving opinions and citing evidence, or extend their understanding of the information by generating questions and/or doing research. When students select key words, make connections, note points of view, write notes in the margins, or make plans based on the notes, they are using what Romainville and Noël suggest are the microskills for training students in the process of note taking (as cited in Troia 2007). Equally important, according to Romainville and Noël, is the raised awareness of the subsequent use of the notes. When your students realize that they will be *using* their notes for something, their effort to make them better will increase.

While some school districts have integrated interactive notebooks into their yearlong curriculum, we have found that most teachers prefer to use interactive notebooks for a few specific units during the year. Teachers we have worked with, for example, have designed interactive notebooks for two- to four-week units on topics like poetry, simple machines, and Mexico. In our experience with using interactive notebooks, teachers have seen increased engagement in their most reluctant learners, including children with autism, who up to that point had not written anything in their classes.

One of the benefits to using interactive notebooks is that they become the proud possessions of their owners and are seldom misplaced or lost. The illustrated manuscripts that are developed through this process serve as powerful study tools for students and provide excellent opportunities to teach organizational and study skills.

MY NOTES

Two additional note-taking formats help young students *stabilize their knowledge* or *resolve problems*. These templates help beginners take notes in order to answer a research question, resolve an authentic problem, or develop a more sustained research project. In Figures 3.22a and 3.22b, a first grader uses the "My Notes" format to organize his newly gained knowledge about dinosaurs into three subtopics, illustrate key ideas, and write two essential details for each subtopic. The "My Notes" graphic organizer will help your students research different aspects of a topic and categorize the information they find.

Figure 3.22a "My Notes" Organizer on Dinosaurs

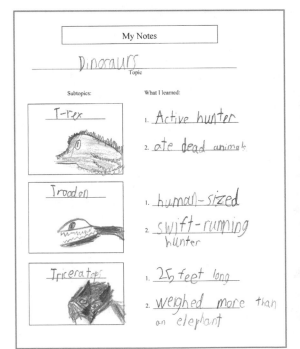

Figure 3.22b First Grader at Work on Researching Dinosaurs and Completing the "My Notes" Organizer Featured in Figure 3.22a

CITEWRITES

Another simple note-taking variation is a CiteWrite, whose main purpose is to help students focus on where they find the evidence to support what they claim. You can see in Figure 3.23 that even in second grade, students can begin to track where information is found in a text. In addition, the CiteWrite helps young learners recognize the importance of giving credit appropriately to sources.

Figure 3.23 A Second Grader's CiteWrite

A CiteWrite

Title: Lift off!

Author: Gare Thompson

Draw a picture to help you remember as much as you can about the topic:

List 3 important details about the topic and on which page you found the information:

1. On page number 5 it says: "Astronauts practice space walking under water."

2. On page number 3 it says: "It takes many years to be an astronaut."

3. On page number 11 it says: "Neil Armstrong placed the United States flag on the moon."

Scaffolding Toolbox: Sentence Frames

Sentence frames are structures that help all students use academic vocabulary and grammar correctly in written and spoken language. The regular use of these frames makes academic content more accessible for learners. Sentence frames guide oral and written fluency so students gain confidence as they build vocabulary and the ability to express themselves in full sentences.

Sentence frames should be used as scaffolds across the disciplines when you introduce a new writing structure. They assist students in making meaning from text, showing understanding in science, expressing complex ideas in math, and so on. They can be used to activate prior knowledge during a do-now activity at the beginning of the class, to guide journal writing or directed freewrites, or for quick formative assessment on an exit card. Figure 3.24 shows a fourth grader summarizing what she has learned by completing an exit card in social studies. She has the option of using sentence frames that are available to the class on anchor charts posted around the room.

Figure 3.24 Writing a
Summary Exit Card

We offer sentence frames as a tool for
your scaffolding toolbox because of the ubiqui-
tous nature of their application. Whether your
students are working with freewrites, recording
in their opinion logs, or writing as scientists or
historians, sentence frames can scaffold their
learning as well as their writing.

COACH'S NOTES

*So as not to overwhelm your students, model and make use of one type of sentence frame
at a time, over a span of several weeks. After modeling for your class how to complete the
frame, invite students to complete one with you. Then, have partners prepare one together.
Finally, give students the opportunity to work independently on one. After all that practice,
most students will be prepared to use the sentence frames as models for their independent
writing. Keep them posted on anchor charts so that English learners and others have access
to them, if still needed.*

The sentence frames we have chosen apply to a set of common organizational patterns that are
inherent in content area texts:

- **description**
- **comparison and contrast**
- **cause and effect**
- **sequence or chronology**
- **problem and solution**
- **opinion or persuasion.**

For each type of organizational pattern, Billmeyer (1996) suggests we provide questions to guide
student thinking, language to assist in expression, and a sentence frame to give direction to their
writing (or speaking).

Students in grades K and 1 should be given a one-sentence summary frame, while students in grades 2–5 can use multiple sentence frames to write a paragraph (or multiple paragraphs). Part of the frame for older students should require them to find evidence in the text for what they write (according to CCSS goals). These writing frames can be used as a follow-up to reading a short informational text or seeing a brief video clip on any topic. Full-page, printable versions of these sentence frames can be downloaded from our online companion resources at heinemann.com /products/E05661.aspx.

COACH'S NOTES

To make these sentence frames even more effective, add the specific graphic organizer that goes along with each organizational pattern that you introduce (Billmeyer 1996). By presenting the graphic organizer and tying the language to it, you will offer students a framework or architecture (Hyerle 2008) for constructing knowledge with help of a visual tool or thinking map. Add this idea to your repertoire of instructional practices and watch students have an aha moment as they finally acquire the skill to express their ideas in logical, coherent fashion, with appropriate academic language.

Teacher-2-Teacher

We use a three-column graphic organizer to collect information about animals: "Appearance," "Habitat," and "Movement." We have used this organizer in many ways over the years, but most recently we have used it successfully with our first graders to learn about nonfiction writing and text structure. The "Habitat" section works perfectly for teaching the text structure some-and-other. For example, "Some bats live in caves. Other bats live under bridges." This text structure is used frequently in nonfiction books, and the graphic organizer along with appropriate sentence frames prepare young students to write about what they are learning.

Rose Doran, grade 1 teacher, and Amy Cooke, ESL teacher

Description Sentence Frames

Questions:

What is being described?

What are some of its characteristics?

What does it do? What is it like?

Language:

First,   Also,

For example,   In addition,

For instance,   Too

Another

One-Sentence Description Frame:

The ____ is a kind of ____ that ____.

Examples: The owl is a kind of bird that hunts at night.

The tornado is a kind of violent storm that happens over land.

Additional Description Sentence Frames:

In addition, the ____ ____.

It also ____.

We know this because on page ____, it says ____.

Cause–Effect Sentence Frames

Questions:

What happens? What is the effect?

What causes it to happen? What are the important factors that cause this effect?

Language:

Because   If ____, then ____.

This led to   For this reason

As a result   Another reason

So   Consequently

Therefore

One-Sentence Cause–Effect Frames:

If ____, then ____.   ____ results in ____.

If ____, it will lead to ____. The effect of ____ is ____.

Additional Cause–Effect Sentence Frames:

One reason ____ happens(ed) is that ____.

Another reason is ____.

These factors can lead to ____.

We know this because on page ____, the author states ____.

Opinion or Persuasion Sentence Frames

Questions:

What is the general topic or issue?

What viewpoint(s) is the author presenting?

What details, facts, and data is the author supplying to support his claim?

Which viewpoint do you agree with and support?

What is your opinion? Can you support it with evidence?

Language:

You should

You should not

I agree

I disagree because

Based on the evidence the author presents,

Instead,

Some believe

Others believe

Most agree

One-Sentence Opinion or Persuasion Frames:

In my opinion ____ because ____.

It is my viewpoint that ____ because ____.

You should ____ because ____.

You should not ____ because ____.

Additional Opinion or Persuasion Sentence Frames

I believe that ____ because here in the text on page ____, the author says ____. Another reason for this opinion is that the author states on page ____ that ____.

Some people don't believe this. Instead, they believe ____.

But, based on the evidence that the author presents, I agree that ____.

Based on the evidence, the best course of action to take is ____.

Problem–Solution Sentence Frames

Questions:

What is the problem?

Who has the problem?

What is causing the problem?

What are the effects of the problem?

Who is trying to solve the problem?

What solutions are recommended or have been tried?

What are the results?

Language:

Problem	One answer is
Wanted	If ___, then ___.
Solution	Because

One-Sentence Problem–Solution Frames:

___ (somebody) wanted ___, but ___, so ___.* (Use with a character in a book.)

Example: Little Red Hen wanted to bake bread, but no one would help her, so she did it herself.

The problem is ___, and one solution is ___. (Use with nonfiction text, topics, and issues.)

Additional Problem–Solution Sentence Frames:

The problem described in this text is ___.

The author suggests on page ___ that one solution might be ___.

If ___, then ___. Although ___, the problem could be solved by ___.

*See Macon, Bewell, and Vogt (1991).

Comparison–Contrast Frames

Questions:

What is being compared and contrasted?
How are things alike or similar?
How are things not alike? How are they different?

Language:

Same as	Both
Similar to	Instead of
Alike	While
Different from	Some ___, but others ___.

One-Sentence Comparison–Contrast Frames:

___ and ___ are alike because they both ___.

___ and ___ are different because ___.

Some ___ ___, but others ___.

Additional Comparison–Contrast Sentence Frames:

While some ___ ___, others ___.

Example: While some storms start over land, others start over water.

Both ___ are ___, but ___ ___.

On one hand, ___ ___, but sometimes ___.

We know this because on page ___, it says ___, and on page ___, it says ___.

Sequence or Chronological Sentence Frames

Questions:

What is being described in this sequence?

What are the major steps in this sequence?

What happens at each stage of the sequence, process, or cycle?

Why is this sequence important?

Language:

First	Before
Next	Following that
Then	Later
After that	After
Finally	Now
Earlier	The final result

One-Sentence Sequence or Chronological Frames:

At first, ___, but finally, ___.

In the beginning ___, but by the end ___.

Before ___, but after ___.

Then, ___, but now, ___.

Additional Sequence or Chronological Sentence Frames:

I want to explain how ___.

First of all/To begin with, ___.

Then, ___.

After that, ___.

Finally/As a result of this/Now, ___.

I know this to be true because the author describes ___ on page(s) ___.

How to Differentiate Writing Instruction

Figure 3.25 offers a quick guide for tiered writing practices to address the readiness levels and varied needs of diverse learners. Please note that there are some overlapping suggestions for ELLs and students with disabilities, whereas their unique needs are also considered.

Figure 3.25 Differentiating Writing Instruction

ELLs	SWDs	Advanced Learners
• Continue to offer scaffolds and sentence frames when they are removed for general education students. • Spend more time on prewriting, drafting, revising, and editing. • Structure writing tasks into shorter, more manageable subtasks. • Offer step-by-step directions and samples (exemplars). • Guide student writing with questions and prompts. • Have students manipulate sentence strips you provide to construct paragraphs. • Provide models of the type of writing expected. • Support writing with visuals, diagrams, or pictures. • Supply a word bank, definitions, or list of words. • Highlight text or provide page numbers, line numbers, paragraph numbers, or section subheadings to make finding evidence easier.		• Require more complex expression of ideas: stronger vocabulary; figurative language; idiomatic expressions; varied sentence structure. • Ask for text-to-text or text-to-world connections. • Ask students to consider "What if?" scenarios. • Call for students to note *multiple* perspectives. • Have students "imagine" or "pretend," placing themselves in the time period, event, or scene and writing from that perspective. • Ask students to *create* their own story, poem, or book. • Require students to include dialogue and quotation marks. • Request additional research and connections. • Have students predict how the conflict will play out ten years from now and write a brief account. • Have students predict in writing what the main character will be doing ten years from now. • Have math students write about a problem that requires them to work backward. • Have science students consider other variables and "What if?" scenarios in their writing.
• Provide word boxes targeting basic (Tier 1) vocabulary as needed. • Use bilingual glossaries and dictionaries if child is bilingual. • Offer native language support through bilingual peer bridges, teaching assistants, and print and electronic resources. • Allow recently arrived students to write in their native languages if they have high levels of literacy skills; ask them to offer an illustration, a glossary of key ideas, or a brief summary in English.	• Follow the specifics of students' Individualized Education Programs (IEPs). • Offer accommodations and modifications based on IEPs. • Offer assistive hardware and software. • Allow students to dictate their ideas if needed. • Help students set individual goals, engage in self-regulation, and evaluate their own performance. • Allow students to alternate the use of conventional, adapted, and alternative writing tools during and across writing sessions.	

A Final Thought

With sharpened pencils, colorful crayons or markers, and leaking pens in their hands, the students in your classroom come to you with varied levels of readiness and willingness to write. They come from diverse linguistic and cultural backgrounds, and they need different types of support to develop into the kind of writers that the College and Career Readiness Standards require. As Kelly Gallagher (2011) reminds us, writing "has become a gatekeeping skill across the workforce" (3). Thus, attention to writing instruction has never been more important than it is now. Once you have committed yourself to providing abundant opportunities for your students to write routinely in your classroom, you can offer variety to meet this goal. Whether writing opinions, recording ideas in journals, summarizing key ideas, or taking notes, students will improve their writing skills each time they write. The routines suggested in this chapter are not the only ones that can help you achieve success. However, we believe that they will enhance your writing instruction and make your students more confident and competent writers. Just as importantly, we trust that many of the ideas presented here can help you reconcile the writing demands of the standards with your desire to nurture creativity and curiosity in your students.

Essential Questions for Individual Reflection, Collegial Circles, and Group Discussions

- *What is the central idea running through this chapter that informs your instruction?*

- *Why do you need writing routines?*

- *How can you reconcile the writing demands of the College and Career Readiness Standards with the desire for nurturing creativity, curiosity, and personal connections?*

- *How often do students write in your class? How often should they be writing to develop new skills and competencies?*

- *What are the most useful takeaways from the writing routines suggested in this chapter?*

- *How can you support your struggling learners as you continue to raise the rigor of the classroom?*

- *How can you support ELLs' literacy development in light of the rigor of high expectations?*

- *How can you challenge advanced learners while continuing to provide support for on-grade learners as well as struggling learners?*

*Reading and writing float on a sea
of talk.*

James Britton, "Writing and the Story of the World"

Whoever explains, learns.

David Sousa, *How the Brain Learns*

*We need more talk and we need
more productive noise—the sounds of
students talking and learning together;
the sounds of learning.*

Nonie Lesaux, "Turn Up the Volume on Academic Talk!"

Chapter 4

SPEAKING AND LISTENING ROUTINES

Overview

In this chapter, we

- summarize research support for the speaking and listening routines we suggest
- examine the expectations of the Common Core State Standards for speaking and listening
- establish routines for whole-class participation, for small-group and partner collaboration, and for presentations by small groups and individual learners
- present examples, templates (available online), resources, and classroom vignettes along with recommendations from coaches and teachers to support the implementation of the speaking and listening routines

- add rubrics to the scaffolding toolbox
- offer differentiated practices for English learners, students with disabilities, and advanced learners.

Speaking and Listening Routines at a Glance

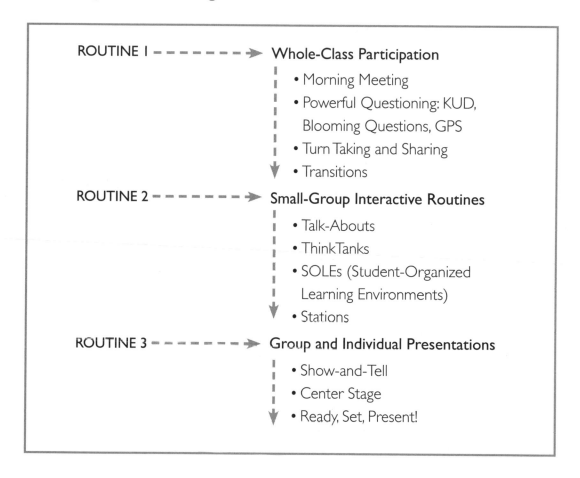

ROUTINE 1 - - - - - - → **Whole-Class Participation**
- Morning Meeting
- Powerful Questioning: KUD, Blooming Questions, GPS
- Turn Taking and Sharing
- Transitions

ROUTINE 2 - - - - - - → **Small-Group Interactive Routines**
- Talk-Abouts
- ThinkTanks
- SOLEs (Student-Organized Learning Environments)
- Stations

ROUTINE 3 - - - - - - → **Group and Individual Presentations**
- Show-and-Tell
- Center Stage
- Ready, Set, Present!

What Does the Research Say About Oral Language Development and Student Interaction?

Celia Genishi (1988) observes that "the development of oral language is one of the child's most natural—and impressive—accomplishments" (1). Childhood first-language acquisition begins at birth in the social context of the home, and then it expands to the larger community, where the child has opportunities to interact with others. The typical progression of childhood oral language results in the following listening and speaking skills—as established by the American Speech-Language-Hearing Association (ASHA)—by the time most children start kindergarten:

Listening

- Follow one to two simple directions in a sequence.
- Listen to and understand age-appropriate stories read aloud.
- Follow a simple conversation.

Speaking

- Be understood by most people.
- Answer simple yes-or-no questions.
- Answer open-ended questions (e.g., "What did you have for lunch today?").
- Retell a story or talk about an event.
- Participate appropriately in conversations.
- Show interest in and start conversations.

(Excerpted from www.asha.org/public/speech/development/kindergarten.htm.)

Yet oral language acquisition—just as many other complex developmental skill sets—can be highly idiosyncratic, resulting in a rather broad range of variances. Some kindergartners will be more communicative, having developed a larger vocabulary and having had more practice in actively listening and interacting with peers and adults than others.

In fact, according to the findings in Betty Hart and Todd Risley's (1995) study—as well as several other research publications—children hear a significantly different amount of oral language spoken to them depending on the households in which they grow up. The frequently quoted multi-million word gap refers to the difference in the number of words heard by age three, or consequently by age five, and so on. While in a typical, middle-class household, the average three-year-old will hear roughly twenty million words, children growing up in poverty will hear less than half this amount. On the other hand, in a more interactive, professional family context, a three-year-old might hear over thirty-five million words in the same time frame. Based on these and other similar startling findings, Andrew Biemiller concludes that

> *early delays in oral language come to be reflected in low levels of reading comprehension, leading to low levels of academic success. If we are to increase children's ability to profit from education, we will have to enrich their oral language development during the early years of schooling.* (2003, para. 7)

Since it is widely recognized that "children's speaking and listening skills lead the way for their reading and writing skills, and together these language skills are the primary tools of the mind for all future learning" (Roskos, Tabors, and Lenhart 2009, vii), a considerable body of research has emerged focusing on classroom discourse or communicative patterns in the classroom context. The questioning framework most used by teachers is known as IRE, during which the teacher *initiates* a question, one student *responds*, and then the teacher *evaluates* the response (Edwards and Westgate

1987). The IRE interaction pattern still seems to dominate many classrooms. For example, you might hear verbal exchanges like this:

Teacher: Why do we need to eat fruits and vegetables?
Student: Because it's healthy.
Teacher: Good. Why else?

Though it might be used productively in skill-oriented, teacher-directed types of lessons, the inherent challenge and problem with the overuse of the IRE sequence is that it typically assesses low-level recall and leads to the teacher taking two out of every three turns to speak. Additionally, it does nothing to stimulate a naturally flowing conversation or productive, academic discourse among learners. As Cazden (1988) observes, "the teacher controls both the development of a topic (and what counts as relevant to it) and who gets a turn to talk" (30). If we want students to engage in conversation for the purpose of learning—and Vygotsky (1978) reminds us that learning is a process that occurs through interaction between people in social, cultural, and historical contexts—then we have to augment the IRE sequence by adding teacher revoicing (restating what a student said for clarification or affirmation: "If I heard you correctly, you think . . ."), which positions the students as thinkers who can agree or disagree with others or find a better way of expressing ideas.

Instructional conversations (Goldenberg 1992; Tharp and Gallimore 1991) and other structured academic interaction frameworks have been researched for over three decades. See, for example, Kate Kinsella's work (2012) on structured academic discourse, or the Intentional Interaction Model discussed by Nicole Marie Sanchez and Lynn Darene Harper (2012). One similarity these models offer is that they recognize the learner as an autonomous thinker who is actively engaged in the learning process along with his or her teacher. As Tharp and Gallimore (1991) observed, when teaching occurs through conversation, a classroom is transformed into a "community of learners" (5).

Building on classroom discourse research, in "How to Start Academic Conversations," Jeff Zwiers and Marie Crawford (2009) suggest ways to engage young learners, particularly ELLs, in meaningful conversations with their peers. Zwiers and Crawford urge teachers to show their students how to use these effective Academic Conversation techniques to discuss worthwhile topics:

- **elaborate and clarify**
- **support one's ideas**
- **build on or challenge another's ideas**
- **apply ideas to life**
- **paraphrase and summarize.**

Lauren Resnick and her colleagues at the University of Pittsburgh Institute for Learning have developed a set of talk moves known as Accountable Talk. Sarah Michaels, Mary Catherine O'Connor, Megan Williams Hall, and Lauren Resnick define what makes talk *accountable*: "For classroom talk to promote learning it must be accountable: to the learning community, to accurate and appropriate knowledge, and to rigorous thinking" (2010, 1).

Their list of Accountable Talk indicators (see Michaels et al. 2010) is similar to the list of features of Academic Conversations mentioned previously. They describe student-to-student questioning, probing, and the use of evidence in a typical Accountable Talk interaction. What's unique about teaching students to engage in either of these conversational processes is that when you use these protocols, even young students can learn to listen to one another, rather than to talk in parallel. With these routines, you can teach them to engage in back-and-forth discussions and conversations. See the following "Check This Out" section for more detailed information regarding the specific and necessary features of Accountable Talk.

 CHECK THIS OUT

Features of Accountable Talk

Students must be *accountable to their learning community* by

listening carefully to others;

adding on to what others have stated;

asking questions and seeking proof;

disagreeing respectfully; and

paraphrasing and summarizing.

Students must be *accountable to accurate knowledge* by

using factual information and providing evidence;

using precise, academic language;

stopping themselves from saying just anything that comes to mind; and

asking others to provide evidence for their claims.

Students must be *accountable to rigorous thinking* by

making connections and synthesizing ideas;

making clear statements and providing related evidence;

building justifications, arguments, explanations, and reasons; and

evaluating the claims and arguments of others.

Adapted from the Accountable Talk Sourcebook (Michaels et al. 2010).

Cooperative learning has also been widely researched and validated by a range of studies. Cooperative learning has been found to promote active student engagement, peer motivation, and increased achievement (Johnson and Johnson 1999; Slavin 1995) and, at the same time, to provide opportunities for meaningful communication and oral language development for at-risk learners (McGroarty 1993). John Hattie (2012) reports that peer interactions and peer support have a positive impact on learning and socializing into the school culture. More specifically, he concludes,

Cooperative learning is most powerful after the students have acquired sufficient surface knowledge to then be involved in discussion and learning with peers—usually in some structured manner. It is then most useful for learning concepts, verbal problem-solving, categorizing, spatial problem-solving, retention and memory, and guessing-judging-predicting. (78–79)

In sum, research supports the notion that the *talking* classroom is the *learning* classroom. For students to develop literacy skills and new understanding in the content areas, they need opportunities for processing through speaking and listening with their peers about what they are learning.

What Are the Speaking and Listening Demands of the Common Core?

Speaking and listening play an important part in promoting student-to-student interactions in the classroom, involving a great deal more student talk than was typically expected prior to this latest standards movement. There are three anchor standards for speaking and listening that emphasize developing comprehension and collaboration skills and three others that focus on student presentation of knowledge and ideas. Suggested participation in critical academic conversations with different partners and using a range of tools, including technology, clearly indicates that these standards go beyond foundational speaking and listening skills. Yet we must also recognize that *everything* that is spoken and heard in the classroom will significantly contribute to students' oral language development, their listening comprehension skills, and formal and less formal academic contributions in the classroom. The two major sections of the Speaking/Listening Anchor Standards are as follows (NGA Center for Best Practices and CCSSO 2010, 22):

Comprehension and Collaboration

1. Prepare for and participate effectively in a range of conversations and collaborations with diverse partners, building on others' ideas and expressing their own clearly and persuasively.
2. Integrate and evaluate information presented in diverse media and formats, including visually, quantitatively, and orally.
3. Evaluate a speaker's point of view, reasoning, and use of evidence and rhetoric.

Presentation of Knowledge and Ideas

4. Present information, findings, and supporting evidence such that listeners can follow the line of reasoning and the organization, development, and style are appropriate to task, purpose, and audience.
5. Make strategic use of digital media and visual displays of data to express information and enhance understanding of presentations.
6. Adapt speech to a variety of contexts and communicative tasks, demonstrating command of formal English when indicated or appropriate.

Speaking and listening skills are closely tied to communicative and literacy development, as well as to academic tasks (Fisher, Frey, and Lapp 2013). The routines we suggest in this chapter align with these standards while also addressing the need for active, engaged student participation in all aspects of learning in every content area throughout the school day.

Speaking and Listening Routines

In this chapter we make a case for establishing routines for speaking and listening for academic purposes within the context of literacy as well as content area learning. As Courtney Cazden (2001) reminds us, "classrooms are complex social systems" (54), with a range of purposes for talking, with often well-established speaking rights, with cultural differences is speech styles, and a lot of other variances that need consideration. We suggest some critical routines to help youngsters engage in a full spectrum of oral language experiences that will expand their linguistic repertoires, enhance their academic language use, and, ultimately, strengthen their reading and writing skills.

ROUTINE *1* Whole-Class Participation

In the K–5 classroom, students need opportunities for meaning making (listening and understanding) as well as for responding and interacting with the teacher and each other. We recommend establishing whole-class routines for (1) morning meeting, (2) questioning, (3) turn taking and sharing, and (4) transitioning.

MORNING MEETING

Based on research and practitioner knowledge from their own classrooms, coaching, or observing others, Maureen Boyd and Sylvia Smyntek-Gworek (2012) claim that "patterns of teacher talk shape student language, reasoning, and critical thinking . . . , that good teaching builds on what students know, and that good teachers seize teachable moments to negotiate and personalize content and student learning in a meaningful, relevant fashion" (4). The morning meeting lends itself to such good teaching. Establishing a routine for the morning meeting—discussed in depth by Roxann Kreite and Lynn Bechtel (2002)—affords a structure for gathering the entire class for a language, literacy, and community-building event. It also significantly contributes to developing academic and social skills through an ongoing conversation guided by a predictable routine. Though it takes only about ten to twenty minutes, if practiced daily, the morning meeting can add up to approximately forty-five hours of class time in a year.

Kreite and Bechtel (2002) suggest including four essential components in the morning meeting routine:

1. **Greeting:** After students are seated in a circle so everyone can see each other, have your students greet each other. Vary the style and format of the greeting, and allow for cultural habits, including handshakes, movements, and so on.

2. **Sharing:** In this critical step, invite a select number of students to reflect on something about their lives—experiences in or outside of school.

3. **Group Activity:** Design a literacy or content-based group activity that allows the entire class to participate. Gamelike, relatively fast-paced, low-risk activities that also respond to the varied cultural experiences in the class best serve the purpose of being highly engaging and effective. Songs, chants, guessing games, movement, wordplay, and other brief activities work well.

4. **News and Announcements:** Leave time for a morning message each day to share note-worthy news items as well as special announcements that pertain to the members of your classroom community.

This type of morning meeting goes beyond the typical calendar and weather routines that many teachers have been using. It invites students to get to know the teacher and each other. It creates a safer environment for taking risks with learning. It promotes respect for individual differences and increased tolerance of others. It evokes a sense of community and engagement with one another. These ingredients contribute to the recipe for success in any elementary classroom.

Teacher-2-Teacher

Figure 4.1 Lisa Zomback shares a morning message about an important class event: a new student coming to join the class.

I write a note to my class a few times a week. This morning message has been an effective way for me to review phonics, sight words, vocabulary, verb tense, and syntax and, most important, to motivate students to want to read. The content of my letters varies from a report about what I did over the weekend, to a description of an upcoming school event, to an announcement about the addition of a new student to the class. Often the students are literally leaning forward out of their chairs to read the note. This is information they need, so they're motivated to read. After students read

continues

the note silently, I read it aloud to them. We then read the note together. Students are invited to ask questions about words they don't know.

The morning message allows for variation and differentiation. I can ask some of my students to identify letters or sight words while asking the more advanced students comprehension questions. Sometimes I ask students to count and identify "mistakes" in the letter. This is always a big hit! The morning message is an opportunity for me to model fluency and for students to read chorally. Throughout the year, my most advanced students often ask to write their own morning messages to the class and conduct their own "lessons" with them. The morning message is a relaxed and natural routine for incorporating listening, speaking, reading, and writing.

Lisa Zomback, grades 4–6
Newcomer Program teacher

POWERFUL QUESTIONING

Margaret Wang, Geneva Haertel, and Herbert Walberg (1993/1994) analyzed fifty years of research and concluded that "positive student responses to questions from teachers and other students" (76), academic interactions that allow for sustained student responses, as well as student engagement in learning were among the most influential factors contributing to academic achievement. Additionally, questioning is one of the nine categories of instructional strategies that Robert Marzano, Debra Pickering, and Jane Pollock (2001) identify as consistently leading to improved student achievement. They also note that cuing students (providing students with hints or prompts) and questioning are "at the heart of classroom practice" (113). Most teachers spend up to 80 percent of class time engaging students with cues and questions. It has also been estimated that teachers may ask over one hundred questions a day, or eighteen thousand a year, which means "18,000 opportunities to develop a student's productive thinking during the school year, and more than a quarter of a million opportunities during the course of a child's 13-year school career" (Tienken, Goldberg, and DiRocco 2009, 40). So, what should be our questioning routine and what sorts of questions should we be asking in order to take advantage of such a critical opportunity?

Whether our learners are in whole groups, small groups, or alone with us, we guide and facilitate their learning by asking questions. Jim Knight (2010) reminds us that there are a number of taxonomies available for consideration when you want to plan the types and levels of questions to use with your students, including the KUD, Blooming questions, and GPS routines.

The KUD Routine

One frequently utilized questioning framework originates from the work of Grant Wiggins and Jay McTighe (2005) and is also discussed by H. Lynn Erickson (2006) and Carol Ann Tomlinson (2008). After establishing carefully crafted essential questions, these authors suggest, teachers should take a trifold approach to day-to-day questioning, addressing what students must *know*, *understand*, and *do* (KUD), and focus on at least these three dimensions of learning.

In the KUD routine, developed as part of Wiggins and McTighe's (2005) backward design, you might generate important questions that fall into the three categories. In fact, by creating a chart for yourself with a column for each of these three categories, you can be sure that you are designing high-quality questions that address exactly what you want students to know, to understand, and to be able to do by the end of your instruction. Once you frame these questions for yourself (and, ultimately, for your students), you will articulate specific learning goals for a lesson. Now, you are ready to plan the learning activities that will help students reach these learning goals.

1. ***Know:*** Ask questions that invite students to demonstrate what they know and remember.
2. ***Understand:*** Pose questions that invite students to demonstrate what they comprehend.
3. ***Do:*** Raise questions that invite students to move beyond their knowledge and understanding and apply what they know and understand to new contexts.

Types of questions that fall into these categories include knowledge questions, understanding questions, and application questions.

Knowledge questions prompt students to demonstrate that they can recall information they have learned. Knowledge questions are frequently closed-ended.

- **Who is the author of *Caps for Sale*?**
- **How did Cinderella get to the ball?**
- **How do you spell *courageous*?**
- **What are three things plants need to survive?**
- **Where is Canada located?**

Understanding questions prompt students to demonstrate that they comprehend the implications of the information they have learned. Understanding questions communicate the big ideas of content being learned. They can be open-ended or closed-ended.

- **How is living in a rural community different from living in the city?**
- **How does using punctuation help readers understand our writing?**
- **What are some examples of the theme of friendship that can be found in this book?**
- **What happens to the environment when we don't recycle?**

Application questions prompt students to extend their knowledge and understanding to new situations or settings.

- Given what you know about the main character, what do you think he'll be doing five years from now?
- Do you think the author would favor school in the summer? Why do you say this?
- What do you think would happen if there were no rain?
- What might be a plan for getting our school to do a better job with recycling?

The Blooming Questions Routine

We believe that, by far, the easiest and most useful questioning taxonomy is still Bloom's taxonomy. Teacher- and kid-friendly, Bloom's taxonomy can be understood even by younger students. Though young learners may not comprehend *six* levels of thinking, they can learn to make sense of multiple levels of thought. Combining levels two at a time, we suggest a routine that shows students how different types of questions evoke different levels of thinking. With this routine, we can demonstrate for learners how, by asking different levels of questions, we move from concrete or basic thinking processes, through interpretation of information, to more abstract ways of thinking.

You can help students climb the taxonomy and begin to think more critically by modeling and using the Blooming questions routine, as illustrated in the following examples. To assist you in guiding your students to *think about thinking*, you can place posters around your room that identify each of the three levels of thinking noted here:

Level A: *Concrete* Thinking Skills and Processes

recalling, recognizing, summarizing, explaining, describing, paraphrasing, identifying, matching, defining

> Who is the main character?
>
> What are three states of matter?
>
> What is the central idea of this text?
>
> How would you summarize this paragraph?
>
> Where do you find mountains on this map?

Level B: *Interpretive* Thinking Skills and Processes

applying, selecting, solving, demonstrating, showing, comparing, contrasting, classifying, categorizing, separating, breaking apart, providing examples, providing evidence, analyzing, examining, connecting

> What does the author believe? How do you know?
>
> What strategy would you use to solve to this problem? Why would you choose this one?
>
> What examples can you give of a healthy lifestyle?
>
> How could you sort these examples of transportation?
>
> How does the style of this author compare with the style of the last author we studied?

Level C: *Critical and Creative* Thinking Skills and Processes

creating, designing, building, planning, composing, inventing, inferring, supporting, defending, judging, rating, prioritizing, justifying, predicting, hypothesizing, arguing, considering

What does it mean when someone tells you, "Don't count your chickens before they hatch?"

What plan could you make to have your class recycle?

How would you argue for getting a new pet at home?

Based on what you know, what will the main character be doing five years from now?

Which of the suggestions made about anti-bullying in this article would work in our classroom? Why or why not?

To lay the foundation for this questioning routine, begin by modeling these types of questions and drawing attention to your posters for a week or two in your class. When students seem to grasp the idea that different questions call forth different levels of understanding, you might place students in pairs to start generating their own Blooming questions. Provide each pair with a sheet of Blooming question starters (see Figure 4.2) and encourage them to generate one question at each of the three levels. A complete one-page chart can be found in the online resources. Have the pairs present their questions for responses from the rest of the class. After additional practice with creating and answering these types of questions, pair-square these partners (place two groups together) and let them challenge other groups with their questions.

Figure 4.2 Blooming Question Starters

Level A Concrete Questions	Level B Interpretive Questions	Level C Critical, Creative, or Abstract Questions
Can you list ___?	Can you illustrate the conflict?	What if ___?
Can you describe ___?	How does ___ compare with ___?	Can you create your own ___?
Can you name ___?	What evidence can you provide for ___?	How can this article help you in your own life?
What are the steps in ___?	Can you describe the motivation of the main character when she ___?	How is ___ still felt today?
Can you give some examples of ___?	Can you explain how ___? Can you explain why ___?	Where will the main character be in ten years?

continues

Figure 4.2 Blooming Question Starters, *continued*

Level A Concrete Questions	Level B Interpretive Questions	Level C Critical, Creative, or Abstract Questions
Can you relate personally to what the main character did?	How is the character's problem in this book similar to/different from the character's problem in another book we've read?	How is the theme/conflict/problem in this story like something we experience today in our community?
Can you define ___?	Can you describe what happened in the beginning, the middle, and the end of this story?	What does it mean when someone says, ___?
Can you paraphrase what I just read?	What was the effect on others when ___?	Would this character/author agree with the following statement: ___? How do you know?
How many days/seasons/months are there in a year?	What does the author believe about ___?	If this character lived in your community, how would his/her life be different? Explain why.
What is the total of 2 + 5?	Why do you think ___?	How would you argue for ___?

The GPS Routine

To provide students additional opportunities to generate their own questions about a topic, we turn to Dan Rothstein and Luz Santana's (2011) work based on a protocol they called Question Formulation Technique (QFT). We suggest students follow three steps when navigating this less familiar territory of asking their own questions. To help them remember how to develop these questions, we've coined the acronym *GPS* (generate, polish, sort).

Generate as Many Questions as Possible
- Don't second-guess yourself; just write down what comes to mind. It is just like a quick-write activity; keep the pencil on the paper.
- Every idea counts; do not throw out any question you might have at this stage.
- Statements and wonderings are acceptable; you will turn them into questions later.
- Don't slow down by trying to think about or answer the questions.

Polish Your Questions
- Revisit your list.
- Review your questions and ideas for clarity: do they ask what you intend?
- If the ideas are not written as questions, change them into questions now.

- Have you climbed the Blooming question taxonomy? (Do you have questions for levels A, B, and C?)
- Do you need to add higher-level questions?

Sort Your Questions

- Organize your questions by type: open-ended or closed.
- Choose two or three of the most important questions.
- Justify your selection: why do you need to seek answers to your chosen questions?
- Plan on how you are going to find answers to your questions.

The GPS routine can be used with learners of any age—as a whole class, with small groups, or as a paired activity—with your guidance. As your students become more independent, encourage them to practice generating questions so that they can become more self-directed, inquisitive learners.

Teacher-2-Teacher

As coteachers, we spend a lot of time on planning our questions. Knowing the needs of our bilingual students gives us the opportunity to create questions that engage all students and maintain a flowing discussion. Some students lack the language skills to fully participate in whole-class discussions. Other students feel too afraid or shy to contribute their thinking because they might say something incorrect. We usually grab these students' attention by asking a big-idea question about a topic of the day. After we give them time to discuss it with their peers for a couple of minutes, we ask them to volunteer their answers. We don't evaluate their answers during this part of the lesson because we want them to say anything and everything they know about a topic.

We usually begin our in-depth discussions with comprehension questions that require simple answers. We tend to paraphrase or revoice students' responses using Standard English and academic terminology. In this way, students gain enough information and get prepared for the more challenging questions we'll ask afterward. We take the simple questions to the next level by providing students with the opportunity for more in-depth thinking. The results? Our students frequently come back and ask their own rigorous questions. In a recent lesson on the four types of germs, students' curiosity was piqued. One boy asked, "How did fungi get its name?" Another student posed an even more complex question: "What would happen if all four types of germs were in the body at the same time?"

When our students have questions like these, we have a routine: Stop, think, speak! We throw those questions right back to the students instead of answering them ourselves. This routine (where we stop our large-group discussion; invite students to think about the questions raised by their peers; and ask them to discuss possible answers in pairs and small groups) activates their knowledge of the topic and promotes higher-order thinking skills. It also makes for a more interesting discussion because the questions come from their peers.

Elena Kushins and Sicilia Valenzuela, grade 2 coteachers

TURN TAKING AND SHARING

Courtney Cazden (2001) observed that "frequently, the teacher chooses to direct verbal traffic by asking students to raise hands and then select someone to speak" (82). When you allow students to assume more speaking rights and take responsibility for their participation, turn taking might be governed by some additional explicit or implicit rules.

Turn taking and sharing are integral parts of the morning meeting routine described earlier in this chapter. Students learn and practice daily how to respectfully engage in a conversation in the large-group setting, how to actively listen to what the speaker is saying, and how to build upon and add to previous comments. Further, sharing and turn taking also play an important role in academic conversations that take place in literacy classes and every other content area. Paul Bambrick-Santoyo, Aja Settles, and Juliana Worrell (2013) suggest that "changing the habit of discussion in your classroom is no cosmetic shift. It sets the stage for deeper discussion, peer-to-peer probing, and authentic conversations" (52). Harnessing the power of well-established and internalized discussion habits will achieve the following:

- **maximize the amount of thinking students do when answering questions**
- **maximize the amount of support students get from their peers**
- **minimize the direct intervention of the teacher**
- **train students to self-monitor and be metacognitive about their learning. (54)**

After you teach the fundamentals, such as speaking audibly, keeping eye contact with peers, not just the teacher, and offering feedback to each other, Bambrick-Santoyo and his colleagues suggest, introduce and practice what they call *universal prompts*. The more students hear you using prompts such as, "Tell me more." "What makes you think that?" "Why do you think that is?" and "Why is this important?" the more students will use the same prompts with their peers.

One way to engage in a rich, structured conversation is for students to make learning as authentic as possible. To achieve that goal, Maureen Boyd and Lee Galda (2011) also promote *real talk* in the classroom so as to engage students in genuine discussions. They note that students need to learn

how to enter into a conversation; how to take turns without explicit permission from [the teacher]; and how to listen to each other so that they [can] move from individual contributions without much uptake to talk that [is] truly conversational, with students responding to one another's comments. (34)

It is necessary to establish and practice discussion patterns that facilitate student-to-student interaction early on in the school year, rather than maintain a teacher-run and teacher-centered classroom environment. Here are further suggestions on how to achieve that in a large-group setting:

- **Encourage students to respond to one another rather than to you all the time.**
  - *Jackie, didn't you have a similar experience to the one that Haley is describing?*

- **Redirect student contributions that seem to be slipping off track with authentic questions.**
  - *When earlier you said _____, I was wondering _____.*

- **Position yourself as a seeker of knowledge rather than as the primary knower.**
  - *I've heard about _____, but have never known that _____. (Or I know _____, but I didn't know _____.) Kamal, can you explain to us _____?*

- **Validate student input when necessary with positive feedback and compliments that resemble real-life acknowledgments.**
  - *Well, that is really impressive; I wish I had _____.*

- **Become a better listener.**
  - *Let me see if I heard it correctly.*
  - *Let me repeat what you said just to make sure I understood it correctly.*

- **Request elaboration from students when needed.**
  - *So as a person just learning about _____, can you tell me what else I should really know about _____?*

- **Show students how to build on prior comments as opportunities to sustain the flow of the conversation.**
  - *When Rickie said _____, I couldn't help thinking of _____.*
  - *Li, your comments about _____ made me think about _____.*

- **Help them participate in co-constructing knowledge about the topic you and the class are exploring.**
  - *So in other words, Ron, Kelly, and Taisha can all be correct about _____. They just defined different aspects of it.*

Within a whole-class setup, create opportunities for dyads or triads to talk about the target subject matter before sharing out with the whole class. This way more students will have a voice. Even though they will be talking at the same time, which might take getting used to at first, this preliminary share will provide essential rehearsal time to those who need it. Well-established practices include turn-and-talk, think-pair-share, and triad talk. See Figures 4.3 and 4.4,

Figure 4.3 Kindergartners Turn and Talk to Discuss Details About a Picture Projected on an Interactive Board

Figure 4.4 Grade 4 Students Participate in Think-Pair-Share

picturing kindergartners and fourth graders, respectively, who are highly engaged in conversation and paying close attention to one another.

Teacher-2-Teacher

Turn-and-talk is a big part of my routine. I will ask the students to turn and talk to their neighbors several times throughout the minilesson. This ensures all students have the ability to speak and be heard. When students finish talking to their partners, I ask for volunteers to tell us who their partners were and what their partners said. For example: "My partner was Joshua and he said today he's going to go back into his old stories in his writing folder and he will add dialogue to his stories." This strategy promotes engagement of all students and is also a part of our routine. Routines give the students a sense of comfort, as they know what is expected of them.

Mary Lou Weymann, kindergarten teacher

COACH'S NOTES

To facilitate successful participation in think-pair-share while students are gathered on the floor in front of you, try some of these tips.

- We learned a great classroom management tip from literacy consultant Kim Yaris: When you invite your student to come to the rug, seat them as if they were on a school bus. Each of them will have an instant partner, and you will have an aisle to walk down to listen in on the conversations. No one will be left without a buddy.
- Give wait time for students to think before turning to their partners. Establish a nonverbal reminder, such as holding your index finger to your forehead.
- Use anchor charts to support reporting back to the class with sentence starters such as the following:
- My partner was _____ and we discussed _____.
- My partner said _____. We agreed _____.

See Figure 4.5 for an anchor chart that guides small-group discussions, whose purpose is to engage several partners in an academic discussion. This configuration allows for more diverse perspectives, more negotiation of ideas, and additional skill development in active listening and turn taking. Also see Figure 4.6, which shows a triad discussing their notes from a close read.

Figure 4.5 Small-Group Discussion Guidelines from a Third-Grade Class

Figure 4.6 Triad Discussion

Small group discussion guidelines

1. Everyone should contribute.
2. Take turns talking.
3. Make eye contact.
4. Listen respectfully.
5. Ask for input or comments from each other: "Can you tell me what you are thinking?" "Would you like to add to my idea?"
6. Ask for clarification: "Can you explain that to me?" "Can you add some more detail?" "Would you tell me more about that?"

TRANSITIONS

Recitations, memorization, and rote learning sound like ghosts of classrooms from the past. Yet we have found that chants and choral presentations of familiar poems, songs, or even the multiplication table fill the air with productive noise *during transition times*. As students gather their notebooks to join the teacher at the front of the room, as they get up one table at a time and line up for lunch, recess, gym, or for any other reason, there is bound to be chatter or other noise. Why not fill that unused, found time with a learning opportunity? Counting off in unison by twos, threes, fours, fives, and so on will improve mathematical fluency. Singing a song or reciting a poem from the literacy unit will offer safe, low-risk rehearsal time for an upcoming assembly performance and improve fluency as well. Chanting a rhyme about the seven continents, the three states of matter, algorithm rules, or other hard-to-remember information will help solidify content knowledge and make the application of new learning more successful.

ROUTINE 2 Small-Group Interactive Routines

Earlier in this chapter, we provided evidence for why you should develop greater student-to-student interaction with diverse learners and engage them in a range of conversations and collaborations. However, we realize that if your students are not used to a sophisticated level of small-group interaction and discourse, you will need to scaffold these conversation skills by modeling.

Try the fishbowl technique. Choose a few of your more verbal, ready-to-interact students, and form a small group with them. Have the rest of the class surround you and simply watch how you all participate in a small-group academic conversation. Afterward, debrief and elicit from your learners the characteristics of effective small-group discussions.

Use scaffolding as well. As mentioned earlier, by prompting students orally with questions that promote richer and deeper conversation, you provide a model for students to engage in this type of conversation eventually on their own. By listing prompts, sound bites, or "This sounds like . . ." on anchor charts around your room, you offer students reference tools for additional support in expressing themselves when they are on their own in small groups. See Figure 4.7 for an anchor chart with discussion prompts.

Figure 4.7 Claudia Martinez's Discussion Prompts Anchor Chart from PS 228 (Queens, New York)

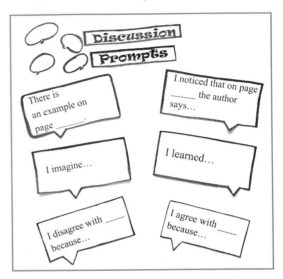

COACH'S NOTES

As Frey, Fisher, and Nelson (2013) point out in "Todo tiene que ver con lo que se habla: It's All About the Talk," teacher talk alone can't elevate student language. We must provide multiple opportunities for students to use and apply academic language on their own. Keep in mind, research suggests as your students become better speakers and listeners, they will also improve their reading and writing skills (Harste, Short, and Burke 1988). You can use the Talk-About routine, SOLE activities, stations, and ThinkTanks to provide frequent speaking and listening opportunities for small groups in your classroom.

✔ CHECK THIS OUT

Cooperative learning has been explored and embraced by both researchers and practitioners for decades. Explore current work on this approach in the following resources.

Books

Johnson, D. W., and F. Johnson. 2009. *Joining Together: Group Theory and Group Skills.* 10th ed. Boston: Allyn and Bacon.

Johnson, D. W., and R. T. Johnson. 1991. *Learning Together and Alone.* Englewood Cliffs, NJ: Prentice Hall.

Kagan, S. 2013. *Kagan Cooperative Learning Structures.* San Clemente, CA: Kagan Cooperative.

Williams, R. B. 2007. *Cooperative Learning: A Standard for High Achievement.* Thousand Oaks, CA: Corwin.

Wincel, M. 2013. *Cooperative Learning for Primary: Grades PreK–2.* San Clemente, CA: Kagan Cooperative.

Websites

Kagan Publishing and Professional Development (Spencer Kagan's Website): www.kaganonline.com/index.php

The International Association for the Study of Cooperation in Education: www.iasce.net

The Cooperative Learning Institute (David and Roger Johnson's Website): www.co-operation.org

The Jigsaw Classroom (Elliot Aronson's Website): www.jigsaw.org

Success for All (Robert Slavin's Website): www.successforall.org

Concept to Classroom (PBS Online Professional Development on Cooperative and Collaborative Learning): www.thirteen.org/edonline/concept2class/coopcollab/index.html

Video Clips

Teaching Channel Clips:

www.teachingchannel.org/videos/jigsaw-method

www.teachingchannel.org/videos/think-pair-share-lesson-idea

www.teachingchannel.org/videos/independent-and-group-work

Kagan YouTube Channel: www.youtube.com/user/kaganvideo

TALK-ABOUTS

Once you have established rules and protocols for classroom interactions, you will find that using small groups will evoke much enthusiasm from elementary learners in grades 2 to 5.

Given the opportunity to converse with their peers, your students will look forward to the moment when you ask them to get into groups for a Talk-About. Combining the best features of Academic Conversations (Zwiers and Crawford 2009) and Accountable Talk (Michaels et al. 2010), described earlier in this chapter, a Talk-About sets up a framework for using academic language in a small-group setting to help your students make sense of information and retain it.

Before releasing students to engage in a Talk-About (a small-group Academic Conversation) on their own, read a short text together and model the types of questions that promote such a conversation. Co-construct an anchor chart of the question and sentence starters that your students come up with to place on your wall for future reference.

When students are ready to try these conversations without your guidance (to talk about, e.g., good nutrition, the comparison of life in different communities, life of the Native Americans, or why people moved westward), place them into heterogeneous groups of four to five members. Then follow these steps:

1. First, remind students that the goal of this group conversation is to promote *a dialogue where all students are involved* in discussing main ideas and/or themes.

2. Tell them beforehand that they will be evaluating their own participation, as well as their group's ability to collaborate, after the Talk-About is over. To develop shared ownership of this step, consider creating a simple rubric or checklist for evaluating the group's interaction (see Figure 4.15 for a Talk-About Self-Evaluation Checklist).

3. As needed, provide students with a note-taking page that you have developed in advance. The page might include written questions that will guide the conversation. It might include a graphic organizer or a page with sections and boxes for recording what each student learns from his or her conversation with peers. The handout can be blank, or you can fill it in partially to scaffold younger students or other learners who might benefit from partial notes.

4. Provide the Talk-About Sentence Starters Foldable (see Figure 4.8) to scaffold your students' conversation and to keep all students more fully engaged.

5. Keep the conversations short at first (no more than five to seven minutes) until students get comfortable with the routine. Rotate among the groups, refocusing learners who need it and modeling good conversational skills.

6. After the set amount of time, regroup as a whole class and share out main ideas and details about the topic. (It is during this time that you will be able to check for accuracy and point out any misconceptions that you may not have picked up as the groups talked separately.)

Figure 4.8 Talk-About Sentence Starters Foldable

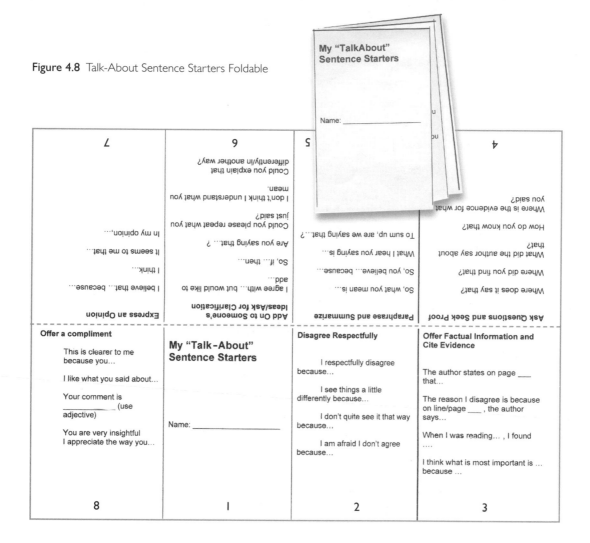

THINKTANKS

In Chapter 1, we suggested using a ThinkTank as an effective approach for assessing and activating prior knowledge. Now, we recommend using this same five-minute routine for bringing students together to make sense of any topic or idea, *after* it has been explored or studied in class. Try this activity to help your learners make meaning and deepen their understanding through conversation. Use it to quickly assess your class' grasp of or misunderstandings about a concept. Use it to reinvigorate your learners when they seem a bit lethargic.

- **Group students randomly, by simply counting off around the room, any time you want to give students five minutes to process information. (By counting off in different directions whenever you do a ThinkTank, you can ensure that different groups will be formed each time.)**

- Ask students to go to their numbered ThinkTank location to *put their heads together* in order to discuss, record, and/or illustrate their understanding of the topic, theme, or concept.

- Alternatively, you can pose a question for the groups to answer. For example:

  - *What operation and strategy would you use to solve this word problem? How do you know?*

  - *Discuss how the author develops the theme of perseverance in this story.*

  - *What types of occupations and recreation would you find in this region? Why do you say that?*

- Have each group record its consensus on chart paper (for shared viewing) or on students' own individual note-taking pages (to be used for future class work, homework, or study).

- Require that the conversation include the use of two to three *academic words* that you have highlighted on your word wall with sticky notes or listed on the board. (See Chapter 5 for a discussion of word walls and academic language.)

- Follow up the group ThinkTank with an individual assessment or written summary.

- Tell students ahead of time what type of assessment will follow to identify a purpose for engaging in the conversation and taking notes. (This "feed-up," which Hattie [2009] describes, provides students with goals and information about where they are headed, and is, as he points out, a necessary component of the learning experience if you want students to take control of their own learning.)

COACH'S NOTES

To make the ThinkTank routine simple to implement, place numbers around your room, where they will permanently remain visible. Consider choosing spots where you can post pieces of chart paper, should you want students to use them. If you don't have enough wall space to post numbers, consider using a table, a desk, and/or a place on the carpet as additional locations for a ThinkTank. Be sure to place enough ThinkTank numbers around your room so that your groups have no more than four to five students. After posting these numbers, you will be able to spontaneously call for a ThinkTank activity, and it will require no additional prep time!

Students will welcome the opportunity to get up and move around for a few minutes. The use of ThinkTanks will engage all of your learners by encouraging collaboration. Not only will students retain more information, but they will also be able to write with greater elaboration after participating in this routine.

Our fifth-grade students participated in a summative assessment using the ThinkTank routine. The class had recently completed the novel Esperanza Rising (Ryan 2002). As a culminating activity, students formed small collaborative ThinkTanks to discuss questions based on their reading. The questions they explored promoted rich discussion among the participants in each group, making students think beyond the text by predicting, making inferences, and analyzing questions. After the discussions, students recorded their opinions on chart paper and shared them with the class as a whole.

Anne Logan, teacher on special assignment/peer coach,
and Catherine Spiller and Claudine Loria, grade 5 teachers

When grouping students for ThinkTanks, consider placing your most verbal students together in one or two groups. Then, the remaining groups will have an opportunity to share without the same students always taking over the conversation. It's great to watch as the cream rises to the top, and formerly quiet students speak up because they are not intimidated by their more loquacious peers. Figure 4.9 shows fourth graders putting their heads together to talk about Native Americans.

Figure 4.9 A ThinkTank Group Generating Ideas About the Iroquois

SOLES

The SOLE (self-organized learning environment) routine is an exciting global project and classroom routine that is being supported by the TED community (a nonprofit devoted to sharing ideas from the technology, entertainment, and design worlds that has expanded to include the educational world). You can try it in your own classroom, even as teachers around the world are engaging in the very same activity with their learners. Requiring only one laptop per four students, SOLEs engage students in researching their own questions or questions that you might pose at first. Requiring Internet research and group presentations, SOLEs encourage collaboration among group members as well as self-directed learning.

Conducting his first "hole in the wall" experiment in New Delhi, Sugata Mitra, a professor from New Castle University in the United Kingdom, watched as students, motivated by curiosity, taught themselves by using one computer with Internet access, despite coming from remote geographical areas in India and having no experience with either English or the Internet (O'Connor 2002).

The SOLE inquiry-based teaching approach that evolved from that experiment, where four students share one computer as they go on intellectual explorations and prepare for classroom presentations, supports our listening and speaking standards. Mitra's team is now building the School in the Cloud, a learning lab in India where rural students will engage in learning activities using the Internet and online mentoring.

Why would you choose to use the SOLE routine with your students? While we have no definitive answer as to what students will *need to know* in the coming decades, we do know that they will need to know *how to learn* and that they will "need to be good at searching for information, collating it, and figuring out whether it is right or wrong" (Mitra 2010, 4). Because SOLEs focus more on process than on content, you can feel satisfied that you are preparing students with twenty-first-century skills when you engage them in SOLE explorations.

When learners collaborate on a SOLE, they use critical thinking skills and problem-solving skills. No longer able to be passive about their learning, students must engage with others and communicate ideas in a variety of formats. Motivation is at an all-time high because students are intrinsically driven when exploring answers to their own questions. "Children will learn to do what they want to do," Mitra (2010, 7) assures us. Creating opportunities for your students to learn about their world in this way will help them develop habits that will lead to lifelong learning. Take the following steps to create a SOLE for math, science, social studies, health, or for any topic or concept you would like students to investigate. Coach your students to research big questions and engage their hearts and minds with this activity.

1. At first, you will pose the big questions for your students: What does it mean to be a family? How does living in one type of community affect who you are? Why do people have revolutions? What factors contribute to a healthy lifestyle and a longer life? How can people live in peace? Why do people leave their homes and travel elsewhere? Eventually, your students will be able to pose their own questions.

2. Then, give your groups of learners anywhere between fifteen and forty minutes to engage with information on the Internet (or on teacher-provided sites) in order to answer the question.

3. Tell students they must answer the question and create a visual representation, as well. (Students must assign themselves roles: Who will navigate the computer? Draw the visual? Lead the group? Keep time for the group during the routine?)

4. Your job at this point is to facilitate the groups by rotating around the classroom, asking questions that will lead students further down the path to self-discovery.

5. After a set amount of time, bring the groups back together to share out and present their learning as a group.

See the following "Check This Out" section for more details about how you can become involved.

The SOLE routine is somewhat similar to the Question Kiosk and WonderQuests, shared in Chapter 1, in that it sparks kids' curiosity and provides them a format for researching their own questions. However, it is different in that the SOLE routine expects *group* interaction, collaboration, and shared presentation, rather than individual research. While students engage in these inquiries, they will be building background knowledge from their extensive reading on the Internet. In Figure 4.10, students work with one laptop to research answers to a problem about which they are curious.

Figure 4.10 Sharing a Laptop for Research

Once students are seeking answers to their *own* questions, they will truly be on their way to self-directed learning and becoming lifelong learners. What a perfect routine to work in weekly or biweekly to support the expectations of the listening and speaking standards while building other literacies at the same time.

Teacher-2-Teacher

I have used project-based learning in my classroom and it is similar to the SOLEs. I usually have my student researchers looking to solve a problem or answer a question on their own. However, I like Mitra's suggestion of allowing the students to organize themselves into groups, to move from group to group, to borrow and share ideas, and then to present together as a group. This type of organization actually mirrors how people in the workplace come to consensus and share information in the real world. **Grade 4 teacher**

Inquiry-based or project-based learning rests on the foundation of student collaboration. Explore current work on project-based learning in the following resources.

Books

Bender, W. N. 2012. *Project-Based Learning: Differentiating Instruction for the 21st Century.* Thousand Oaks, CA: Corwin.

Hallermann, S., J. Larmer, and J. Mergendoller. 2014. *PBL in the Elementary Grades: Step-by-Step Guidance, Tools and Tips for Standards-Focused K–5 Projects.* Novato, CA: Buck Institute for Education.

Krauss, J. I., and S. K. Boss. 2013. *Thinking Through Project-Based Learning: Guiding Deeper Inquiry.* Thousand Oaks, CA: Corwin.

Laur, D. 2013. *Authentic Learning Experiences: A Real-World Approach to Project-Based Learning.* New York: Routledge.

McKenzie, W. N. 2012. *Intelligence Quest: Project-Based Learning and Multiple Intelligences.* Waynesville, NC: International Society for Technology in Education.

Websites

Edutopia Resources: www.edutopia.org/project-based-learning

Buck Institute for Education: http://bie.org

PBS Online Professional Development on Inquiry-Based Learning: www.thirteen.org /edonline/concept2class/inquiry/index.html

Video Clips

Buck Institute YouTube Channel: www.youtube.com/user/BIEPBL

Teaching Channel Clips:

www.teachingchannel.org/videos/students-teaching-themselves

www.teachingchannel.org/videos/teaching-hurricanes-video?fd=1

www.teachingchannel.org/videos/learning-through-experiences

In addition, archived Twitter chats about project-based learning can be found at #PBLChat, where you can also participate in real time in the robust discussions on this topic.

STATIONS

As a collaborative activity, the stations routine ranks high in student popularity. Students rotate through a set of teacher-designed stations with engaging names (the quotation station, the manipulation station, the visualization station, etc.) and complete essential tasks. See the next "Coach's Notes" section in this chapter for ideas for other stations. Elementary students love the movement that the routine provides, as well as the opportunity to talk (albeit academically) with their peers. Teachers enjoy the freedom to work with students who need additional attention, as small groups busily move through a set of review or practice activities.

As we have mentioned several times, routines can incorporate several literacy skills at once and are sometimes used with one set of skills or another. The "Teacher-2-Teacher" vignette describes one fourth-grade teacher's exciting set of stations where students used the skills of speaking and listening as they interviewed immigrant visitors to their classroom. However, a set of stations might be developed that involve less speaking and listening and more reading and independent writing. The possibilities are endless.

For Social Studies: Set up stations for students to gain practice in analyzing authentic documents. Rotating through multiple stations, groups look at the document (chart, graph, map, photo, political cartoon, etc.) that they find at each station, discuss together what conclusions they draw (perhaps guided by teacher-prepared questions), and individually record notes for future reference.

For ELA: Have students take the first draft of an individual piece of writing they have been working on and move through five editing stations. At each station they might find an example of a particular writing craft or skill to try in their own piece of writing. For example, the task card at one station might read:

Identification Station

Reread your paragraph to check for capital letters. Remember to capitalize the first word in each new sentence. Names, places, holidays, and other proper nouns must be capitalized. Circle the capital letters in green.

For Science: In a classroom where students have been studying buoyancy, for example, have them rotate through a set of stations at the end of the unit. While one station might ask them to sort pictures into groups of items that will sink and items that will float, another station could ask them to annotate an illustration and use the following terms in the caption: *sinking, floating, displacement,* and *density.* A third station might ask students to make a prediction about whether the item on the table will sink or float in the bowl, to test their hypothesis, and to explain in writing why they were right or wrong.

Most of the teachers we have worked with choose to use the stations routine at the end of a unit to make reviewing a more dynamic and meaningful process than the usual review-sheet method. However, stations can also be used to activate prior knowledge *before* a unit or to provide practice *during* a unit. Regardless of how you choose to use them, we know they will enliven your classroom, maximize engagement, and increase opportunities for collaboration.

- Observation/Identification Station: Students describe, analyze, sort, categorize, and so on.
- Justification Station: Students tell why, cite evidence, support with details, persuade others, and so on.
- Documentation Station: Students analyze and interpret primary source documents, charts, graphs, maps, and so on.
- Experimentation Station: Students conduct an experiment, design an experiment, draw conclusions from given data, and so on.
- Evaluation Station: Students judge the actions of others, prioritize the needs, rate the importance of, and so on.

Follow these steps to implement a set of stations:

1. Label index cards with numbers (1, 2, 3, 4, etc.) to identify your stations.
2. At each station (several desks grouped together, a table, a space on the carpet, a few desks situated just outside your door, etc.), place a task card that contains written instructions for what students must do at the station.
3. Design the task for each station to take about the same amount of time. To address this very issue, some teachers include an early finisher's activity (a bonus or challenge question, a creative task, an extension activity, or an assessment that will be assigned for homework) that students can work on for a minute or two if they complete any station before time is up.
4. Signal that it's time to move to the next station by using a chime, a bell, or a light.
5. Make sure that each student has his or her own clipboard, Foldable, graphic organizer, or notebook to record information.
6. Encourage the group to discuss the task or question together and to share their ideas out loud.
7. Although the conversation is collaborative, the resulting finished product is individual. Each student must complete his or her own responses in writing.

Some teachers execute a set of stations over the course of a week, having students go to one station a day. Other teachers prefer to design short tasks (five to eight minutes) and have students complete them all in one or two days. Most teachers plan activities that last anywhere from five to twenty minutes. The shorter the activities, the more frequently you will tend to use stations as a routine (for practicing different math or language skills, for example).

Each time students engage in this routine, they will transition more smoothly from station to station and they will focus more quickly on the task at hand. This routine is an excellent way for students to talk about what they have learned in a unit or to practice a skill by discussing it with someone else.

Teacher-2-Teacher

During a lesson about why different families immigrate to the United States, my students had many thought-provoking questions. Some of these questions were so insightful and detailed that I didn't feel comfortable answering them without doing a little research. Prior to this discussion, we had also talked about the variety of countries that their families were from. Remembering this part of the conversation, one of my students asked if we would be able to invite their immigrant relatives to our class for the purpose of interviewing them about their experiences. We prepared the interview questions as a class and set up stations so students could interact with several guests in small groups. This turned into a wonderful day, filled with stories about immigration travel and the newcomers' experiences once they reached the United States, and excited kids eager to learn about the process immigrants went through to become United State citizens.

Danielle Shine, grade 4 teacher

COACH'S NOTES

If you have a large class (anywhere between twenty-five to thirty students), it's easier to create three stations and repeat the same three stations on the opposite side of the classroom. Students on one side of the room rotate through three stations numbered 1A, 2A, and 3A. Students on the opposite side of the room rotate through the same three tasks but at stations 1B, 2B, and 3B. Have students count off around the room (1A, 2A, 3A, 1B, 2B, 3B, repeating until every student has a number and a letter), and, when you give the signal, have them all move to their stations. Students will learn to rotate from the first to the second station, from the second to the third station, and from the third back to the first station on their side of the room. (See the classroom stations flowchart in Figure 4.11 for a visual of this rotation.) Run in this fashion, the entire rotation will take half the time (students rotate through only three stations, instead of four to six), group size will be smaller, and you will have time to bring the class together at the end to share out as a whole group.

Figure 4.11 Classroom Stations Flowchart

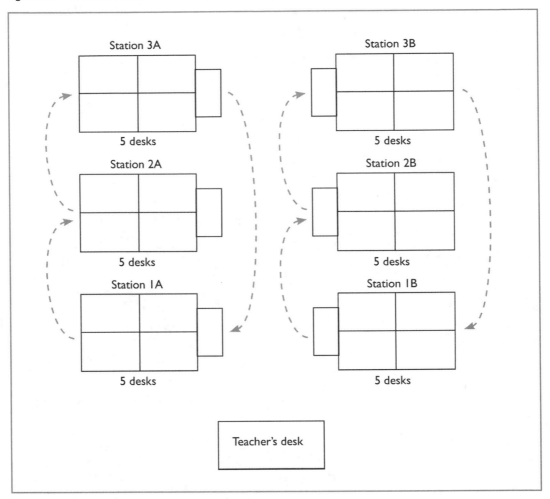

ROUTINE 3 **Group and Individual Presentations**

Students in kindergarten through grade 2 need ample opportunities to speak publicly and develop confidence in their academic oral language skills (using accurate vocabulary, complete sentences, and so on). Students in grades 3 to 5 are ready to report on a topic or text in an organized manner, using appropriate facts and details to support main ideas. In addition, students are expected to use audio recordings and visual displays when appropriate and to speak in clear, complete sentences, at an understandable pace. To help students achieve these goals, we suggest that you use several age- and grade-appropriate presentation routines, such as show-and-tell, the center stage, and Ready, Set, Present!

SHOW-AND-TELL

An elementary classroom favorite, show-and-tell entices students to do a brief presentation of a special object or offer an account of an event based on firsthand experiences. When you set up a routine for show-and-tell, keep in mind some logistical questions:

- Will you establish the guidelines for the show-and-tell routine collaboratively with your class?
- When will you hold show-and-tell sessions: beginning, middle, or end of the day?
- How often can students share? Weekly, monthly, or only on special occasions?
- What type of rotating schedule will you create? Weekly or monthly?
- What types of objects are acceptable or desirable?
- How will the parents be informed about the expectations?
- How long will students be presenting about what they brought to the class?
- What language support will be given to the speaker?
- What expectations will you establish for the listeners?

We've found that show-and-tell encourages students to tell the stories behind the objects and allows children to expand their descriptive vocabulary and precise use of language. During these short sessions, non-presenters learn to be receptive audience members who are ready to discuss, ask questions, and make connections.

Show-and-tell sessions can be open-ended and spontaneous or structured and organized around curricular goals. Some of our favorites include the following:

- **My Life in a Bag:** Students bring personally meaningful items at the beginning of the year so they can get to know each other. Have one student display his or her objects and invite others to make educated guesses about the significance of the selections.
- **The Antique Show-and-Tell:** Students share a household item that is older than they are. They discuss what the object is and how it was used. A few sentence frames might support this type of presentation:
    - *This was used by my grandmother but today we use ___.*
    - *Before I was born, people used to ___.*
- **Family Fair:** Students share something special about their family by bringing in an object of cultural significance or retelling a story that is often heard at home. This form of show-and-tell adds an appreciation for diversity and helps build respect for differences in the classroom. See a second grader getting ready to present a *samovar* (Russian teapot) and other cultural items in Figure 4.12.

Figure 4.12 Presenting Cultural Heritage Items from Home

CENTER STAGE

If Shakespeare is correct that all the world's a stage, then the classroom may certainly be considered a rehearsal for that larger stage. Unlike show-and-tell, center stage presentations—whether content- or literacy-based—are prepared ahead of time and even rehearsed. Michaels and her colleagues (2010) insightfully note that "in student presentations, the presenters are positioned as 'experts' on their own work, and critiqued and questioned by both teachers and other students" (26). Luis Moll (1992) has also suggested giving students time and space for showcasing their *funds of knowledge* and to be recognized for their out-of-school expertise.

Center stage is a special routine that calls for advanced planning and preparation. Depending on your curricular goals, you can require individual or group presentations. These opportunities will build students' oral language skills and confidence in preparing and presenting their expertise to their classmates. See Figure 4.13 for a selection of presentation types, what these might look like in the classroom, and how they will benefit learners. Figure 4.14 shows a fourth-grade student narrating a familiar story to her classmates as she occupies a special speaker's chair.

Figure 4.13 Individual and Group Presentations for Center Stage

Individual Presentations and Their Benefits		Group Presentations and Their Benefits	
Author's Chair: Students present original short stories or poetry.	These presentations support the development of independence, public speaking skills, and fluency.	Group Research Presentations: Students present their findings on a topic, using posters or technology.	In addition to fostering public speaking skills, these presentations also enhance project organization skills. Students learn to apply the use of technology such as recording devices or multimedia presentation tools (audio recordings, music clips, sound effects, or video recordings can be added to these presentations).
Research Projects: Students present their findings on self-selected topics (closely or loosely connected to the curriculum).	Students get accustomed to taking the stage and taking pride in their own work.	Readers Theater: Students perform a dramatic presentation of a published or student-written script.	
Book Reports: Students recount assigned or self-selected fiction or nonfiction pieces.	When these presentations are short and accompanied by peer feedback, the entire class benefits.	Role-Plays or Skits: Students reenact scenes from stories you've read together as a class.	
Current Events: Students give local, regional, national, or international news reports.			

Figure 4.14 Fourth Grader Presenting to Her Class

Teacher-2-Teacher

My students participate in a "Climb into Black History" project. They choose a person and research him or her. Students are required to write letters from a first-person point of view to either a friend or a relative from that time period. The letter has to describe an important event in that person's life and how he or she felt when it happened. When students present their letters, some add speeches, dancing, or singing.

Lisa Peluso, grade 4 teacher

READY, SET, PRESENT!

The Ready, Set, Present! routine will give your students another focused classroom opportunity to informally converse about what they have been learning. Rather than have students engage in new research, as the SOLE routine does, this collaborative practice asks small groups of students to work together to elicit the key points of a lesson. This impromptu discussion and reporting out will help your learners review their notes, reflect on your class discussions, and focus on what's important to know and remember. Each group is expected to record, and then present, the essential understandings to the rest of the class. While we recommend using this routine at the end of a unit, it can also be used during the course of a unit, after a few concepts have been explored.

Before you begin this routine, do the following activities to prepare the kids:

- Model for your class how to complete a summary report on a topic you have previously studied. Summarizing does not come easily to students.
- As a guide, complete one or two summary reports with your students.
- Since students will need to work together to decide what tasks must be completed and who will complete each task, be sure to coach them on how to make these decisions in their groups. (Would Damen prefer to work on the visual because he is artistic? Would Li like

to type up the notes because he is so good with computers? Would Rachel like to take down the notes on the graphic organizer because she writes neatly with ease?)
- Let partners prepare a summary report together.
- Model how to make audio recordings and visual displays and how to use multimedia components. Your students must be familiar with each presentation tool before you ask them to use it independently.

COACH'S NOTES

Some students might struggle with certain tasks, so be ready to offer scaffolds (graphic organizers, lists of questions, sentence frames, opportunities for students to brainstorm verbally in pairs or with you before they start taking notes, etc.) in case some students get stuck and don't know what to do when working independently. Assign a student leader for each group or assign a few for the class. Give these leaders ideas for how to help their peers with their presentations.

Once you have modeled sufficiently for your class and guided the students through practice, try these steps to implement the routine:

1. Divide your students into small groups (three to four students) and ask them to determine the key ideas and supporting details for the topic you have been studying.
2. Give them between fifteen and twenty minutes to work together to prepare a summary report. Allow students to revisit their notes and any other resources they feel they need to complete the task. (While fifteen minutes is not a long time to gather new information for a report, keep in mind that these summaries are about information and concepts *already explored and examined* by your class.)
3. The first few times you do this, consider scaffolding the note-taking portion of the presentation by providing a graphic organizer that helps students briefly note the main ideas and details of their presentation (See the "Scaffolding Toolbox" section in Chapter 2 for more on graphic organizers.)
4. Require groups to include a visual display to enhance the meaning behind their presentation. Encourage them to consider making audio recordings or include multimedia components (graphics and sound), when appropriate.
5. After a set amount of time, bring the groups together to share.

At this time, you'll be able to assess your students' grasp of the key ideas and identify any gaps in understanding.

Providing an environment that puts the students in a position to take ownership of their learning has always been a guiding principle in my philosophical approach towards education. To that end, I have incorporated a "Chime In" routine that allows academic discussions within my student-centered learning environment to flourish. Integral to the structure of my class is affording students the latitude to "chime in" and share elements of significant learning or questions they believe can assist in furthering the academic conversation. When the soothing sound of the chime is initiated by a group of students, the focus, intent, and active listening of the entire class is immediate. Students value and recognize the potential benefits that the insight or question being shared can provide for their experience. Similarly, this routine provides me the opportunity to formatively assess and engage from the background, allowing the academic discussions to be at the forefront of the learning and the vehicle for deeper understanding. Inspiring depth of skill and knowledge acquisition, it is evident to me, through the emergence of academic vocabulary and meaningful discussions, that growth abounds when students "chime in."

Timothy Miller, grade 5 teacher

Scaffolding Toolbox: Rubrics and Checklists

John Hattie (2009) identified formative assessment to be among the top three instructional practices with the highest level of impact on student learning. We suggest adding some unique types of formative assessment tools that will serve multiple purposes and achieve multiple goals. The rubrics and checklists that you develop with your students will

- scaffold their oral language development
- establish the criteria for target performance
- raise metalinguistic awareness about their participation (listening and speaking) and presentation skills
- help develop ownership of the process and product.

A rubric is both a scaffolding tool and a formative assessment measure that can be used by students to plan or monitor their performance or to assess each other or by teachers to assess the learners. Brookhart (2013) suggests that the criteria in classroom rubrics should be

- appropriate for the goals and objectives as well as for the students' level of understanding
- understandable by students and teacher
- observable (seen or heard) by a person other than the performer
- distinct from one another
- as a whole, descriptive of the entire performance
- descriptive of a range of performance levels.

Whether you create checklists or rubrics, keep in mind that they can be used as scaffolding tools, so creating and reviewing them with students is an important step. Students must feel ownership of the checklists and rubrics used in the class and see them as serving a number of important purposes—clarifying expectations for listening and speaking, supporting them in setting their own goals for participation, and offering and using feedback. Consider using the rubrics and checklists in the sections that follow for self-evaluation, peer evaluation, and teacher assessment in your classroom.

Self-Evaluation Connected to the Talk-About Routine and Academic Conversations

Self-evaluation invites students to become reflective about their own learning and helps develop metacognitive awareness. Look back at the Talk-About routine discussed earlier in this chapter. While the Talk-About routine establishes a set structure for summarizing and discussing classroom learning, you can use the checklist in Figure 4.15 for any type of academic conversation. Students answer the questions to evaluate their own participation in a conversation.

Figure 4.15 A Talk-About Self-Evaluation Checklist

Check	Questions for Self-Evaluation	Reflections on My Participation
☐	Did I offer a compliment?	
☐	Did I disagree respectfully?	
☐	Did I offer factual information and cite evidence?	
☐	Did I ask questions and seek proof?	
☐	Did I paraphrase and summarize?	
☐	Did I add on to someone's ideas or ask for clarification?	
☐	Did I express an opinion?	
What should I focus on during my next conversation? 1. 2. 3.		

Peer Evaluation Checklist and Rubric for Presentations

In this chapter, we suggest creating multiple and varied opportunities for students to do formal presentations. Whether they do so individually or collaboratively, students require time to reflect on what they have learned both inside and outside of class. Peers become engaged when asked to become active listeners and evaluators of the presentations. Figure 4.16 is a checklist students can use when they act as critical friends and perform peer evaluations. Students indicate the frequency of each criterion that is observable during the presentation. In the final column, they jot down warm feedback (compliments and other positive comments) as well as cool feedback (suggestions for improvement). Figure 4.17 is an example of an analytic rubric where several criteria have been established with three levels of performance. This type of rubric is rather challenging to develop with students, so we suggest you brainstorm all the important dimensions of an oral presentation first (see the column named "Criteria") and then work on the highest levels of performance for students to help establish the target goals for themselves. If you can, demonstrate, model, or even role-play the difference between the levels of performance so students get a better grasp of the continuum along which they will evaluate each other. Developed this way, the rubric also serves as a scaffolding tool, allowing students to see where they are headed.

Figure 4.16 Checklist for Peer Evaluating an Individual Presentation

Did the presenter ...	🙂🙂🙂	🙂🙂	🙂		Warm and Cool Feedback (Comments and Suggestions)
Speak loudly and clearly?					
Maintain eye contact?					
Use visual aids?					
Summarize the main ideas?					
Show knowledge of his/her subject by providing specific details?					
Answer questions from the audience?					

Figure 4.17 Group Research Presentation Rubric

Criteria	Proficient	Acceptable	Needs Work
Content	The presentation includes many important facts and details.	The presentation includes some important facts and details.	The presentation includes information that is not relevant or not important.
Organization	Information is presented in a clear, well-structured, easy-to-follow manner.	Information is presented in an organized way.	Information lacks clear organization.
Group Participation	All group members contribute equally.	All group members contribute, but some more than others.	Some group members contribute; others do not.
Clarity of Speech	All group members speak clearly. Everyone is easy to understand.	Most group members speak clearly. Not everyone is easy to understand.	Some group members speak clearly. Some members are difficult to understand.
Use of Visual Aids	The group keeps referring to the visual throughout the presentation.	The group uses a visual that supports the presentation.	The group does not connect a visual to the presentation.

Class Assessment Tools

Rubrics and checklists can provide the kinds of formative assessment that partner teacher and student (Brookhart 2013) during the learning process. When accompanied by a class checklist used by the teacher, rubrics may also be helpful for gathering data that informs teacher planning and tracks student progress over time. See Figure 4.18 for an example of a holistic conversation rubric that describes student participation along a continuum and creates a solid framework for feedback to students. The conversation checklist that complements this rubric allows teachers to assess the same listening and speaking skills that students are peer evaluating (see Figure 4.19). Both tools were developed by New York City literacy coaches Eileen Hughes and Darlin Diaz, from PS 228Q.

Figure 4.18 Conversation Rubric with Four Levels of Performance

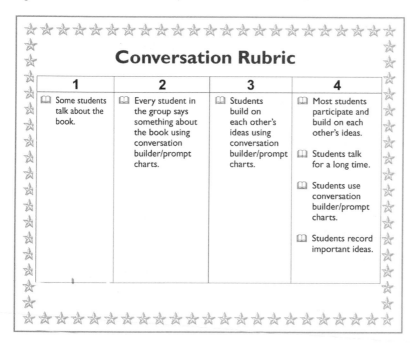

Conversation Rubric

1	2	3	4
📖 Some students talk about the book.	📖 Every student in the group says something about the book using conversation builder/prompt charts.	📖 Students build on each other's ideas using conversation builder/prompt charts.	📖 Most students participate and build on each other's ideas. 📖 Students talk for a long time. 📖 Students use conversation builder/prompt charts. 📖 Students record important ideas.

Figure 4.19 Conversation Checklist for Peer and Teacher Evaluation

Conversation Checklist

Text: _____ Date: _____

Name	Participates in the discussion	Builds on ideas	Uses conversation builders/prompt chart	Talks a long time	Records important ideas
1.					
2.					
3.					
4.					
5.					
6.					
7.					
8.					
9.					
10.					

Notes:

How to Differentiate Speaking and Listening Instruction

Figure 4.20 offers a quick guide for differentiated practices to address the readiness needs of diverse learners. Please note that there are some overlapping suggestions for ELLs and students with disabilities, whereas their unique needs are also considered.

Figure 4.20 Differentiating Speaking and Listening Instruction

ELLs	SWDs	Advanced Learners
• Incorporate structured, extended wait time (such as stop-and-jot activities) before students are expected to talk. • Allow these students to record their voices or present to you after class, if they are too shy at first to speak in front of others. • Offer linguistic scaffolds and verbal encouragement to students as they participate in public speaking or large-group presentations. • Provide partially completed scaffolds for listening and note-taking tasks. • Assign these students to specific groups and specific roles during the SOLE routine, rather than letting them self-organize. • During stations, pair these learners with partners who might assist in the task or record notes for the pair.		• Group these students together occasionally for collaborative activities, so that you can provide a more complex level of research (or expect a more rigorous academic conversation). • When grouping advanced learners together for any of the routines, ask them to make connections, not just to summarize (e.g., compare this new lesson to something previously learned, note a cause and multiple effects, state a problem and possible solutions, point out the sequence of events, mention multiple points of view).
• Allow ELLs to share their varied life experiences. • Use native language support (such as a bilingual buddy system) for clarification. • Integrate all four language skills so ELLs listen, speak, read, and write about the same ideas.	• Use assistive technology (both low-tech options, such as pictures, photographs, and symbols, as well as high-tech ones, such as computer programs and augmentative communication devices).	• When designing stations that include content that these students have already mastered, add a challenge-level question or advanced task to one or two of the stations. Encourage these students to work on the alternative tasks found at these stations. • Ask these students to develop their own questions for SOLE research.

A Final Thought

As Cazden (1988) noted over two decades ago, conversing with peers improves comprehension and engagement with texts. Conversing does a lot more than that. Talking is exploring, questioning, sharing, reporting, engaging the mind, engaging each other, thinking out loud, rehearsing and practicing . . . talking is learning. We need to reduce teacher talk and increase student talk so learners can speak their own thoughts, listen to and process each other's ideas, and develop a confident, academic voice during their primary and elementary years. When you provide students with ongoing, varied, and authentic opportunities to collaborate with each other, to engage in academic discussions, and to share and present what they have learned, school becomes an exciting place where learning is socially and developmentally appropriate.

Essential Questions for Individual Reflection, Collegial Circles, and Group Discussions

- *What is the central idea that runs through this chapter?*

- *How do the listening and speaking standards confirm, modify, or augment the listening and speaking routines you have had up until now in your classroom?*

- *What opportunities can you provide routinely so that your students' reading and writing "float on a sea of talk" (Britton 1983, 11)?*

- *What are the benefits of students working with Talk-Abouts, SOLE activities, stations, and ThinkTanks?*

- *If reading and writing continue to be the most assessed skills in state exams, why is it necessary to build speaking and listening skills?*

- *What are some of the challenges that you anticipate when you group students for academic conversations?*

- *What are some of the ways you will provide support for your students so that they are successful with academic conversations?*

- *How often and where during a lesson or unit will you integrate speaking activities into your classroom routines?*

Chapter 5

ACADEMIC LANGUAGE ROUTINES

When children learn language, they are not simply engaging in one kind of learning among many; rather, they are learning the foundation of learning itself.

M. A. K. Halliday, "Towards a Language-Based Theory of Learning"

As children develop new knowledge, they also need support in using language in new ways.

Mary J. Schleppegrell, "Academic Language in Teaching and Learning: Introduction to the Special Issue"

As colleagues, we need to have a united, sustained, and informed vision about how we're going to tackle this monster of academic language. It will take more than rhetoric.

Kate Kinsella, *Teaching Academic Vocabulary*

Overview

In this chapter, we

- summarize research support for the routines we present
- examine the expectations of the Common Core State Standards for language
- establish routines for academic language development at the word, sentence, and text levels
- present examples, templates, resources, and classroom vignettes along with recommendations from coaches to support the implementation of the academic language routines
- add anchor charts to the scaffolding toolbox
- offer differentiation of academic language instruction for English learners, students with disabilities, and advanced learners.

Academic Language Routines at a Glance

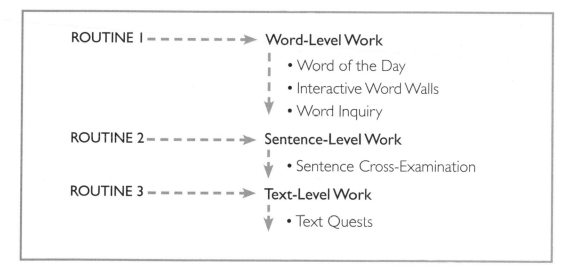

ROUTINE 1 - - - - - - → **Word-Level Work**
- Word of the Day
- Interactive Word Walls
- Word Inquiry

ROUTINE 2 - - - - - - → **Sentence-Level Work**
- Sentence Cross-Examination

ROUTINE 3 - - - - - - → **Text-Level Work**
- Text Quests

What Does the Research Say About Academic Language?

A comprehensive literature review on academic English and its implication for instruction was conducted by a research team at the George Washington University Center for Equity and Excellence in Education (CEEE) (Anstrom et al. 2010). The report synthesized research studies that focused on one of three target areas: what academic English is, how to teach it, and how to prepare teachers to incorporate it in their practice. Highlights of the findings that are particularly helpful and important for K–5 teachers include the following:

1. Academic English (AE) is conceptualized differently by different researchers and practitioners, which, in turn, impacts what recommendations are made for teaching AE.
2. It is critical to distinguish academic English from everyday language use and also to consider how AE is used differently in each subject matter.
3. Academic English develops in social contexts, so teachers should establish opportunities for students to be engaged in social interactions that focus on the use of academic discourse.
4. For academic English proficiency to develop, teachers should consider both the academic content and the language necessary to communicate about the target content.
5. For academic literacy to develop, teachers should help their students understand text organization and the multiple meanings of words unique to each discipline, as well as how to use the language patterns specific to each content.
6. Most researchers agree that it is important to teach essential features of academic English, including the "academic vocabulary, grammar, and discourse structures common to specific content areas" (Anstrom et al. 2010, v); restricting academic language teaching mainly to vocabulary instruction would, however, be limiting and less effective.

Others who investigated the nature and importance of academic language for student success focused on various related findings in their reports. Most recently, members of the Academic Language Development Network team (O'Hara, Zwiers, and Pritchard 2013) published a research brief that included a framework for academic language and literacy development. Based on a synthesis of their literature review and classroom observations, they established three dimensions of academic language (see Figure 5.1). We adapted the academic language features they listed and added related CCSS goals to create clearer connections to the Common Core.

In addition to describing the three dimensions of academic language and features of each, the team also identified several foundational language development practices that will accomplish the following:

1. Acknowledge and build on students' own linguistic and cultural strengths while also addressing their unique academic language needs (How to do it: Pre-assess for language skills, not just for background knowledge; learn about the language variations and cultural experiences your students have outside school.)
2. Expect students to master content and develop the most important language skills related to the content (How to do it: Design content objectives as well as matching language objectives that support the acquisition of the content for your lessons.)
3. Require students to use academic language with appropriate complexity in an authentic way on a regular basis (How to do it: Model and scaffold complex language structures that push students beyond their everyday linguistic comfort zones. Integrate word wall activities as a daily routine.)

Figure 5.1 Academic Language Dimensions, Features, and CCSS Goals

Dimension	Academic Language Features	Select Examples from the CCSS
Vocabulary (Word or Phrase)	• General academic terms • Content-specific terms • Figurative expressions • Collocations • Words with multiple meanings • Roots and affixes (prefixes and suffixes) • Idiomatic expressions • Shades of meaning • Precision of expression • Metaphors and similes	• Determine or clarify the meaning of unknown and multiple-meaning words and phrases based on *grade-level reading and content*, choosing flexibly from an array of strategies. • Demonstrate understanding of word relationships and nuances in word meanings. • Acquire and use accurately grade-appropriate general academic and domain-specific words and phrases. • Interpret words and phrases as they are used in a text, including determining technical, connotative, and figurative meanings, and analyze how specific word choices shape meaning or tone.
Syntax (Sentence)	• Sentence structure • Sentence length • Verb tense • Active and passive voices • Pronouns • Context as a clue to meaning of vocabulary • Proverbs	• Demonstrate command of the conventions of Standard English grammar and usage when writing or speaking. • Expand, combine, and reduce sentences for meaning, reader/listener interest, and style. • Use sentence-level context as a clue to the meaning of the word or phrase.
Discourse (Text or Message)	• Text organization • Text craft and structure • Text density • Clarity and coherence • Text types and genres	• Use knowledge of language and its conventions when writing, speaking, reading, or listening. • Compare and contrast the varieties of English (e.g., dialects, registers) used in stories, dramas, or poems. • Analyze the structure of texts, including how specific sentences, paragraphs, and larger portions of the text (e.g., a section, chapter, scene, or stanza) relate to each other and the whole. • Produce clear and coherent writing in which the development and organization are appropriate to task, purpose, and audience.

Adapted from O'Hara, Zwiers, and Pritchard (2013).

I put my first-grade students into small groups to act out, or use puppets to act out, vocabulary words. While the students are engaged in these activities, the ESL teacher and I have mini-conferences with each group of students (only a minute or two). During these conferences we ask students to describe what they are doing and why they are doing it. Letting students act out words gives them a deeper understanding of the meaning of each word. It also helps them remember the words. Then students practice using the words over and over again during the group activities. As new concepts are introduced, students have the vocabulary and experience to formulate questions and make connections. Words such as echolocation, migrate, *and* predator *simply become a part of their working vocabulary.*

Rose Doran, grade 1 teacher, with Amy Cooke, ESL teacher

Furthermore, three cross-cutting practices (implemented across all content areas and grades) were also introduced by O'Hara, Zwiers, and Pritchard (2013): *clarifying* complex language to ensure understanding; *modeling* standard language use by the teacher and through the use of mentor texts or other resources; and *guiding* students' language learning to move from building receptive language skills to strengthening their language production appropriate for the instructional context.

Finally, they also recommended three high-impact practices:

1. Using complex text (How to do it: Have high-level texts available for reading, analysis, and discussion as a regular part of your instruction.)

2. Fortifying complex output (How to do it: Make sure your students are not just the recipients of complex language input—which might naturally come from using high-level texts—but also *producers* of such language both orally and in writing with necessary support.)

3. Fostering academic interactions (How to do it: Create opportunities not just for teacher-to-student but for student-to-student academic dialogues. Support your students' communication, social, and collaboration skills while they complete content-based assignments or engage in interactive tasks that require academic language use. Figure 5.2 shows second graders engaged in an academic conversation about a text on germs, which was followed by a collaborative writing task.)

Figure 5.2 Second Graders Listen, Speak, Read, and Write About Germs

No matter how demanding and challenging these academic language development practices may appear, we hope that by the end of the chapter you will agree: we need to reexamine and adjust our instruction to integrate academic language on multiple levels and in a variety of contexts.

What Are the Academic Language Demands of the Common Core?

Even before the publication of the CCSS, Jeff Zwiers (2008) observed that "academic language is (1) intricately linked to higher-order thinking processes, (2) developed by extensive modeling and scaffolding of classroom talk, and (3) accelerated by weaving direct teaching of its features *while* teaching content concepts" (xv). Many other researchers and practitioners have also noted that acquiring the *language of schooling* is vital for academic success (Francis et al. 2006; Wong Fillmore 2009) and, later in life, for socioeconomic well-being (Scarcella 2003).

The importance of academic language is duly recognized by the CCSS. Language has a designated strand of standards in addition to being woven into the reading, writing, and speaking and listening standards. In Appendix A of the standards document, the writers offer the following explanation for this decision:

> The inclusion of Language standards in their own strand should not be taken as an indication that skills related to conventions, knowledge of language, and vocabulary are unimportant to reading, writing, speaking, and listening; indeed, they are inseparable from such contexts.   (NGA Center for Best Practices and CCSSO 2010, 28)

In grades K–5, teaching academic language cannot be separated from teaching the four language skills of listening, speaking, reading, and writing. In fact, academic language—as a register or form of language—must gain a higher level of instructional importance in all grades and all subject matters, since it is typically not acquired and practiced outside of school and most parents rarely use it with their children in the home. For instance, when was the last time you heard parents or peers say, "Please use academic and domain-specific words and phrases"?

✔ CHECK THIS OUT

So what is academic language? If you explore recent publications, you will find some variations and, to some degree, a lack of consensus regarding what AL is. Review the following definitions and notice the differences.

The language that is used by teachers and students for the purpose of acquiring new knowledge and skills . . . imparting new information, describing abstract ideas, and developing students' conceptual understandings. (Chamot and O'Malley 1994, 40)

Academic language is the linguistic glue that holds the tasks, texts, and tests of school together. If students can't use this glue well, their academic work is likely to fall apart. I define academic language as the set of words and phrases that (1) describe content-area knowledge and procedures, (2) express complex thinking processes and abstract concepts, and (3) create cohesion and clarity in written and oral discourse. (Zwiers 2004/2005, 60)

[Academic English] refers to more abstract, complex, and challenging language that will eventually permit you to participate successfully in mainstream classroom instruction. Academic English involves such things as relating an event or a series of events to someone who was not present, being able to make comparisons between alternatives and justify a choice, knowing different forms and inflections of words and their appropriate use, and possessing and using content-specific vocabulary and modes of expression in different academic disciplines such as mathematics and social studies. (Goldenberg 2008, 9)

Academic English is most typically thought of as a register of the language. A register is a variety of the language used in a specific context. Choice of certain words, grammatical features and the organization of discourse of both oral and print forms become the hallmarks of a register. The hallmarks of academic language are those that students will need to acquire, most often in school, for schoolwork and school success. (Bailey 2010, 229)

Academic language is the specialized language, both oral and written, of academic settings that facilitates communication and thinking about disciplinary content.
(Nagy and Townsend 2012, 92)

Notice how each of these definitions expands beyond merely discussing key vocabulary. Academic language is complex and challenging to teach, so we must be intentional about it. Reflect on which of these definitions seem(s) to be closest to your own understanding of academic language and why.

As Mary Schleppegrell (2012) notes, "For many teachers, language is so transparent in its meanings that it is challenging to talk about explicitly and make expectations for language use clear to children" (412). Would you agree that most native speakers of English, including many teachers, might not be consciously thinking about the word choices, grammatical features, or any particular linguistic structures that they are using when they speak or write in English? They implicitly apply their knowledge of English to their own language processes. Teaching academic language explicitly may be just as elusive and challenging as teaching a brand-new, difficult concept, such as elapsed time in math. Yet now is the time to embrace this challenge as a new opportunity and make teaching academic language a more purposeful, preplanned, and intentional part of your daily routine.

COACH'S NOTES

The use of academic language shifts as you move from context to context or from one content area to the next. Be sure to offer specific guidance to children on their academic language use in a systematic and routine way. For example, during daily teaching routines, point out key vocabulary, typical sentence patterns, grammatical structures, or unique text features to be used. Also keep in mind what Debbie Zacarian (2013) so accurately points out: some of your students will already be academic language users (and carry AL from home), whereas others will be academic language learners (requiring your direct instruction).

Academic language users will come to school with a rich vocabulary tied to literacy, with early exposure to a dialect that matches what is used at school, and with experiences using complex language forms for problem solving and decision-making.

Academic language learners, on the other hand, will arrive in school with exposure to oral storytelling, vernacular speech (a dialect that does not match what is used in school), rich personal and cultural experiences with oral language, and experiences rooted in following parents' specific directions.

Don't look at this dichotomy from a deficiency perspective, though. Instead, consider ways of building on what students come with, and expand upon their existing knowledge of English and linguistic skill base. Think of this as an opportunity to construct a language-rich learning environment that will support your students in all academic areas.

Academic Language Routines

When academic language use becomes routine in the classroom, students internalize the form and function of standard American English and apply their knowledge in all four language skills. The academic language routines we suggest are built on the most current work by the Academic Language Development Network (www.aldnetwork.org), the WIDA Consortium (www.wida.us), and Stanford University's Understanding Language initiative (http://ell.stanford.edu), all of which advocate for all learners to develop a deep understanding of how language is used in the school environment on the word or phrase, sentence, and discourse levels of language. According to WIDA's website,

> There is now general agreement that all students are learning to manage new sociocultural and language routines in classrooms and schools and that in each content area, students make use of specialized vocabulary, grammar, language functions and related discourse structures, and text types.   (2013, para. 1)

We, too, advocate for word-, sentence-, and text-level routines to take place in every classroom. In order to support the complexity of academic language development, we suggest moving "beyond teaching words in isolation or presented as vocabulary lists; instead, . . . provide students with multiple varied and meaningful learning experiences for understanding, analyzing, and using academic language at the sentence level as well as the text (or discourse) level" (Dove and Honigsfeld 2013, 18).

ROUTINE *1* Word-Level Work

Teaching vocabulary has been established as a critical part of the K–5 as well as the K–12 ELA curriculum and classroom instruction (Marzano 2005). Research has also found that the key features of effective vocabulary instruction "are frequent and varied encounters with target words and robust instructional activities that engage students in deep processing" (Beck, McKeown, and Kucan 2013, 83). To achieve this engagement, Robert Marzano and Julia Simms (2013) recommend, for example, a six-step process to teaching vocabulary:

1. The teacher offers an explanation, description, or example.
2. Students restate the explanation, description, or example.
3. Students create a picture, symbol, or graphic representation.
4. Students participate in varied, engaging activities with the words using their vocabulary notebooks.
5. Students discuss target vocabulary with others.
6. Students engage in games that invite them to use the target words.

Based on her collaborative work with Isabel Beck and Margaret McKeown, Linda Kucan (2013) promotes a more concise, three-step approach that involves a "thoughtful introduction to a set of words, interesting interactions with the words, and assessments of students' knowledge of the words" (364). The vocabulary routine we recommend based on this work consists of the following three steps:

1. Prepare student-friendly explanations for the words that make sense to students, that build on age-appropriate dictionary definitions but also consider students' prior knowledge and experience with the concepts.

2. Engage students in a range of meaningful activities that allow them to use the words in a variety of ways and in a variety of contexts. See the suggestions that follow, as well as student work samples representing varied vocabulary development tasks, many of which involve students' interaction with the words, with the text, and with each other.

Figure 5.3 Thumbs Up for Words You Know!

3. Use formative assessments to gauge students' understanding as well as productive use of the target words. It's also beneficial to use self-assessment practices such as having students put their thumbs up, sideways, or down to show their levels of understanding for key words. (In Figure 5.3 a fourth grader proudly indicates that she knows the target word.)

Building upon the work of Isabel Beck and her colleagues (2002, 2008), vocabulary instruction is frequently discussed in terms of modes of communication and text types where words are most typically used:

- Tier 1 words appear in everyday communication and are typically acquired with ease by native speakers of English. However, ELLs will need additional opportunities for explicit instruction to learn these words. Examples include *walk, chair, book, school, friend, open,* and *happy.*

- Tier 2 words (also called *general academic* words) can be found across many types of texts, both literary and informational. They are more common in written communication than in speech. Examples include *explain, according to, illustration, author, compare,* and *contrast.*

- Tier 3 words (also called *domain-specific* words) are specific to a subject matter (or domain), are more common in informational texts, and are closely tied to specific content knowledge. Examples include *predator, retractable claws, sphere, surface,* and *hurricane.*

We suggest three classroom practices for word-level work: (1) the word of the day (to introduce and reinforce Tier 2 academic words that travel across the content areas and span grade levels, also referred to as general academic words); (2) interactive word walls; and (3) word inquiry as a process for analyzing essential Tier 2 or Tier 3 words.

WORD OF THE DAY

Each day, introduce a general academic word (Tier 2 word) during the morning meeting (unless the word of the day is part of the routine for the entire school and it is announced by the principal). Define it in a student-friendly way and start using it right away. Make a conscious effort to include it in all content areas, and if possible even during transitional times or noninstructional times (such as arrival, recess, lunch, and dismissal). Figure 5.4 depicts a school-wide effort to establish

Figure 5.4 Word of the Week Displayed in the Lunchroom

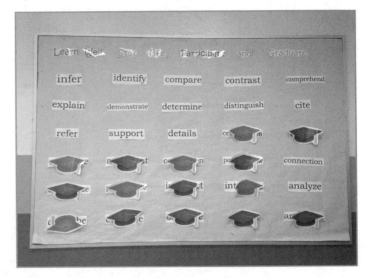

a word of the week initiative with a bulletin board in the lunchroom at Davison Avenue School, Malverne, New York.

After eating, students use the words while drawing, writing, and/or interacting with each other. The words in the lunchroom are Tier 2 academic vocabulary whose usage is further supported by all teachers in their own classrooms, as seen later in this chapter in Figure 5.8b. Use the word in all modalities: have students listen to, speak, read, and write the word in multiple ways at appropriate times during the day. By the end of the day, the goal is for your students to have been exposed to the word and to actually have used it in meaningful and authentic ways. For example, if the word of the day (WOD) is *identify*, plan on engaging students with the word through age- and grade-appropriate activities such as these:

- **Explain that the word means to name, to know, or to recognize something or someone.**
- **Ask your students to *identify* children who are absent.**
- **Have students share if they have seen or heard the word before and invite them to explain their experiences (keep it short and focused).**
- **Ask students if the word looks or sounds similar to other words they know (they might say *identity* or *identical*).**
- **Point the word out to the students when you tell them you are *identifying* the objectives, learning goals, agenda, or plan for the day.**
- **Ask students to *identify* proper nouns (verbs, adverbs, adjectives, punctuation marks, etc.) in a text.**

- Have students look at a map and *identify* the town where they live, the nearest large city, a mountain, a river, and so on.
- Have students *identify* the question word in the math problem.
- Have students *identify* the author and illustrator of the book you read.
- Ask students which character they can most *identify* with in the story.
- *Identify* the choices students have during recess, lunch, free time, and so on.
- If you have Spanish speakers, point out that the Spanish cognate for *identify* is *identificar*.

Implementing the word of the day will lead to varied exposure to critical Tier 2 words 180 days a year. It is a simple, yet powerful reminder for you, as your students' mentor, to consciously use Tier 2 words in your own speech and in a range of collaborative, interactive tasks like those in the previous list. A possible extension of the word of the day is to have students look for the word and listen for the word outside of school. Encourage your students to use the word at home with family members and keep a WOD journal about how the words were used in sentences or longer texts. Revisiting previous words of the day should also be part of your daily practices through games, sentence- and text-level routines (see later in this chapter), and homework connections.

✔ CHECK THIS OUT

What resources are available to help you choose the word of the day? The best approach is to make this a school-wide effort, or at least to decide on a list in collaboration with your grade-level colleagues. But even if you have to choose these words alone, there are online sources to help you establish target words for the year:

Academic Word List (Coxhead 2000) (570 Headwords): www.victoria.ac.nz/lals /resources/academicwordlist

Academic Word List Cross-Referenced with Simple World Families (343 Words): http://textproject.org/assets/library/resources/Academic-word-list.pdf

Jim Burke's Academic Vocabulary List (358 Words): www.englishcompanion.com /pdfDocs/acvocabulary2.pdf

The Top 60 Most Common Academic Words: www.vocabulary.com/lists/23710

SuperKids Vocabulary Builders: www.superkids.com/aweb/tools/words/wod.shtml

Visual Thesaurus General Academic Vocabulary List: www.visualthesaurus.com /wordlists/144473

Visual Thesaurus VocabGrabber: www.visualthesaurus.com/vocabgrabber (analyzes texts for the most useful vocabulary words)

Teacher-2-Teacher

Our school has many bulletin boards interspersed throughout the hallways and students continually pass them on their way to and from classes (see Figures 5.5 and 5.6). Hoping to capitalize on student exposure to these boards, I polled teachers as to what vocabulary was giving students the most difficulty and designed Math Billboards to visually represent some of the Tier 2 and Tier 3 math vocabulary words with which students struggle. My colleagues explicitly use the boards to teach these words, either in passing, or by conducting classes in the hallway, in front of the boards.

Christine Pearsall, Teacher on Special Assignment, Peer Coach

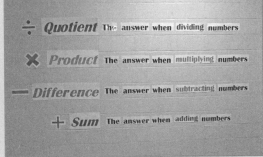

Figure 5.5 Math Billboard to Teach Descending and Ascending Numbers

Figure 5.6 Math Symbols and Definitions in the Stairwell

INTERACTIVE WORD WALLS

A word wall is one of the easiest and most useful tools for building literacy in any classroom. Many primary teachers use word walls to teach and review basic vocabulary words and sight words (Tier 1 words), to list word families (e.g., words that end in -ink), and to record important content area vocabulary. Upper-elementary teachers tend to use them more for academic words (Tier 2 words) or discipline-specific vocabulary (Tier 3 words), grouping words by theme or topic.

A word wall is an organized group of words that is visibly displayed so you and the students can refer to it over and over again. Sometimes, the words are written on dry-erase boards or blackboards, but frequently they are typed and laminated on card stock, so they can be manipulated and used in different ways. The cards can be placed in pocket charts, pinned to bulletin boards, or even taped to windows or doors, if space is limited. We have seen many teachers include visuals to enhance their word walls and help students make memorable connections. Just make sure the words are visible and easily accessible; many times, we have walked into classrooms where teachers have posted word walls in the back of the room or in one of the corners of the room, where they are unlikely to be used for learning.

We believe that using word walls as a *daily routine* will build the vocabulary and, in effect, the background knowledge of your students. It will provide your learners with the language of the discipline that you are studying. Yes, you will need different word walls for different subjects, but start slowly with one subject area at a time so that students can use domain-specific words in conversation. Equally important, word walls serve as a resource or reference tool when your students are reading or writing independently. You should expect them to spell any word on the word wall correctly. Model for students how to use the word wall words when giving presentations or demonstrations and encourage them to use the words in classroom discussions.

Once you have posted a list of terms or concepts, you might want to create an extra set of word cards that you duplicate and attach to recipe cards or index cards for easy student use. Brian Cambourne (2000) argues "that the artifacts [on a word wall] are only valuable when students are actively engaged in meaningful tasks with the artifacts" (as cited in Harmon et al. 2009, 398). See the next "Teacher-2-Teacher" section for several activities that will help your students make use of word wall vocabulary more often.

Many authors and researchers have recommended the use of games and partner (or small-group) activities as a route to building robust vocabulary. Isabel Beck et al. (2013), Douglas Fisher and Nancy Frey (2009), Donald Bear and colleagues (2012), as well as Jennifer Cronsberry (2004) and others make the case that vocabulary learning must be interactive and playful, and we agree. Many teachers integrate occasional games to review something that has been taught. But, as part of the regular routine of using word walls, we suggest some meaningful partner and small-group activities that these authors recommend, as well.

Teacher-2-Teacher

I like to use the following partner (or small-group) activities:

Visual Vocab: Each team creates a visual for a specific word and shows it to other teams. If another team guesses the word correctly, it earns a point. (After the game, post the visuals on the word wall.)

Word Connections: Everyone gets one word card. Partners are asked to create a meaningful connection (compare and contrast, show cause and effect, sequence the order, etc.) to share. Pairs square; i.e., two pairs share and try to explain a four-part relationship.

Sort–Group–Label: Give students a few minutes to organize the words into a certain number of categories. Teams share the groupings and the other groups try to guess the category or label that underlies the sorting.

Frayer Model Activity: Partners are given a specific term from the word wall. Using the Frayer model (Frayer, Frederick, and Klausmeier 1969), they write the term in the center and decide upon a definition, a list of characteristics, examples, and nonexamples.

Grade 5 teacher

Coach's Notes

We encourage you to provide individual word wall lists for students to keep in their notebooks or to post the words on your classroom website so that they will have the resources they need to include this important vocabulary in their homework. The more students use these words in their summaries, quick writes, and answers to questions, the more they will own them.

Finally, you might like to assess your students' use of the word wall words as part of a larger performance task at the end of a unit of study. Jennifer Cronsberry (2004) suggests the use of an observation checklist to help your students focus on the importance of using the word wall. In Figure 5.7 we present our own checklist, heeding Cronsberry's advice.

Figure 5.7 Word Wall Assessment

The student . . .
_____ refers to the word wall when answering questions in class.
_____ looks to the word wall when engaged in partner activities.
_____ uses the word wall during class to enhance independent writing tasks.
_____ checks spelling of written words to make sure they are accurate.
_____ makes connections between or among terms when speaking.
_____ shows evidence of having learned the terms through fluency and frequency of use.

Adapted from Cronsberry (2004).

Word walls are as varied as the different classrooms in a school. They contain Tier 1, 2, or 3 words, depending on what the teacher believes will serve the students' vocabulary development needs best. You can see examples of word walls in the following classroom snapshots: Figure 5.8a depicts a word wall to support high-frequency word development in a newcomer program. Figures 5.8b and 5.8c are both interactive word walls that display Tier 2 words in multigrade inclusion classes. Figure 5.8d depicts a math-ab-ulary word wall in a third-grade classroom that supports disciplinary vocabulary development. Some unique ways of using the word walls include offering stars to students as they use the words (see Figure 5.8c) and allowing students to take the words back to their seats as they work on an independent writing task (see Figure 5.8a).

WORD INQUIRY

Janet Allen (1999) recommends word questioning as a practice that involves (1) examining Tier 3 words in the context in which they appear, (2) asking questions about the word on all levels of Bloom's taxonomy, and (3) helping students form habits of closely examining complex words for

Figure 5.8a Word Wall to Support High-Frequency Word Development in a Newcomer Program

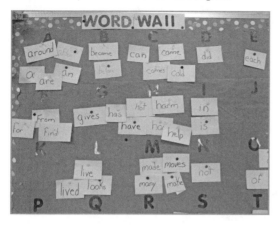

Figure 5.8b Interactive Word Wall from an Inclusion Class

Figure 5.8c Interactive Word Wall from an Inclusion Class

Figure 5.8d Math-ab-ulary Word Wall from a Third-Grade Classroom

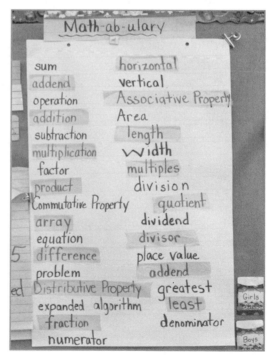

meaning and form. Inspired by Allen's work, we have used a similar approach to build a more robust vocabulary for students.

As part of a word inquiry, select a Tier 3 word that gives students power to tackle challenging content matter. Engage students in a thorough word analysis that helps them understand how words are made up of smaller parts (root, prefix, suffix) and how making associations with other words can help them figure out word meanings. Figure 5.9 is a template with questions to guide students in their word inquiry. Figure 5.10 contains an example of a word inquiry chart completed by a fifth-grade class exploring the word *government*. Feel free to develop additional questions or to modify some of those we provide in order to match the subject matter and grade or readiness levels of your students.

Figure 5.9 Word Inquiry Template

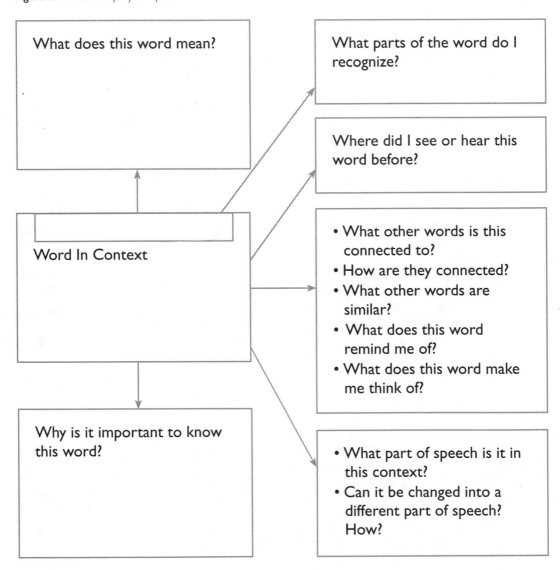

Figure 5.10 Word Inquiry Chart That Examines the Term Government

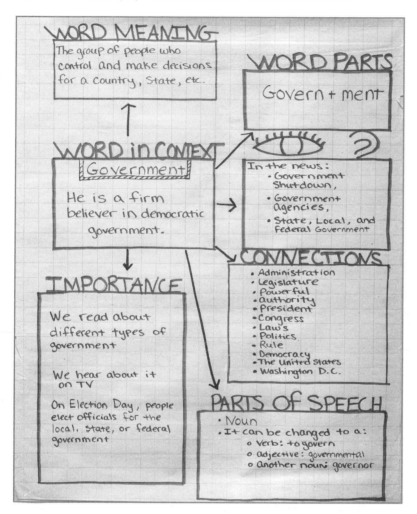

Another way to take a global, big-picture approach to word meaning is to create a visual, linguistic representation of how the target word is connected to other words. A word web (like a wheel and spokes) can show complex relationships (parts and whole, synonyms, antonyms), free word associations, or even grammatical connections such as the word with various suffixes to indicate different parts of speech or inflections. Following are two examples that you can model for your students. In the first case, put the word *friend* in the middle, and in a think-aloud, show students how adding prefixes and suffixes changes the meaning and the form of the word. In the second example, place the word *buddy* in the center of the web (for example, connected to reading the book *Bud, Not Buddy*) and put synonyms with different shades of meaning on spokes around it. Also see Figure 5.11 for an example of a third grader's elaborate word web that examines the term *weather*. Figure 5.12 depicts a fifth grader's word associations for the term *industry*.

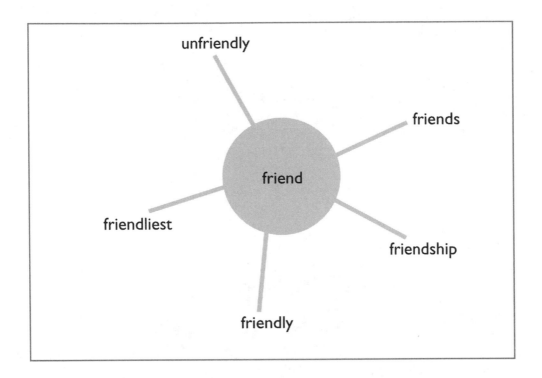

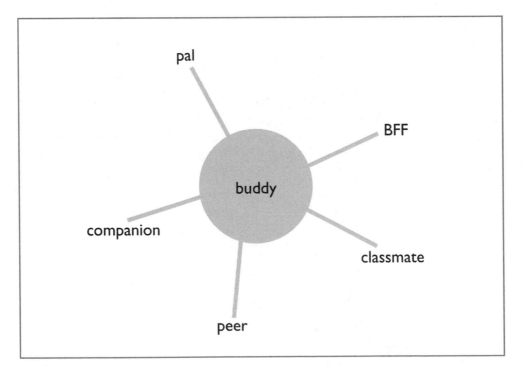

Figure 5.11 A Third Grader's Word Web for the Concept *Weather*

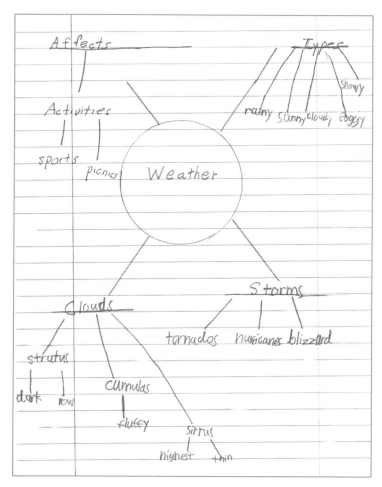

Figure 5.12 A Fifth Grader's Word Associations for *Industry*

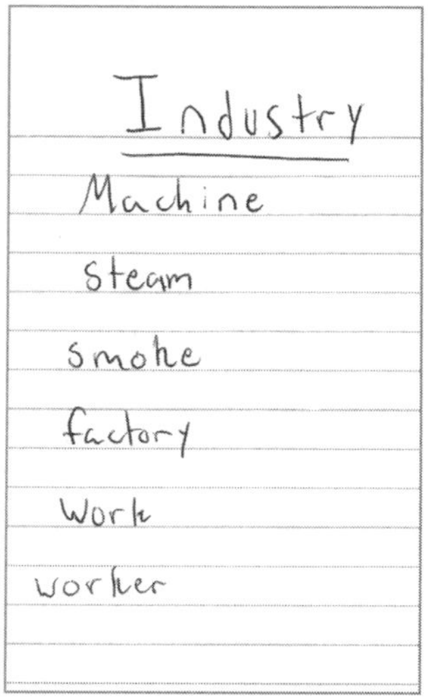

Industry
Machine
Steam
Smoke
factory
Work
worker

Build your own professional library of essential books or help develop one in your school. Explore the following print resources for a variety of meaningful vocabulary-building activities.

Beck, I. L., M. G. McKeown, and L. Kucan. 2013. *Bringing Words to Life: Robust Vocabulary Instruction.* 2nd ed. New York: Guilford. (A critical resource on tiered vocabulary instruction, this is an updated version of the 2002 classic.)

Frey, N., and D. Fisher. 2009. *Learning Words Inside and Out, Grades 1–6: Vocabulary Instruction That Boosts Achievement in All Subject Areas.* Portsmouth, NH: Heinemann. (Provides hands-on examples for making vocabulary learning intentional, transparent, usable, personal, and above all a priority within a school-wide focus on word learning.)

Graves, M. F. 2006. *The Vocabulary Book: Learning and Instruction.* New York: Teachers College Press. (Offers a four-part comprehensive plan for vocabulary instruction including providing rich and varied language experiences, teaching individual words, teaching word learning strategies, and fostering word consciousness.)

Marzano, R. J., and J. Simms. 2013. *Vocabulary for the Common Core.* Denver, CO: Solution Tree. (Describes Marzano's classic six-step approach to vocabulary instruction, along with recommendations for integrating Tier 2 and Tier 3 vocabulary from the CCSS document itself.)

Overturf, B. J., L. Montgomery, and M. Holmes Smith. 2013. *Word Nerds: Teaching All Students to Learn and Love Vocabulary.* Portland, ME: Stenhouse. (Offers a strategic vocabulary plan and comprehensive vocabulary instruction.)

COACH'S NOTES

Don't forget to have your learners ponder the shades of meaning as they expand their vocabulary. Synonyms have similar meanings, yet each word suggests subtle differences that help the writer or speaker use more precise or more nuanced language. By placing synonyms on a continuum, you can help students better understand such subtleties in meaning.

1. *First, model several examples and guide students through a process of deciding where on a continuum a set of synonyms should be placed.*

2. *After modeling and some additional guided practice, your students will be ready to work collaboratively on this task. Assign students to small groups and provide each group of students a set of synonyms, such as cold, freezing, icy, chilly, and cool. (You can give each group the same set of words or a different set of words.)*

3. *Ask the groups to discuss the words and decide where to place the words on a continuum from least to greatest intensity. The group discussion prompted by this task helps students learn about the nuances of words.*

Hardware stores carry a useful tool you can pick up for free to help students understand shades of meaning and how synonyms compare with each other. "Using a paint chip," Fisher and Frey (2008) suggest, "students identify a continuum of words and then write the words in the colored sections of the paint chip" (82). This visual tool provides a powerful image for students to see that synonyms have similar meanings that can be placed along a continuum. Some teachers post these paint chips to encourage students to use more precise words in their speech and writing (also see the Teaching Channel episode titled "Vocabulary Paint Chips" at www.teachingchannel.org). The vocabulary paint chips in Figure 5.13 depict shades of meaning at various grade levels.

The ultimate goal is to help students become self-directed, independent learners of new words and to help them develop ownership of vocabulary. We have seen many teachers introduce their students to (and regularly work on) personal dictionaries or word-study books. In a personal dictionary, students self-select words that they come across in their readings or content area studies. Have them

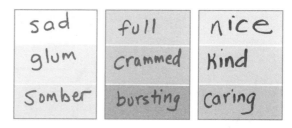

Figure 5.13 Shades-of-Meaning Paint Chips

organize the words alphabetically and use student-friendly definitions. A word-study book is organized by content or theme. For example, in the lower-elementary grades, tabs for each subject matter could be inserted into a marble notebook to separate the subjects. In upper-elementary classes, a word-study book can be dedicated to just the science topics or social studies topics covered.

Whether you choose to introduce personal dictionaries or word-study books— based on students' grade and readiness levels—invite your students to write a sentence with each word, illustrate it, and add synonyms or word family words or other related words. (See the sample pages from several students' notebooks in Figures 5.14, 5.15a, 5.15b, and 5.16.)

In summary, Blachowicz, Fisher, Ogle, and Watts Taffe remind us of the critical role that teachers play in helping students become curious and enthusiastic about learning words:

> *Students need your help and encouragement in attending to and learning academic vocabulary. Teachers are role models and guides in helping students learn how to be "vocabulary-smart." It is up to you to regularly note new and interesting words, as well as new uses of somewhat familiar terms, and to "think aloud" about these with students.* (2013, 12)

Figure 5.14 A Second Grader's Word-Study Page

Figure 5.15a A Fourth Grader's Word Quilt

Word	Word	Word	Word	Word	Word
accomplish	apparent	civilian	conceal	duplicate	keen
Definition	**Definition**	**Definition**	**Definition**	**Definition**	**Definition**
to do, make happen, succeed in, carry through	open to view; easy to understand	a person not in a military, police, or firefighting force	to hide or keep a secret, to place out of sight	an exact copy	having a sharpened edge; eager
Part of Speech	**Part of Speech**	**Part of Speech**	**Part of Speech**	**Part of Speech**	**Part of Speech**
verb	adjective	noun adjective	verb	noun, verb, adjective	adjective
Antonym(s)	**Antonym(s)**	**Antonym(s)**	**Antonym(s)**	**Antonym(s)**	**Antonym(s)**
to fail, undo, fall short	concealed, uncertain, hidden, difficult	military	to uncover, open, reveal	an original	dull, blunt, lazy, unwilling
Synonym(s)	**Synonym(s)**	**Synonym(s)**	**Synonym(s)**	**Synonym(s)**	**Synonym(s)**
to perform, fulfill, achieve, complete	clear, obvious, visible, plain, likely	non-military	to cover, disguise, mask, tuck away	to reproduce, clone, replica, identical, a reproduction	razor-edged, acute, alert, ready
Example	**Example**	**Example**	**Example**	**Example**	**Example**

Figure 5.15b A Fourth Grader's Word Quilt

WORD	MY CONNECTION	WORD	MY CONNECTION
myth	fairy tales	continuous	infinity sign God's love circle
WHAT IT MEANS	**HOW IT LOOKS**	**WHAT IT MEANS**	**HOW IT LOOKS**
something imaginary		going on without a stop or break	
WORD	**MY CONNECTION**	**WORD**	**MY CONNECTION**
capacity	weight	vast	giant
WHAT IT MEANS	**HOW IT LOOKS**	**WHAT IT MEANS**	**HOW IT LOOKS**
the amount of space that can be filled		very great or very large	
WORD	**MY CONNECTION**	**WORD**	**MY CONNECTION**
nomad	tourist	luxurious	Hawaii
WHAT IT MEANS	**HOW IT LOOKS**	**WHAT IT MEANS**	**HOW IT LOOKS**
a person who roams aimlessly		providing ease or comfort far beyond what is ordinary or necessary	

Figure 5.16 A Second Grader's Work with Synonyms

delicious tasty yummy mouthwatering

ROUTINE 2 **Sentence-Level Work: Sentence Cross-Examination**

Similar to the word of the day, the sentence cross-examination routine creates a framework for examining academic language at the sentence level. A similar practice is discussed under several other names, such as *juicy sentences* (Wong Fillmore 2012), *syntax surgery* (Herrell and Jordan 2008), and *sentence dissection* (Dove and Honigsfeld 2013). In the routine that we suggest, the focus is somewhat different in that it attends to *both* the meaning communicated at the sentence level as well as the grammatical and stylistic form of the sentence. We believe that creating a routine that combines both sentence-level concerns will improve academic language in students.

Each day, or as frequently as your curriculum allows or your students need it, set aside approximately eight to ten minutes to examine a carefully selected, sufficiently complex sentence (or two). During this structured session devoted to sentence cross-examination, take your students through a guided exploration of the target sentence both for meaning and for logistic and grammatical form. Lily Wong Fillmore (2012) reminds us that students need a preplanned instructional conversation, "focused on various aspects of a sentence or two chosen . . . for their grammatical features or complexity" (10). The sentence should come from the text you are using for literacy or content-based instruction and ideally it should be rich in information as well as opportunities for discussing word choice, phrases, sentence structure, grammar, and usage.

Follow these steps with as much differentiation as necessary based on your students' needs and the actual sentence you have selected:

1. Present the sentence on chart paper, a sentence strip, the whiteboard, or an interactive whiteboard.
2. Facilitate an in-depth discussion of what the sentence means, how the author expresses his or her idea, and so on by first inviting student input into meaning making.
3. Ask guiding questions about the *who*, *what*, *when*, and *where* of the sentence.
4. Move on to discussing the *how* and *why* of the sentence, especially focusing on how and why the writer used certain words, phrases, language conventions, or grammar structures.
5. Use color coding or other visually engaging methods to chunk the sentence into clauses or phrases.
6. Make note of one or more unique linguistic features of the sentence (active versus passive voice, relative clauses, heavy noun phrases, present or past participles, and so on) to call students' attention to select language complexities.
7. Think aloud as you pinpoint grammatical or stylistic choices in some (but not all) of the language chunks.

8. Invite students to use the sentence as a mentor text and to create similar sentences of their own to be able to internalize the linguistic complexity represented in the sentence. Encourage them to select their favorites to include when they are writing. See Figure 5.17 for an example of a first grader using a mentor text to produce her sentences in the conditional mood.

The following examples illustrate how to conduct sentence cross-examination with guiding questions at various grade levels.

A favorite in kindergarten and first grade is the Little Bear series, by Minarik and Sendak (1992). Consider both the simplicity of this target sentence and the opportunities for complex linguistic conversations with young learners directly tied to the sentence, as shown in Figure 5.18:

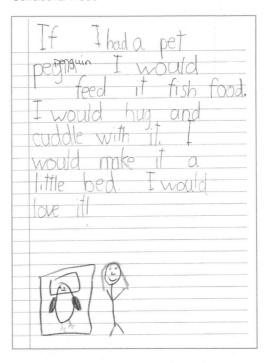

Figure 5.17 First Grader Emulating Sentences in the Conditional Mood

Birthday Soup
is good to eat,
but not as good as Birthday Cake.

Figure 5.18 Cross-Examination Example Based on an Excerpt from Little Bear

Guiding Questions for Meaning	Guiding Questions for Form and Usage
• What is Little Bear thinking about eating? • What is Birthday Soup? • According to this sentence, which is better to eat: Birthday Soup or Birthday Cake? Do you agree? Why?	• Which words are capitalized? • Why do you think Birthday Soup and Birthday Cake are capitalized in this sentence? • Why does the author use the word *but* in the middle of this sentence? • What other ideas would make sense after *but*? How else could you finish this sentence: Birthday Cake is good to eat but … • What if we changed the word *but* to *and*? How could you finish the sentence then?

During sentence cross-examination, this sentence allows for a discussion of rules for capitalization and punctuation, the use of the coordinating conjunction *but*, and how compound sentences are formed.

For grades 2–3, try the following sentence from *A Medieval Feast*, by Aliki (1986). Think of a few guiding questions that you would plan for meaning and form and then compare them with our suggestions in Figure 5.19.

It was announced
from the palace
that the King
would soon make a long journey.

Figure 5.19 Cross-Examination Example Based on an Excerpt from *A Medieval Feast*

Guiding Questions for Meaning	Guiding Questions for Form and Usage
• Who is going to make a long journey? • Where does the king live? • How do we know? • What does the word *announce* mean?	• What does the author mean by "it was announced"? (Answer: Someone made an announcement.) • Can we tell who actually made the announcement? (Answer: We know someone from the palace made the announcement, but we don't know who.) • How can you say "make a long journey" differently? (Answer: Take a long trip.) • When will the king make a journey? Which part of the sentence tells us when the journey will take place? (Answer: *Soon* and the helping verb *would*.)

This excerpt makes an interesting choice for sentence cross-examination. Passive voice is a complex grammatical structure that is routinely used in informational text, so it is helpful for students in the younger grades to develop receptive language skills of this structure. Only then will they be prepared to move on to produce the same structures independently in later grades.

Finally, we selected the following sentence to illustrate a possible sentence cross-examination for grades 4 and 5 from *Quest for the Tree Kangaroo: An Expedition to the Cloud Forest of New Guinea*, written by Sy Montgomery (2009; see also Figure 5.20).

The European explorers
who saw kangaroos
for the first time in Australia
reported they had discovered
a two-headed animal—
with one head on the neck
and another in the belly.

Figure 5.20 Cross-Examination Example Based on an Excerpt from *Quest for the Tree Kangaroo*

Guiding Questions for Meaning	Guiding Questions for Form and Usage
• Whom is the sentence about? • Where did the Europeans go? • How many times had the European explorers visited Australia? • What did they think they discovered in Australia? Why did they think that? • How did the Europeans describe kangaroos?	• The author uses the relative pronoun *who*. Find the noun this pronoun refers to. (Answer: The European explorers.) • How many prepositional phrases can you find in this sentence? (Answer: Five—*for the first time, in Australia, with one head, on the neck,* and *in the belly*.) • Why does the author use the past perfect verb form *had discovered* in this sentence? (Answer: It shows that the discovery took place and was completed before reporting about the kangaroos.)

This sentence is a perfect match for the grades 4 and 5 grammatical structures. Several of the target grammar points are concentrated in this sentence, including relative pronouns, prepositional phrases, and the perfect verb tense. While the actual meaning of the sentence is relatively easy to comprehend, complex grammatical terms and structures can be introduced and discussed.

In sum, sentence cross-examination lends itself to explicitly talking about sentence-level meaning and the grammatical forms that are behind the meaning. In an academic conversation, the five Ws + H questions help address the meaning of the sentence, while the guided discussion on grammar and usage every day focuses on a grade-appropriate convention and a standard-aligned structure.

COACH'S NOTES

Once students are used to the sentence cross-examination routine, they will need to apply what they have learned independently. One way they can practice their newly acquired grammatical understanding is the use of the target sentence—after careful examination and analysis—as a mentor text. The goal is for students to use, unassisted, one or more of the grammatical structures analyzed together in class.

Birthday Soup is good to eat, but not as good as Birthday Cake was presented as an ideal sentence for cross-examination. Not only does it allow for analyzing some basic language convention elements, but it can also serve as a great mentor text. Students offer their own ideas and words by completing the frame based on the original sentence:

_____ is good to eat, but not as good as _____.

_____ is good to drink, but not as good as _____.

CHECK THIS OUT

If you need a crash course or a refresher on your working knowledge of grammatical terms and concepts, check out the following books and websites. These are some of the best we have found, which inform our own work.

Grammar Books

Anderson, J. 2005. *Mechanically Inclined: Building Grammar, Usage, and Style into Writer's Workshop.* Portland, ME: Stenhouse.

Lester, M., and L. Beason. 2012. *McGraw-Hill Handbook of English Grammar and Usage.* 2nd ed. New York: McGraw-Hill.

Seely, J. 2012. *Grammar for Teachers: Unlock Your Knowledge of English.* Cheltenham, UK: Oxpecker.

Straus, J. 2007. *The Blue Book of Grammar and Punctuation: An Easy-to-Use Guide with Clear Rules, Real-World Examples, and Reproducible Quizzes.* New York: Wiley.

Thurman, S., and L. Shea. 2003. *The Only Grammar Book You'll Ever Need: A One-Stop Source for Every Writing Assignment.* Cincinnati: Adams Media.

Websites

http://grammaropolis.com

www.roadtogrammar.com

www.grammarbook.com

Teacher-2-Teacher

Some of the most challenging aspects of language learning revolve around academic vocabulary and sentence structure. In order to help my students overcome these challenges, I've set up two weekly routines: word of the week and sentence of the week.

Every Monday, I write a new academic vocabulary word on the board. I try to choose words that will help students with an upcoming topic in their general education classroom. For example, if the fourth graders are about to learn about the scientific method, the word might be hypothesize. Students will start the activity by discussing whether they've ever heard, seen, or used the word before. Then I give students a graphic organizer to define the word using a dictionary, use the word in a sentence, compare it with other words (It is like x. It is not like y.), identify the part of speech, indicate where they might see the word next, and draw a picture of the word. I differentiate the process based on the word and the level of the students' English proficiency. As a bonus challenge, I ask the students to use the word five times over the course of the week in their daily lives and report back to me. By the end of the school year, students have a binder filled with academic vocabulary words that they can use as a reference guide!

continues

ROUTINE 3 Text-Level Work: Text Quests

The routine we recommend for fostering students' academic language development at the text level builds on inquiry-based learning. Create meaningful opportunities for your students to interact with the text by questioning not only its content and meaning but also its linguistic features.

Text-level work—whether you focus on a paragraph or longer chunks of text such as a short article, an excerpt from a longer selection, a chapter, or an entire book—will contribute to developing sophisticated linguistic understanding and skills. Regular use of the text quest routine will not only help your students develop better reading habits but also help them see how a text is constructed linguistically. See Figure 5.21 for generic guiding questions as well as specific examples for *Throw Your Tooth on the Roof: Tooth Traditions Around the World* (Beeler 2001).

Nagy and Townsend (2012) "suggest potential guiding questions that teachers can ask themselves and their students as they work to derive meaning from academic texts" (104). We modified these questions to better match the elementary instructional context but urge you to further adapt the text analysis questions to help your students understand how a text works as a unit of communication or discourse.

Teacher-2-Teacher

I set up the ABCs of text features early in the year, because I feel identifying text features is vital to unlocking the mystery to many reading passages. My students (K–6) help create a bulletin board with numerous text features, all with examples that they have found. Students become text feature detectives throughout the year. Working on specific lessons, students pull out their magnifying glasses as well as their detective notebooks and write down the clues that help them identify text features. By year's end, students are able to glance at a reading passage and identify multiple text features.   Judy Harkins-Diede, K–6 ESL teacher

Figure 5.21 Text Quest Schema

Text Quest Categories	General Guiding Questions	Examples for *Throw Your Tooth on the Roof*
Author's Identity (Author's Point of View)	• Who is the speaker? • Who is telling the story? • Who is reporting about facts/events? • How do we know who is talking? • Is the first or third person used? • What is the speaker's opinion, belief, or feeling? How do we know?	• Who are the two speakers on the introductory page? • Who is the speaker in each of the paragraphs in the rest of the book? • Who is reporting about what happens to a lost tooth in each country? • Why is the first-person-singular "I" used to tell about tooth traditions in different countries or regions in the world?
Information Load (Text Density)	• What is the main idea of the text? • What kinds of details are given in each paragraph? • Why is there so much information in the first (second/last) paragraph? • Which paragraph/section is most loaded with information?	• What is the main idea of the book *Throw Your Tooth on the Roof?* • What kinds of details are given in each paragraph? • Which paragraph is most loaded with information about what happens to a lost tooth?
Text Structure (Organization of the Information)	• What is the purpose of this text? How do we know? • What is the structure of this text? Are there stanzas (a poem)? Is there dialogue? Are there stage directions (a play)? Are there captions and photos, headings, bold print (nonfiction text)? • Is this text organized as a description, a sequence, a comparison and contrast, or a problem and solution? • What signal words help us understand this text? • What else in the text helps us understand the organization of the text? • What word/phrase/expression/text feature is repeated in a purposeful way throughout the text? • Can you draw a text structure map for this text?	• What is the purpose of this book? How do we know? • What is the structure of this book? • Is this book organized as a description, a sequence, a comparison and contrast, or a problem and solution? • Are there any signal words that help us understand the organization of each paragraph? • What else in the text helps us understand the organization of the entire text? • What words or phrases get repeated throughout the text? Why?

continues

Figure 5.21 Text Quest Schema, *continued*

Text Quest Categories	General Guiding Questions	Examples for *Throw Your Tooth on the Roof*
Grammatical Choices	• Can you find phrases and grammatical structures in the text that we don't usually use when we speak? • Why are there longer, more complex sentences in this text? • Why does the author choose one grammatical structure over the other?	• Can you find phrases and grammatical structures in the text that we don't usually use when we speak? • Why does the author use simpler sentences than we usually find in informational texts? • Look for all the future-tense verb phrases in this text, like "will take." Why do these appear in so many paragraphs?

COACH'S NOTES

Keep in mind that not all students will be able to respond to verbal questions about a text. Some of them will require additional wait time in order to respond. Still others could benefit from simple bookmarks that have general guiding questions written on them. That way, students will be able to hear your questions and be able to refer to and read the bookmark questions for additional support.

Dr. Maria G. Dove, Professor of Education

Scaffolding Toolbox: Anchor Charts

Debbie Miller (2008) believes that "the walls of a classroom speak" (13). They reveal what students are learning about, what they are thinking about, and what they have accomplished. "'Come learn with us!', they seem to say" (13). Most teachers believe that creating a print-rich, vibrant learning environment significantly contributes to language and literacy development. We agree that anchor charts can occupy a unique place in the classroom as they make learning visible and remain available for students long after they are created. They scaffold the learning process and serve as reference tools. So what are they and what are they not?

Anchor charts are

- large sheets filled with documentation of student thinking
- constructed together by teachers and their students
- functional and authentic.

Anchor charts might

- focus on language or content (or both)
- display webs or lists of words such as synonyms or antonyms
- offer sentence starters or prompts
- display mentor text samples containing specific lines from readings
- outline graphic representations of text structures
- synthesize new learning and key ideas about a content topic
- recap the strategies brainstormed by the students to solve a math problem
- list the steps needed to apply a reading or writing strategy
- record findings from student research
- summarize prior knowledge, student predictions, and questions
- capture classroom expectations and routines for participation.

Anchor charts

- serve as reference materials for students
- guide students when they work independently.

Remember to add your own ideas!

Anchor charts—as we present them here—are *not*

- purchased in teacher stores
- ready-made posters
- prepared in advance of the lesson by the teacher
- designed with the sole purpose of decorating the classroom
- posted in places where students cannot view or use them easily.

In sum, anchor charts may support academic language development at the word, sentence, and text levels and all aspects of literacy learning (reading, writing, listening, and speaking). This decision belongs to you (and your students).

What essential learning processes should we make visible and accessible? See the two different examples that highlight anchoring reading (Figure 5.22) and anchoring writing (Figure 5.23) for some ideas.

We create charts with the students to encourage them to use talk prompts that facilitate conversations and increase reading comprehension. Examples of effective prompts are I think ____, I wonder ____, I would like to add____, and I agree/disagree because ____. We model how to use each prompt. As the students learn to use each prompt, they refer to prompt charts and prompt cards during conversations to help them develop and share ideas. We also use prompt charts as assessment tools to reflect on conversations and to assess whether or not the students used the prompts during their conversations.

Members of the PS 228Q Professional Learning Community

Figure 5.22 Anchor Chart for Reporting Text-Based Evidence

Figure 5.23 Anchor Chart to Support Paragraph Writing About Sequence of Events

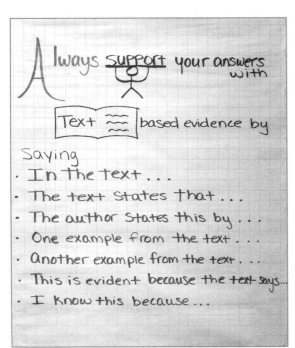

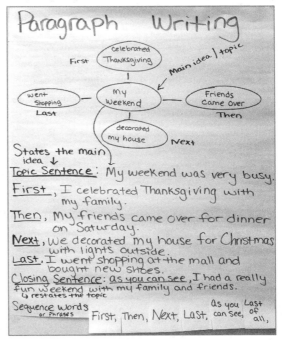

Alycia Zimmermann, third-grade New York City teacher and Scholastic blogger, confessed the internal battle she fights:

> Do I hang this authentic but messy chart up in my classroom, or do I painstakingly rewrite the chart after school ends? While I understand the value of creating anchor charts that my students will actually use, at times it feels like charting is simply an Olympic sport for teachers to create the most photo-worthy "wallpaper." (2012, para. 3)

How about a three-way compromise for anyone concerned about what to display?

1. When the chart fully captures the learning process—including the language and content that your students can easily refer back to—just post it, as is! Even if it does not look fancy, it will serve its purpose of capturing and scaffolding students' academic language. Learning and thinking can be messy; your chart will remind students that reaching new understandings and co-constructing meaning is a complex process.

2. After the chart is completed, you might insert pictures or use color highlights to offer additional visual support that can help students when working independently.

3. When the chart you develop with your students seems too crowded, or when it does not turn out to be as functional as you'd imagined, don't hesitate to rewrite it. For example, if it has too many cross-outs, if it is not legible or clear, or if it contains errors that you discover after the lesson, you should revise your chart. Students will learn that sloppy copies can and should be turned into finished products.

COACH'S NOTES

Look around your classroom. Do your walls speak to you about the shared learning process that takes place daily? Do your anchor charts reflect the academic language that you expect your students to use? Do the charts inform and support your learners as they listen, speak, read, and write about the target content? Do the charts offer linguistic support as students grapple with word choice, sentence structure, and text features? Reflect on these questions. Take a look around other classrooms and see how your colleagues have created anchor charts with their students. Use the best ideas that you find around the building and compose your anchor charts with the guiding principles above.

How to Differentiate Academic Language Instruction

Figure 5.24 offers a quick guide for differentiated practices to address the readiness needs of diverse learners. Please note that there are some overlapping suggestions for ELLs and students with disabilities, whereas their unique needs are also considered.

Figure 5.24 Differentiating Academic Language Instruction

ELLs	SWDs	Advanced Learners
• Chunk it: divide everything (words, sentences, texts) into smaller, more meaningful, more manageable sections. • Don't oversimplify your own language: do offer simpler explanations, comprehensible word choices, or language structures and then build up the complexity. • Don't lower your expectations for language use; instead, scaffold language production through language frames and anchor charts. • Restate: when students make simpler than expected language choices, repeat what they have produced at a higher level of complexity. • Recast: when students use incomplete or grammatically incorrect language, repeat what they have said using the grammatically correct or more complete, expanded version of the same idea. • Offer word and phrase banks, sentence starters, sentence frames, and other scaffolding tools, such as anchor charts.		• Offer these learners more complex mentor texts. • Ask these learners to compare two words, two sentences, or two texts and explain the differences. • Introduce advanced students in grades 3–5 to tone, and ask them what word in the text describes the tone. • Ask these students to change words in the text in order to create a different tone. • Give these learners more sophisticated vocabulary terms and expect them to use these terms in writing and in speech. • Expect more advanced vocabulary and grammatical structures to be used orally and in writing.
• Rely and capitalize on students' native language skills. • Help students find and use cognates. • Encourage students to make explicit connections between the rules and conventions of their home languages and English. • Teach and regularly practice dictionary skills.	• Follow the IEPs. • Permit students to listen to recordings of instructions or readings so they can hear them again. • Keep students focused by engaging them in frequent oral and written summaries. • Give students the opportunity to jot down or sketch an idea before having to respond verbally. • Make use of assistive technology as needed.	• Encourage these students to work independently (or with another advanced learner) on sentence cross-examination or other language-based tasks while you work with the rest of the class. • Have these students find their own synonyms for a given word and order them on a continuum to reinforce shades of meaning. • Ask these students to choose their own sentences to present to the class in a sentence cross-examination.

A Final Thought

As Kucan (2012) so eloquently states, "the classrooms of teachers who support the vocabulary development of their students are *energized verbal environments*—environments in which words are not only noticed and appreciated, but also savored and celebrated" (361). Similarly, we praise the classrooms of teachers who support students' word-level, sentence-level, and text-level academic language development. Their classrooms are *supercharged linguistic environments*—environments in which complex academic language is recognized, considered, valued, and nurtured. If you cultivate a classroom where your students' academic language will flourish and grow, you will be helping them become more sophisticated readers and writers, as well as more proficient listeners and speakers.

Essential Questions for Individual Reflection, Collegial Circles, and Group Discussions

- *How can word-, sentence-, and text-level routines be integrated into specific ELA and content area units?*

- *How can you design meaningful, creative homework assignments to reinforce your word-, sentence-, and text-level routines?*

- *How can you engage learners to use sophisticated academic language?*

- *How can you incorporate students' out-of-school experiences with intriguing words, challenging sentences, and complex texts into class routines?*

- *What are two strategies presented in this chapter that you can see yourself trying in your classroom?*

- *What materials or resources would you need to accomplish this?*

- *With which colleagues will you discuss these new strategies? Will the change be on a classroom level or grade level?*

- *What role will parents have in supporting academic language development? What resources can you provide them to help at home?*

References

Allen, J. 1999. *Words, Words, Words: Teaching Vocabulary in Grades 4–12*. Portland, ME: Stenhouse.

Allington, R. L. 1984. "Oral Reading." In *Handbook of Reading Research*, ed. P. D. Pearson, 1:829–64. New York: Longman.

———. 2006. *What Really Matters for Struggling Readers: Designing Research-Based Programs*. 2nd ed. Boston: Allyn and Bacon.

———. 2009. *What Really Matters in Fluency: From Research to Practice*. New York: Allyn and Bacon.

Allington, R. L., and R. E. Gabriel. 2012. "Every Child, Every Day." *Educational Leadership* 69 (6): 10–15.

Anderson, R. C., E. H. Hiebert, J. A. Scott, and I. A. G. Wilkinson. 1985. *Becoming a Nation of Readers: The Report of the Commission on Reading, U.S. Department of Education*. Champaign, IL: Center for the Study of Reading.

Anstrom, K., P. DiCerbo, F. Butler, A. Katz, J. Millet, and C. Rivera. 2010. *A Review of the Literature on Academic English: Implications for K–12 English Language Learners*. Arlington, VA: George Washington University Center for Equity and Excellence in Education. http://ceee.gwu.edu/Academic%20Lit%20Review_FINAL.pdf.

Bailey, A. L. 2010. "Implications for Assessment and Instruction." In *The Education of English Learners: Research to Practice*, ed. M. Shatz and L. C. Wilkinson, 222–47. New York: Guilford.

Bambrick-Santoyo, P., A. Settles, and J. Worrell. 2013. *Great Habits, Great Readers: A Practical Guide to K–4 Reading in Light of the Common Core*. San Francisco, CA: Jossey-Bass.

Bear, D. R., M. Invernizzi, S. Templeton, and F. Johnston. 2012. *Words Their Way: Word Study for Phonics, Vocabulary, and Spelling Instruction*. 5th ed. Upper Saddle River, NJ: Pearson.

Beck, I. L., M. G. McKeown, and L. Kucan. 2002. *Bringing Words to Life: Robust Vocabulary Instruction*. New York: Guilford.

———. 2008. *Creating Robust Vocabulary: Frequently Asked Questions and Extended Examples*. New York: Guilford.

———. 2013. *Bringing Words to Life: Robust Vocabulary Instruction*. 2nd ed. New York: Guilford.

Biemiller, A. 2003. "Oral Comprehension Sets the Ceiling on Reading Comprehension." *American Educator* 27 (1). www.aft.org/newspubs/periodicals/ae/spring2003/hirschsboral.cfm.

Billmeyer, R. 1996. *Teaching Reading in the Content Areas: If Not Me, Then Who?* Aurora, CO: McREL Research Laboratory.

Blachowicz, C., P. Fisher, D. Ogle, and S. Watts Taffe. 2013. *Teaching Academic Vocabulary K–8: Effective Practices Across the Curriculum*. New York: Guilford.

Boch, F., and A. Piolat. 2005. "Note Taking and Learning: A Summary of Research." *The WAC Journal* 16: 101–13.

Bower, B., J. Lobdell, and L. Swenson. 1999. *History Alive! Engaging All Learners in the Diverse Classroom*. Rancho Cordova, CA: Teacher Curriculum Institute.

Boyd, M. P., and L. Galda. 2011. *Real Talk in Elementary Classrooms: Effective Oral Language Practice.* New York: Guilford.

Boyd, M. P., and S. Smyntek-Gworek. 2012. "Morning Meeting in a Third Grade Classroom: Literacy and Learning [Standards]." *Journal of Classroom Interaction* 47 (2): 4–12.

Boyles, N. N. 2013. "Closing in on Close Reading." *Educational Leadership* 70 (4): 36–41.

Britton, J. 1983. "Writing and the Story of the World." In *Explorations in the Development of Writing: Theory, Research, and Practice*, ed. B. M. Kroll and C. G. Wells, 3–30. New York: Wiley.

Brookhart, S. M. 2013. *How to Create and Use Rubrics for Formative Assessment and Grading.* Alexandria, VA: ASCD.

Brown, S., and L. Kappes. 2012. *Implementing the Common Core State Standards: A Primer on "Close Reading of Text."* Washington, DC: Aspen Institute.

Bruner, J. 1966. *Towards a Theory of Instruction.* Cambridge, MA: Harvard University Press.

Buehl, D. 1995. *Classroom Strategies for Interactive Learning.* Newark, DE: International Reading Association.

———. 2001. *Classroom Strategies for Interactive Learning.* 2nd ed. Newark, DE: International Reading Association.

———. 2009. *Classroom Strategies for Interactive Learning.* 3rd ed. Newark DE: International Reading Association.

———. 2011. *Developing Readers in the Academic Disciplines.* Newark, DE: International Reading Association.

Burkins, J., and K. Yaris. 2013. "Top Ten Themes of IRA Convention 2013." *Burkins and Yaris: Think Tank for 21st Century Literacy* (blog). April 23. www.burkinsandyaris.com /top-ten-themes-of-ira-convention-2013/.

Burris, C. C., and D. T. Garrity. 2008. *Detracking for Excellence and Equity.* Alexandria, VA: ASCD.

Calkins, L. 1986. *The Art of Teaching Writing.* Portsmouth, NH: Heinemann.

———. 1994. *The Art of Teaching Writing.* 2nd ed. Portsmouth, NH: Heinemann.

Calkins, L., M. Ehrenworth, and C. Lehman. 2012. *Pathways to the Common Core: Accelerating Achievement.* Portsmouth, NH: Heinemann.

Cambourne, B. 2000. "Observing Literacy Learning in Elementary Classrooms: Nine Years of Classroom Anthropology." *The Reading Teacher* 53 (6): 512–15.

Cazden, C. B. 1988. *Classroom Discourse: The Language of Teaching and Learning.* Portsmouth, NH: Heinemann.

———. 2001. *Classroom Discourse: The Language of Teaching and Learning.* 2nd ed. Portsmouth, NH: Heinemann.

Chamot, A. U., and J. M. O'Malley. 1994. *The CALLA Handbook: Implementing the Cognitive Academic Language Learning Approach.* Reading, MA: Addison-Wesley.

Clark, J. M., and A. Paivio. 1991. "Dual Coding Theory and Education." *Educational Psychology Review* 3 (3): 149–70.

Coleman, D. 2011. "Bringing the Common Core to Life." Presentation made in Albany, New York, April 28. Retrieved from New York State Education Department at http://usny.nysed.gov/rttt /docs/bringingthecommoncoretolife/part6transcript.pdf.

Coleman, D., and S. Pimentel. 2012. *Revised Publishers' Criteria for the Common Core State Standards in English Language Arts and Literacy, Grades 3–12*. Retrieved from the Common Core Standards Initiative at www.corestandards.org/assets/Publishers_Criteria_for_3-12.pdf.

Connecticut State Department of Education. 2004. *Core Science Curriculum Framework: An Invitation for Students and Teachers to Explore Science and Its Role in Society*. Hartford, CT: Connecticut State Department of Education. www.sde.ct.gov/sde/lib/sde/word_docs/curriculum/science /framework/sciencecoreframework2005v2.doc.

Costa, A. L., and R. J. Garmston. 1994. *Cognitive Coaching: A Foundation for Renaissance Schools*. Norwood, MA: Christopher-Gordon.

Costa, A. L., and B. Kallick. 2000. Habits of Mind: A Developmental Series. *Book I: Discovering and Exploring Habits of Mind*; *Book II: Activating and Engaging Habits of Mind*; *Book III: Assessing and Reporting Growth in Habits of Mind*; *Book IV: Integrating and Sustaining Habits of Mind*. Alexandria, VA: ASCD.

Coxhead, A. 2000. "A New Academic Word List." *TESOL Quarterly* 34 (2): 213–238.

Cronsberry, J. 2004. *Word Walls: A Support for Literacy in the Secondary School Classroom*. http:// curriculum.org/storage/258/1334340769/World_Walls_-_A_Support_for_Literacy_in_Secondary _School_Classrooms.pdf.

Cunningham, P., D. Hall, and C. Sigmon. 1999. *The Teacher's Guide to the Four Blocks*. Greensboro, NC: Carson-Dellosa.

Dewey, J. 1933. *How We Think*. Boston: D. C. Heath.

Dodge, J. 2006. *Differentiation in Action*. New York: Scholastic.

Dooley, N. 1992. *Everybody Eats Rice*. Minneapolis, MN: Lerner Publishing Group.

Dorfman, L. R., and R. Cappelli. 2007. *Mentor Texts: Teaching Writing Through Children's Literature, K–6*. Portland, ME: Stenhouse.

Dove, M. G., and A. Honigsfeld. 2013. *Common Core for the Not-So-Common Learner, Grades K–5: English Language Arts Strategies*. Thousand Oaks, CA: Corwin.

Duffelmeyer, F. 1994. "Effective Anticipation Guide Statements for Learning from Expository Prose." *Journal of Reading* 37: 452–55.

DuFour, R., and R. Eaker. 1998. *Professional Learning Communities at Work: Best Practices for Enhancing Student Achievement*. Bloomington, IN: Solution Tree.

Duke, N., S. Caughlan, M. Juzwik, and N. Martin. 2011. *Reading and Writing Genre with Purpose in K–8*. Portsmouth, NH: Heinemann.

Edwards, A. D., and D. P. G. Westgate. 1987. *Investigating Classroom Talk*. London: Falmer.

Erickson, H. L. 2006. *Concept-Based Curriculum and Instruction for the Thinking Classroom*. Thousand Oaks, CA: Sage.

Fearn, L., and N. Farrnan. 2001. *Interactions: Teaching Writing and the Language Arts*. Boston: Houghton Mifflin.

Fisher, B., and E. Fisher Medvic. 2000. *Perspectives on Shared Reading: Planning and Practice*. Portsmouth, NH: Heinemann.

Fisher, D., and N. Frey. 2008. *Better Learning Through Structured Teaching: A Framework for the Gradual Release of Responsibility*. Alexandria, VA: ASCD.

———. 2009. *Background Knowledge: The Missing Piece of the Comprehension Puzzle*. Portsmouth, NH: Heinemann.

Fisher, D., N. Frey, and D. Lapp. 2013. "Speaking and Listening Standards." In *Teaching with the Common Core Standards for English Language Arts—Grades 3–5*, ed. L. M. Morrow, K. K. Wixson, and T. Shanahan, 107–29. New York: Guilford.

Fisher, D., N. Frey, and C. Uline. 2013. *Common Core English Language Arts in a PLC at Work*. Bloomington, IN: Solution Tree.

Fountas, I. C., and G. S. Pinnell. 2001. *Guiding Readers and Writers Grades 3–6: Teaching Comprehension, Genre, and Content Literacy*. Portsmouth, NH: Heinemann.

———. 2012. *Genre Study: Teaching with Fiction and Nonfiction Books*. Portsmouth, NH: Heinemann.

Francis, D. J., M. Rivera, N. Lesaux, M. Kieffer, and H. Rivera. 2006. *Practical Guidelines for the Education of English Language Learners: Research-Based Recommendations for Instruction and Academic Interventions*. No. 2. Portsmouth, NH: Center on Instruction.

Frayer, D., W. C. Frederick, and H. J. Klausmeier. 1969. *A Schema for Testing the Level of Cognitive Mastery*. Madison, WI: Wisconsin Center for Education Research.

Frey, N., and D. Fisher. 2013. *Rigorous Reading: 5 Access Points for Comprehending Complex Texts*. Thousand Oaks, CA: Corwin.

Frey, N., D. Fisher, and J. Nelson. 2013. "Todo tiene que ver con lo que se habla: It's All About the Talk." *Phi Delta Kappan* 94 (6): 8–13.

Fuchs, D., L. Fuchs, and P. Burish. 2000. "Peer-Assisted Learning Strategies: An Evidence-Based Practice to Promote Reading Achievement." *Learning Disabilities Research and Practice* 15 (2): 85–91.

Gallagher, K. 2011. *Write Like This: Teaching Real World Writing Through Modeling and Mentor Texts*. Portland, ME: Stenhouse.

Genishi, C. 1988. "Young Children's Oral Language Development." ERIC Digest. ED301361. Urbana, IL: ERIC Clearinghouse on Elementary and Early Childhood Education. http://files .eric.ed.gov/fulltext/ED301361.pdf.

Gersten, R., and S. Baker. 2001. "Teaching Expressive Writing to Students with Learning Disabilities: A Meta-analysis." *The Elementary School Journal* 101: 251–72.

Gewertz, C. 2012. "Common Standards Ignite Debate Over Prereading." *Education Week* April 24. www.edweek.org/ew/articles/2012/04/25/29prereading_ep.h31.html.

Goldenberg, C. N. 1992. *Instructional Conversations and Their Classroom Application*. Educational Practice Report 2. Berkeley, CA: Center for Research on Education, Diversity and Excellence, University of California. http://escholarship.org/uc/item/6q72k3k9.

_____. 2008. "Teaching English Language Learners: What the Research Does—and Does Not—Say." *American Educator* 32 (2): 8–23, 42–44. www.aft.org/pdfs/americaneducator/summer2008/goldenberg.pdf.

Graham, S., D. McKeown, S. Kiuhara, and K. R. Harris. 2012. "A Meta-analysis of Writing Instruction for Students in the Elementary Grades." *Journal of Educational Psychology* 104 (4): 879–96.

Graham, S., and D. Perin. 2007. "A Meta-analysis of Writing Instruction for Adolescent Students." *Journal of Educational Psychology* 99: 445–76. DOI: 10.1037/0022-0663.99.3.445.

Guthrie, J. T., A. Wigfield, N. M. Humenick, K. C. Perencevich, A. Taboada, and P. Barbosa. 2006. "Influences of Stimulating Tasks on Reading Motivation and Comprehension." *Journal of Educational Research* 99 (4): 232–245.

Halliday, M. A. K. 1993. "Towards a Language-Based Theory of Learning." *Linguistics and Education* 5 (2): 93–116.

Harmon, J. M., K. D. Wood, W. B. Hedrick, J. Vintinner, and T. Willeford. 2009. "Interactive Word Walls: More than Just Reading the Writing on the Wall." *Journal of Adolescent and Adult Literacy* 52 (5): 398–408. DOI: 10.1598/JAAL.52.5.4.

Harste, J. C., K. G. Short, and C. Burke. 1988. *Creating Classrooms for Authors: The Reading-Writing Connection.* Portsmouth, NH: Heinemann.

Hart, B., and T. Risley. 1995. *Meaningful Differences in the Everyday Experiences of Young American Children.* Baltimore, MD: Paul H. Brookes.

_____. 2003. "The Early Catastrophe: The 30 Million Word Gap by Age 3." *American Educator* 27 (1): 4–9.

Harvey, S., and H. Daniels. 2009. *Comprehension and Collaboration: Inquiry Circles in Action.* Portsmouth, NH: Heinemann.

Harvey, S., and A. Goudvis. 2013. "Comprehension at the Core." *The Reading Teacher* 66 (6): 432–39.

Hattie, J. 2009. *Visible Learning.* New York: Routledge.

_____. 2012. *Visible Learning for Teachers.* New York: Routledge.

Hayes, D. A., and R. J. Tierney. 1982. "Developing Readers' Knowledge Through Analogy." *Reading Research Quarterly* 17 (2): 256–80.

Herrell, A. L., and M. Jordan. 2008. *50 Strategies for Teaching English Language Learners.* Upper Saddle River, NJ: Pearson.

Hillocks, G. Jr. 1986. *Research on Written Composition: New Directions for Teaching.* Urbana, IL: National Council of Teachers of English.

Hirsch, E. D. 2006. *The Knowledge Deficit: Closing the Shocking Education Gap for American Children.* New York: Houghton Mifflin.

Honigsfeld, A., and M. G. Dove. 2010. *Collaboration and Co-teaching: Strategies for English Learners.* Thousand Oaks, CA: Corwin.

Hyerle, D. 2008. *Visual Tools for Transforming Information into Knowledge.* 2nd ed. Thousand Oaks, CA: Corwin.

Iaquinta, A. 2006. "Guided Reading: A Research-Based Response to the Challenges of Early Reading Instruction." *Early Childhood Education Journal* 33 (6): 413–18. DOI: 10.1007 /s10643-006-0074-2.

International Reading Association (IRA) and National Council of Teachers of English (NCTE). 2013. "Strategy Guide: Implementing the Writing Process." ReadWriteThink. www. readwritethink.org/professional-development/strategy-guides/implementing-writing-process-30386 .html#research-basis.

Jensen, E. 1996. *Brain-Based Learning*. Del Mar, CA: Turning Point.

Johnson, D. W., and R. Johnson. 1999. *Learning Together and Alone: Cooperative, Competitive, and Individualistic Learning*. 5th ed. Boston: Allyn and Bacon.

Keene, E. O., and S. Zimmermann. 1997. *Mosaic of Thought: Teaching Comprehension in a Reader's Workshop*. Portsmouth, NH: Heinemann.

———. 2007. *Mosaic of Thought: The Power of Strategy Instruction*. Portsmouth, NH: Heinemann.

Kinsella, K. 2005. *Teaching Academic Vocabulary*. Aiming High Resource. Santa Rosa, CA: Sonoma County Office of Education. www.scoe.org/docs/ah/AH_kinsella2.pdf.

———. 2012. "Cutting to the Core: Communicating on the Same Wavelength." *Language Magazine* 12 (4): 18–25.

Kirby, D. L., and D. Crovitz. 2012. *Inside Out: Strategies for Teaching Writing*. Portsmouth, NH: Heinemann.

Knight, J. 2010. *Effective Questioning*. Version 3.0. Lawrence, KS: Instructional Coaching, Kansas Coaching Project, University of Kansas. www.instructionalcoach.org/images/big4manuals /EffectiveQuestions.3.0.pdf.

Krashen, S. D. 2004. *The Power of Reading: Insights from the Research*. Westport, CT: Libraries Unlimited.

———. 2011. *Free Voluntary Reading*. Santa Barbara, CA: Libraries Unlimited.

Kreite, R., with L. Bechtel. 2002. *The Morning Meeting Book*. Turners Falls, MA: Northeast Foundation for Children.

Kucan, L. 2012. "What Is Most Important to Know About Vocabulary?" *The Reading Teacher* 65 (6): 360–66.

Kuhn, M. R., P. Schwanenflugel, R. D. Morris, L. M. Morrow, D. Woo, B. Meisinger, et al. 2006. "Teaching Children to Become Fluent and Automatic Readers." *Journal of Literacy Research* 38 (4): 357–88.

Lesaux, N. 2013. "Turn Up the Volume on Academic Talk!" National Geographic Reach. http://ngl .cengage.com/assets/downloads/ngreach_pro0000000005/am_lesaux_rch_acad_talk.pdf.

Lodge, D. 1992. *The Art of Fiction*. London: Penguin.

Macon, J. M., D. Bewell, and M. E. Vogt. 1991. *Responses to Literature*. Newark, DE: International Reading Association.

Malloy, J. A. and L. B. Gambrell. 2013. "Reading Standards for Literature." In *Teaching with the Common Core Standards for English Language Arts*, ed. L. M. Morrow, K. Wixson, and T. Shanahan, 22–49. New York: Guilford Press.

Mandell, N., and B. Malon. 2008. *Thinking Like a Historian: Rethinking History Instruction*. Madison, WI: Wisconsin Historical Society Press.

Marzano, R. J. 2003. *What Works in Schools: Translating Research into Action*. Alexandria, VA: ASCD.

_____. 2004. *Building Background Knowledge for Academic Achievement: Research on What Works in Schools*. Alexandria, VA: ASCD.

_____. 2005. *Building Academic Vocabulary: Teacher's Manual*. Alexandria, VA: ASCD.

Marzano, R. J., D. J. Pickering, and T. Heflebower. 2011. *The Highly Engaged Classroom*. Bloomington, IN: Marzano Research Laboratory.

Marzano, R. J., D. Pickering, and J. Pollock. 2001. *Classroom Instruction That Works: Research-Based Strategies for Increasing Student Achievement*. Alexandria, VA: ASCD.

Marzano, R. J., and J. A. Simms. 2013. "Vocabulary for the Common Core." Bloomington, IN: Marzano Research Laboratory.

McGroarty, M. 1993. "Cooperative Learning and Second Language Acquisition." In *Cooperative Learning: A Response to Linguistic and Cultural Diversity*, ed. D. D. Holt, 19–46. Washington, DC: Delta Systems and Center for Applied Linguistics.

Merkley, D. J. 1996/1997. "Modified Anticipation Guide." *Reading Teacher* 50 (December/January): 365–68.

Michaels, S., M. C. O'Connor, M. W. Hall, with L. B. Resnick. 2010. *Accountable Talk Sourcebook: For Classroom Conversation That Works*. Pittsburgh, PA: University of Pittsburgh, Learning Research and Development Center.

Miller, D. 2008. *Teaching with Intention*. Portland, ME: Stenhouse.

_____. 2009. *The Book Whisperer: Awakening the Inner Reader in Every Child*. San Francisco: Jossey-Bass.

_____. 2013. *Reading with Meaning: Teaching Comprehension in the Primary Grades*. 2nd ed. Portland, ME: Stenhouse.

Miller, D., B. Moss, N. K. Duke, and E. O. Keene. 2013. *No More Independent Reading Without Support (Not This but That)*. Portsmouth, NH: Heinemann.

Mitchell, K. E. 2006. "Getting to the Heart of a Story." *Teaching PreK–8* 37 (1): 66–67.

Mitra, S. 2010. "SOLE: How to Bring Self-Organized Learning Environment to Your Community." TED.com. www.ted.com/pages/sole_toolkit.

Moll, L. C. 1992. "Bilingual Classroom Studies and Community Analysis: Some Recent Trends." *Educational Researcher* 21 (2): 20–24.

Nagy, W., and D. Townsend. 2012. "Words as Tools: Learning Academic Vocabulary as Language Acquisition." *Reading Research Quarterly* 47 (1): 91–108.

National Commission on Writing in America's Schools and Colleges (NCWASC). 2003. *The Neglected "R": The Need for a Writing Revolution*. New York: College Board. www.collegeboard.com/prod_downloads/writingcom/neglectedr.pdf.

National Governors Association (NGA) Center for Best Practices and Council of Chief State School Officers (CCSSO). 2010. *Common Core State Standards for English Language Arts and Literacy in History/Social Studies, Science, and Technical Subjects*. Washington, DC: NGA Center for Best Practices and CCSSO. http://corestandards.org/assets/CCSSI_ELA%20Standards.pdf.

National Institute of Child Health and Human Development (NICHD). 2000. *Report of the National Reading Panel: Teaching Children to Read: An Evidence-Based Assessment of the Scientific Research Literature on Reading and Its Implications for Reading Instruction: Reports of the Subgroups.* NIH Publication No. 00-4754. Washington, DC: US Government Printing Office.

National Writing Project and C. Nagin. 2006. *Because Writing Matters: Improving Student Writing in Our Schools.* Berkeley: University of California, National Writing Project.

O'Connor, Rory, dir. 2002. "India—Hole in the Wall." *Frontline/World.* October. www.pbs.org /frontlineworld/stories/india/thestory.html.

Ogle, D. 2011. *Partnering for Content Literacy: PRC2 in Action.* Upper Saddle River, NJ: Pearson.

O'Hara, S., J. Zwiers, and R. Pritchard. 2013. "Framing the Development of Complex Language and Literacy." Stanford, CA: ALD Network. www.aldnetwork.org/sites/default/files/pictures/aldn _brief_2013.pdf.

Pearson, P. D., and M. C. Gallagher. 1983. "The Instruction of Reading Comprehension." *Contemporary Educational Psychology* 8: 317–44.

Pearson, P. D., and E. H. Hiebert. 2013. "Understanding the Common Core State Standards." In *Teaching with the Common Core Standards for English Language Arts: What Educators Need to Know* (Book 1: Grades PreK–2; Book 2: Grades 3–5), ed. L. Morrow, T. Shanahan, and K. K. Wixson, 1–21. New York: Guilford.

Peregoy, S. F., and O. F. Boyle. 2012. *Reading, Writing, and Learning in ESL: A Resource Book for K–12 Teachers.* 6th ed. New York: Longman.

Pilgreen, J. L. 2000. *The SSR Handbook: How to Organize and Manage a Sustained Silent Reading Program.* Portsmouth, NH: Heinemann.

Pressley, M., C. J. Johnson, S. Symons, J. A. McGoldrick, and J. A. Kurita. 1989. "Strategies That Improve Children's Memory and Comprehension of Text." *Elementary School Journal* 90: 3–32.

Rathvon, N. 1999. *Effective School Interventions: Strategies for Enhancing Academic Achievement and Social Competence.* New York: Guilford.

Renner Del Nero, J. 2013. Introduction. In *Teaching with the Common Core Standards for English Language Arts, Grades 3–5,* ed. L. M. Morrow, K. K. Wixson, and T. Shanahan, xi–xiv. New York: Guilford.

Reutzel, D. R., C. D. Jones, and T. H. Newman. 2010. "Scaffolded Silent Reading: Improving the Conditions of Silent Reading Practice in Classrooms." In *Revisiting Silent Reading: New Directions for Teachers and Researchers,* ed. E. H. Hiebert and D. R. Reutzel, 129–50. Newark, DE: International Reading Association.

Richardson, J. 2009. *The Next Step in Guided Reading: Focused Assessments and Targeted Lessons for Helping Every Student Become a Better Reader.* New York: Scholastic.

Ritchhart, R., M. Church, and K. Morrison. 2011. *Making Thinking Visible: How to Promote Engagement, Understanding, and Independence for All Learners.* San Francisco: Jossey-Bass.

Rosenblatt, L. 1993. *Literature as Exploration.* New York: Modern Language Association of America.

Roskos, K. A., P. O. Tabors, and L. A. Lenhart. 2009. *Oral Language and Early Literacy in Preschool: Talking, Reading, and Writing.* Newark, DE: International Reading Association.

Rothstein, D., and L. Santana. 2011. *Make Just One Change: Teach Students to Ask Their Own Questions*. Cambridge, MA: Harvard Education Press.

Sanchez, N. M., and L. D. Harper. 2012. *Intentional Interaction: Research-Based Model for Content and Language Learning*. Minneapolis, MN: 2030 Press.

Scarcella, R. 2003. *Academic English: A Conceptual Framework*. Technical Report 2003-1. Oakland, CA: University of California Linguistic Minority Research Institute.

Scardamalia, M., and C. Bereiter. 1991. "Higher Levels of Agency for Children in Knowledge-Building: A Challenge for the Design of New Knowledge Media." *Journal of the Learning Sciences* 1 (1): 37–68.

Schleppegrell, M. J. 2012. "Academic Language in Teaching and Learning: Introduction to the Special Issue." *Elementary School Journal* 112 (3): 409–18.

Shanahan, T. 2012–2013. "The Common Core Ate My Baby and Other Urban Legends." *Educational Leadership* 70 (4): 10–16.

Slavin, R. E. 1995. *Cooperative Learning: Theory, Research, and Practice*. 2nd ed. Boston: Allyn and Bacon.

Sousa, D. 2001. *How the Brain Learns*. 2nd ed. Thousand Oaks, CA: Corwin.

_____. 2011. *How the Brain Learns*. 4th ed. Thousand Oaks, CA: Corwin.

Taberski, S. 2010. *Comprehension from the Ground Up*. Portsmouth, NH: Heinemann.

Taylor, B. M. 2011. *Catching Schools: An Action Guide to Schoolwide Reading Improvement*. Portsmouth, NH: Heinemann.

Teachers' Curriculum Institute (TCI). 1999. *History Alive! Notebook*. Rancho Cordova, CA: TCI.

_____. 2013. "The Interactive Student Notebook." TCI.com. www.teachtci.com/interactive-social -studies-notebook.html.

Temple, C. A., D. Ogle, A. N. Crawford, and P. Freppon. 2013. *All Children Read: Teaching for Literacy in Today's Diverse Classrooms*. 4th ed. Upper Saddle River, NJ: Pearson.

Tharp, R. G., and R. Gallimore. 1991. *The Instructional Conversation: Teaching and Learning in Social Activity*. Research Report 2. Berkeley, CA Center for Research on Education, Diversity and Excellence, University of California. http://escholarship.org/uc/item/5th0939d.

Tienken, C. H., S. Goldberg, and D. DiRocco. 2009. "Questioning the Questions." *Kappa Delta Pi Record* 6 (1): 39–44.

Tomlinson, C. A. 2001. *How to Differentiate Instruction in Mixed-Ability Classrooms*. 2nd ed. Alexandria, VA: ASCD.

_____. 2008. *The Parallel Curriculum: A Design to Develop Learner Potential and Challenge Advanced Learners*. 2nd ed. Thousand Oaks, CA: Corwin.

Trelease, J. 2013. *The Read-Aloud Handbook*. 7th ed. New York: Penguin.

Troia, G. A. 2007. "Research in Writing Instruction: What We Know and What We Need to Know." In *Shaping Literacy Achievement: Research We Have, Research We Need*, ed. M. Pressley, A. Billman, K. Perry, K. Refitt, and J. M. Reynolds, 129–56. New York: Guilford.

Tutwiler, M. S., M. C. Lin, and C. Y. Chang. 2013. "Determining Virtual Environment 'Fit': The Relationship Between Navigation Style in a Virtual Field Trip, Student Self-Reported Desire to Visit the Field Trip Site in the Real World, and the Purposes of Science Education." *Journal of Science Education and Technology* 22 (3): 351–61.

Vogt, M. E., and J. Echevarria. 2008. 99 *Ideas and Activities for Teaching English Learners with the SIOP Model.* Boston: Pearson.

Vygotsky, L. S. 1978. *Mind in Society: The Development of Higher Psychological Processes.* Cambridge, MA: Harvard University Press.

Wang, M.C., G. D. Haertel, and H. J. Walberg. 1993/1994. "Synthesis of Research: What Helps Students Learn?" *Educational Leadership* 51 (December/January): 74–79.

WIDA. 2013. "Academic Language and Literacy." WIDA.us. www.wida.us/research/agenda /AcademicLanguage/index.aspx.

Wiggins, G., and J. McTighe. 2005. *Understanding by Design.* 2nd ed. Alexandria, VA: ASCD.

Wolfe, P. 2001. *Brain Matters: Translating Research into Classroom Practice.* Alexandria, VA: ASCD.

———. 2010. *Brain Matters: Translating Research into Classroom Practice.* 2nd ed. Alexandria, VA: ASCD.

Wong Fillmore, L. 2009. *English Language Development: Acquiring the Language Needed for Literacy and Learning.* Upper Saddle River, NJ: Pearson Education. http://assets.pearsonschool.com/asset_mgr /current/201010/English%20Language%20Development.pdf.

———. 2012. *Supporting Access to the Language and Content of Complex Texts for EL and LM Students.* www.cgcs.org/cms/lib/DC00001581/Centricity/Domain/25/ELA_retreat-Wong%20Fillmorepart2 .pdf.

Wood, K. D., D. Lapp, J. Flood, and D. B. Taylor. 2008. *Guiding Readers Through Text: Strategy Guides for New Times.* 2nd ed. Newark, DE: International Reading Association.

Wormeli, R. 2005. *Summarization in Any Subject: 50 Techniques to Improve Student Learning.* Alexandria, VA: ASCD.

Wright, J. 2007. *RTI Toolkit: A Practical Guide for Schools.* Port Chester, NY: Dude Publishing.

Zacarian, D. 2013. *Mastering Academic Language.* Thousand Oaks, CA: Corwin.

Zimmermann, A. 2012. "Anchor Charts: Academic Supports or Print-Rich Wallpaper?" *Top Teaching* (blog). October 17. www.scholastic.com/teachers/top-teaching/2012/10/anchor-charts -academic-supports-or-print-rich-wallpaper.

Zwiers, J. 2004/2005. "The Third Language of Academic English: Five Key Mental Habits Help English Language Learners Acquire the Language of School." *Educational Leadership* 62 (4): 60–63.

———. 2008. *Building Academic Language: Essential Practices for Content Classrooms.* San Francisco, CA: Jossey-Bass.

———. 2014. *Building Academic Language: Meeting Common Core Standards Across Disciplines: Grades 5–12.* 2nd ed. San Francisco: Jossey-Bass.

Zwiers, J., and M. Crawford. 2009. "How to Start Academic Conversations." *Educational Leadership* 66 (7): 70–73.

Online Sources

Intervention Central: www.interventioncentral.com
Teaching Channel: www.teachingchannel.org
Dinah Zike's website: www.dinah.com/faq/faq.php

Children's Books

Aliki. 1986. *A Medieval Feast*. New York: HarperCollins.

Baum, L. F. 2000. *The Wonderful Wizard of Oz*. New York: HarperCollins.

Beeler, S. 2001. *Throw Your Tooth on the Roof: Tooth Traditions Around the World*. New York: HMH Books.

Capeci, A., J. Johnston, E. Moore, A. Schreiber, and J. B. Stamper. 2006. The Magic School Bus Chapter Book Boxed Set. Books 1–8. New York: Scholastic Book Club.

Dooley, N. 1992. *Everybody Eats Rice*. Minneapolis, MN: Carolrhoda Books.

Eastman, P. D. 1960. *Are You My Mother?* New York, NY: Random House.

Hurd, E. D. 2000. *Starfish*. New York: HarperCollins.

Kuklin, S. 2006. *Families*. New York: Disney-Hyperion.

Mayer, M. 2001. *Just Grandma and Me*. New York: Random House Books for Young Readers.

———. 2001. *The New Baby*. New York: Random House Books for Young Readers.

Minarik, E. H., and M. Sendak. 1992. Little Bear Boxed Set. New York: HarperCollins.

Montgomery, S. 2009. *Quest for the Tree Kangaroo: An Expedition to the Cloud Forest of New Guinea*. New York: HMH Books.

Morris, A. 2000. *Families*. New York: HarperCollins.

Pryor, B., and B. Peck. 1992. *The House on Maple Street*. New York: HarperCollins.

Ryan, P. M. 2002. *Esperanza Rising*. Woodland Hills, CA: Scholastic.

Slobodkina, E. 1990. *Caps for Sale: A Tale of a Peddler, Some Monkeys and Their Monkey Business*. New York: HarperCollins.

Thomson, S. L. 2009. *Where Do Polar Bears Live?* New York: HarperCollins.

Young, E. 1996. *Lon Po Po: A Red-Riding Hood Story from China*. New York: Puffin.